life-
m
tidying up

a magical story

marie kondo

author of *the life-changing magic of tidying up*

illustrated by yuko uramoto
translated from the japanese by cathy hirano

TEN SPEED PRESS
California | New York

the life-changing *manga* of

contents

1 decide to tidy up 1

2 visualize your
ideal lifestyle 19

3 finish discarding
first 37

4 tidy by category 55

5 just fold and
stand upright 73

6 choose books
by feel 91

7 papers and
komono 109

8 leave sentimental
items for last 127

9 store things where
they belong 149

10 real life begins
after putting your
house in order. 167

afterword 186

about the author
and illustrator. 187

Chiaki Suzuki

Twenty-nine years old. Sales
rep. Single. Falls in love easily
but loses interest quickly,
which makes it hard for her to
have a lasting relationship.

tidying up — a magical story

introducing the characters

Marie Kondo

Tidying consultant. Nickname: KonMari. Has a winning smile but is an exacting instructor.

Chiaki's Neighbor

Good-looking guy who lives in the apartment next to Chiaki's. Works as a cook at a café. Likes to keep things tidy.

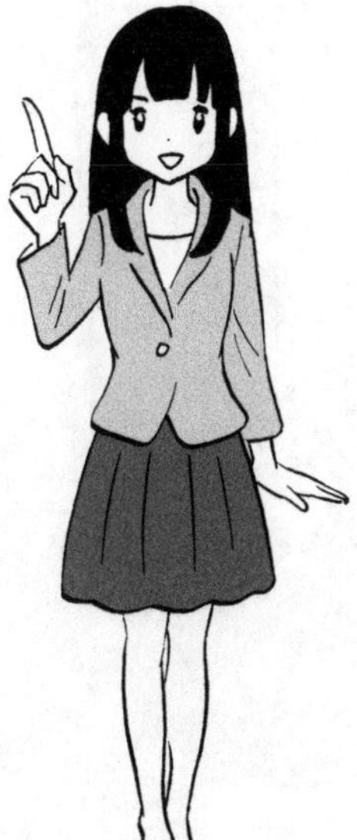

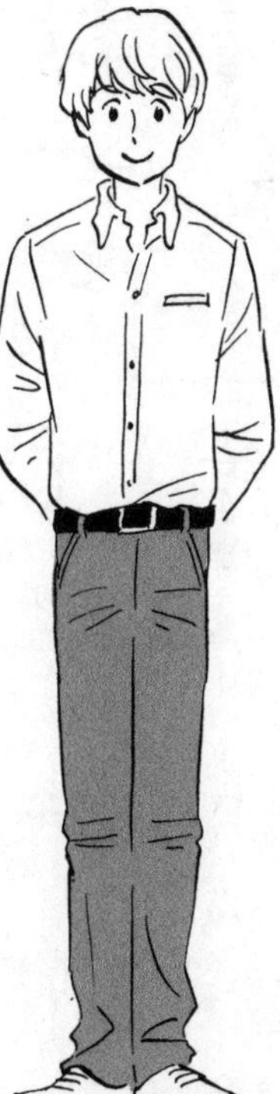

You really want to tidy up, but you don't believe you can. If this describes you, don't worry. You, too, can be just like Chiaki in this story.

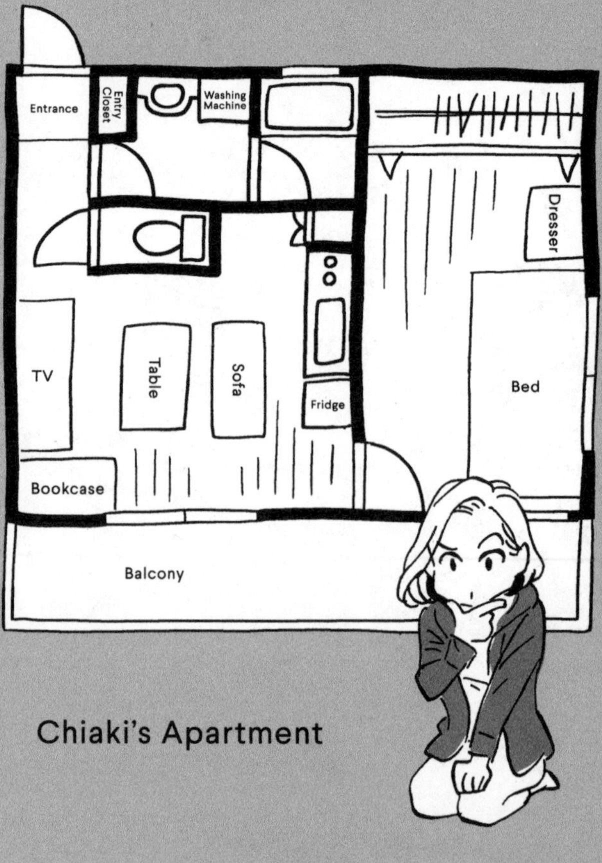
Entrance
Entry Closet
Washing Machine
Dresser
TV
Table
Sofa
Fridge
Bed
Bookcase
Balcony

Chiaki's Apartment

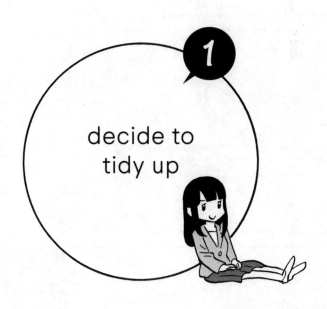

decide to
tidy up

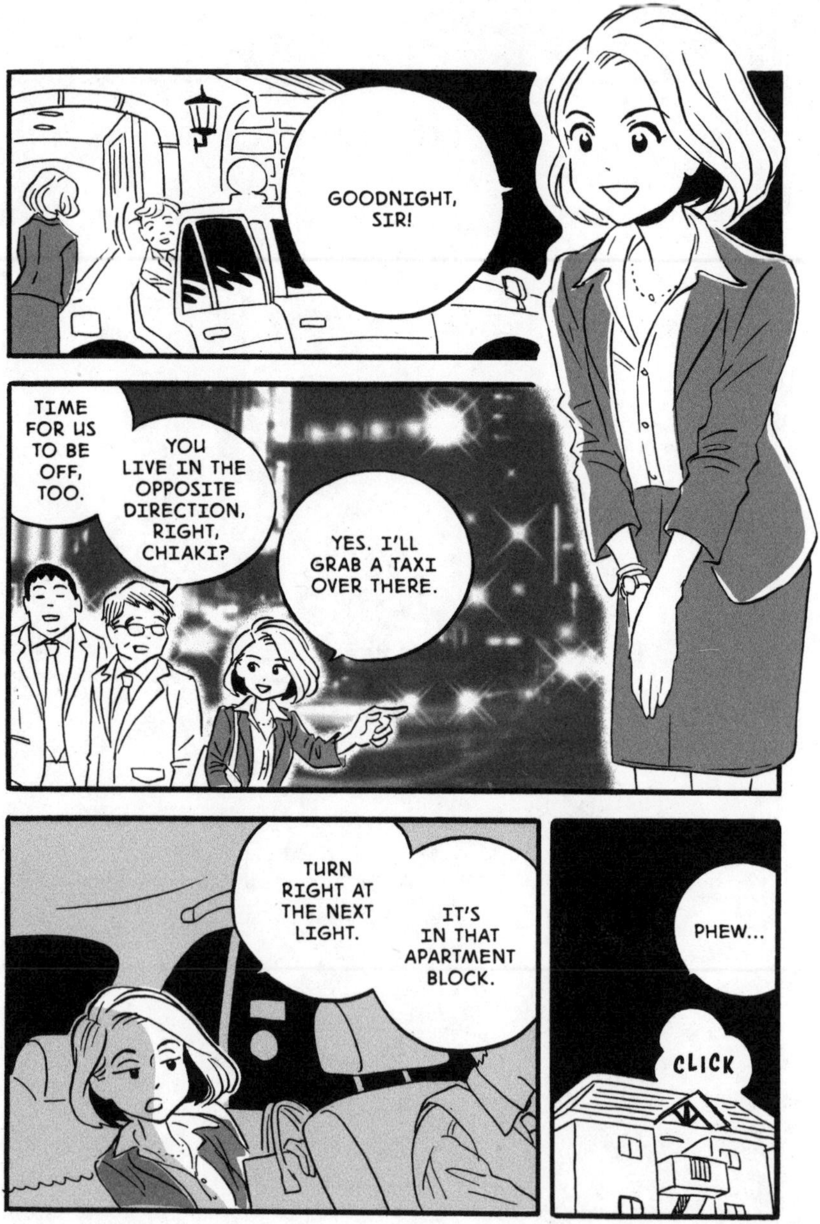
GOODNIGHT, SIR!
TIME FOR US TO BE OFF, TOO.
YOU LIVE IN THE OPPOSITE DIRECTION, RIGHT, CHIAKI?
YES. I'LL GRAB A TAXI OVER THERE.
TURN RIGHT AT THE NEXT LIGHT.
IT'S IN THAT APARTMENT BLOCK.
PHEW...
CLICK

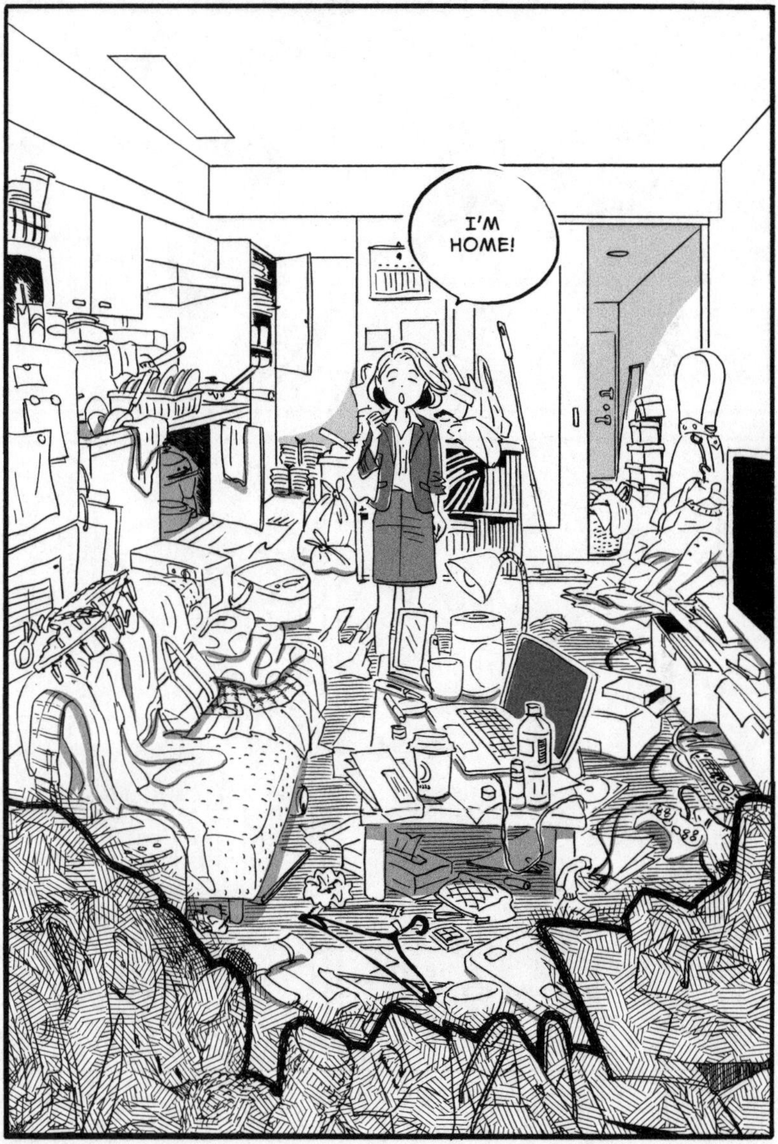
I'M HOME!

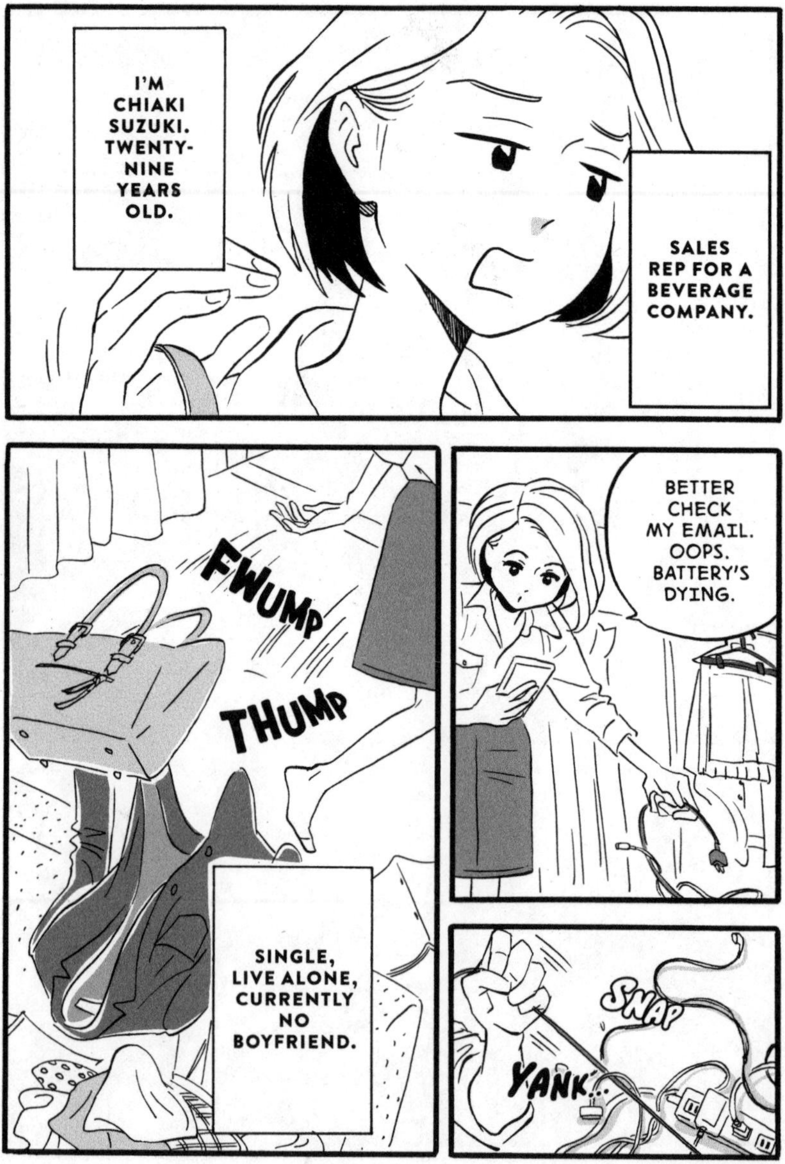
I'M CHIAKI SUZUKI. TWENTY-NINE YEARS OLD.
SALES REP FOR A BEVERAGE COMPANY.
FWUMP
THUMP
SINGLE, LIVE ALONE, CURRENTLY NO BOYFRIEND.
BETTER CHECK MY EMAIL. OOPS. BATTERY'S DYING.
SNAP
YANK...

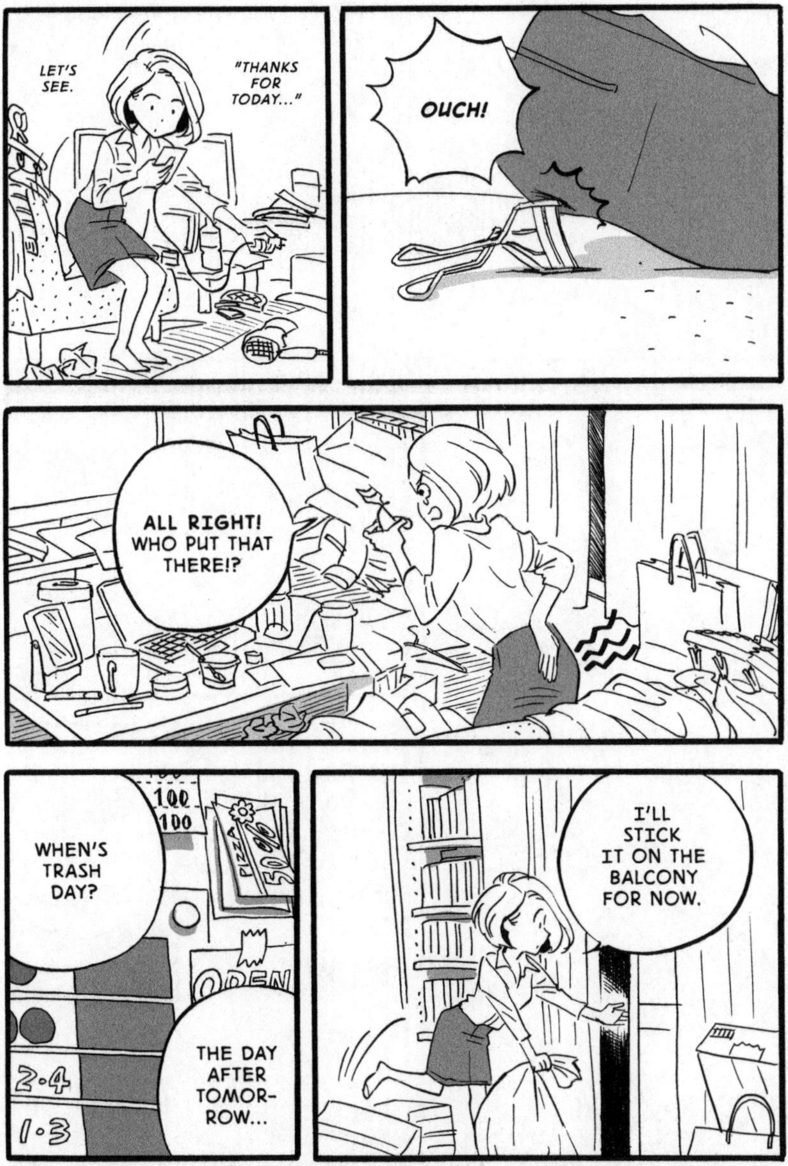
LET'S SEE.
"THANKS FOR TODAY..."
OUCH!
ALL RIGHT! WHO PUT THAT THERE!?
100
100
PIZZA 50%
ODEN
2·4
1·3
WHEN'S TRASH DAY?
THE DAY AFTER TOMORROW...
I'LL STICK IT ON THE BALCONY FOR NOW.

OHHH... LAST WEEK'S GARBAGE IS STILL HERE.

BETTER REMEMBER TO TAKE IT OUT THIS TIME.

PHEW

THAT'LL DO FOR NOW.

CLAP

CLAP

HEY! WHERE'S THE LID TO MY LENS CASE?

FORGET IT. I'LL USE A NEW PAIR.

TIME TO SHOWER AND GO TO BED.

SNAP

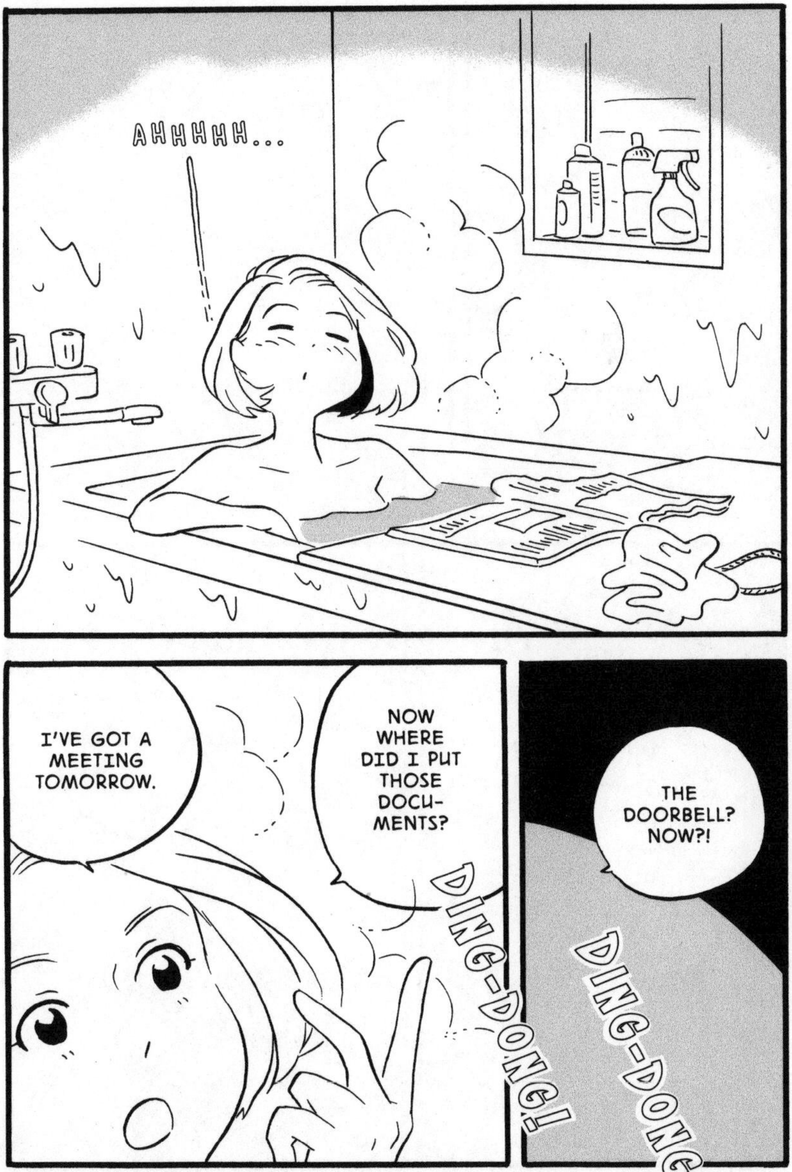
AHHHHH...
I'VE GOT A MEETING TOMORROW.
NOW WHERE DID I PUT THOSE DOCU-MENTS?
DING-DONG!
THE DOORBELL? NOW?!
DING-DONG!

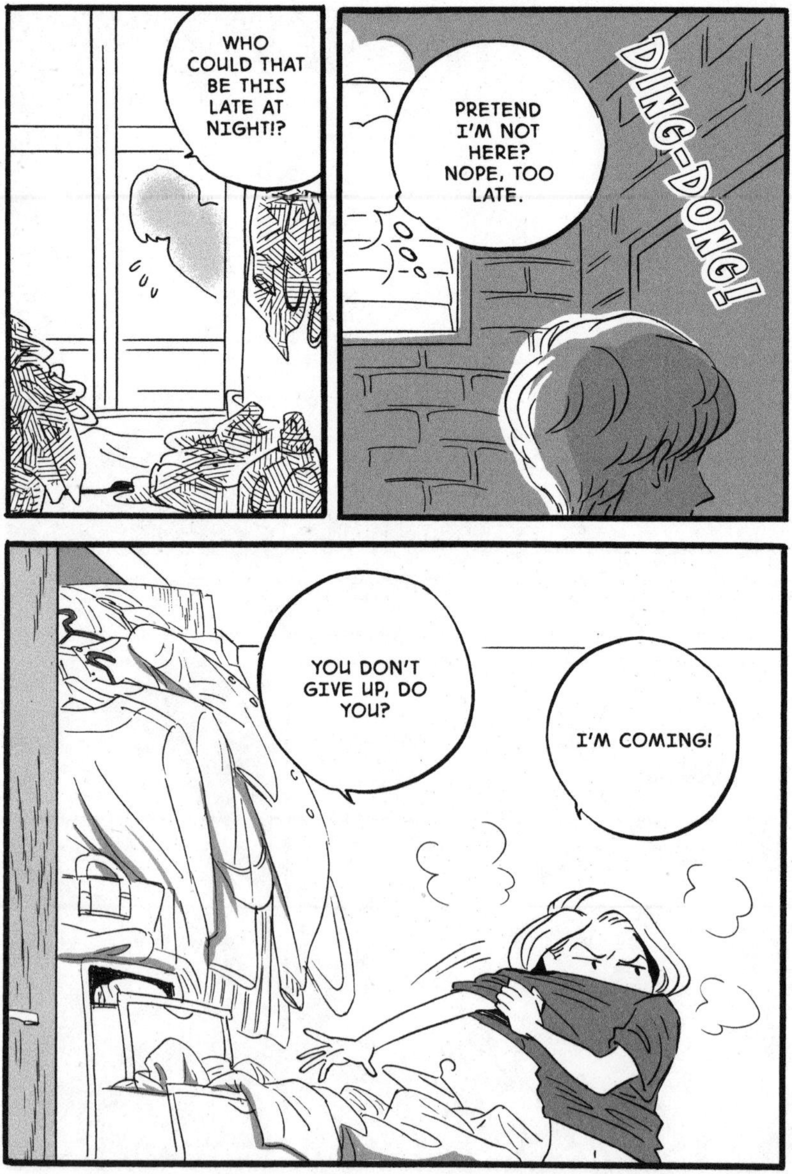
WHO COULD THAT BE THIS LATE AT NIGHT!?
PRETEND I'M NOT HERE? NOPE, TOO LATE.
DING-DONG!
YOU DON'T GIVE UP, DO YOU?
I'M COMING!

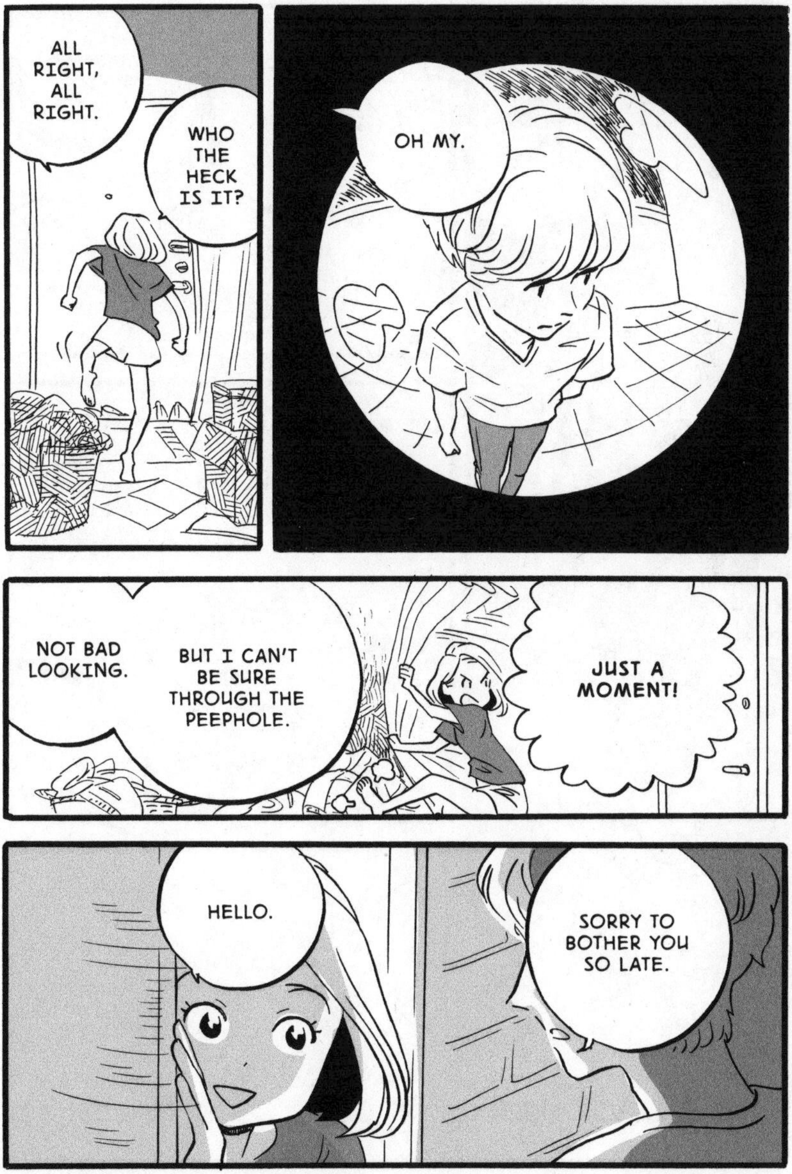
ALL RIGHT, ALL RIGHT.
WHO THE HECK IS IT?
OH MY.
NOT BAD LOOKING.
BUT I CAN'T BE SURE THROUGH THE PEEPHOLE.
JUST A MOMENT!
HELLO.
SORRY TO BOTHER YOU SO LATE.

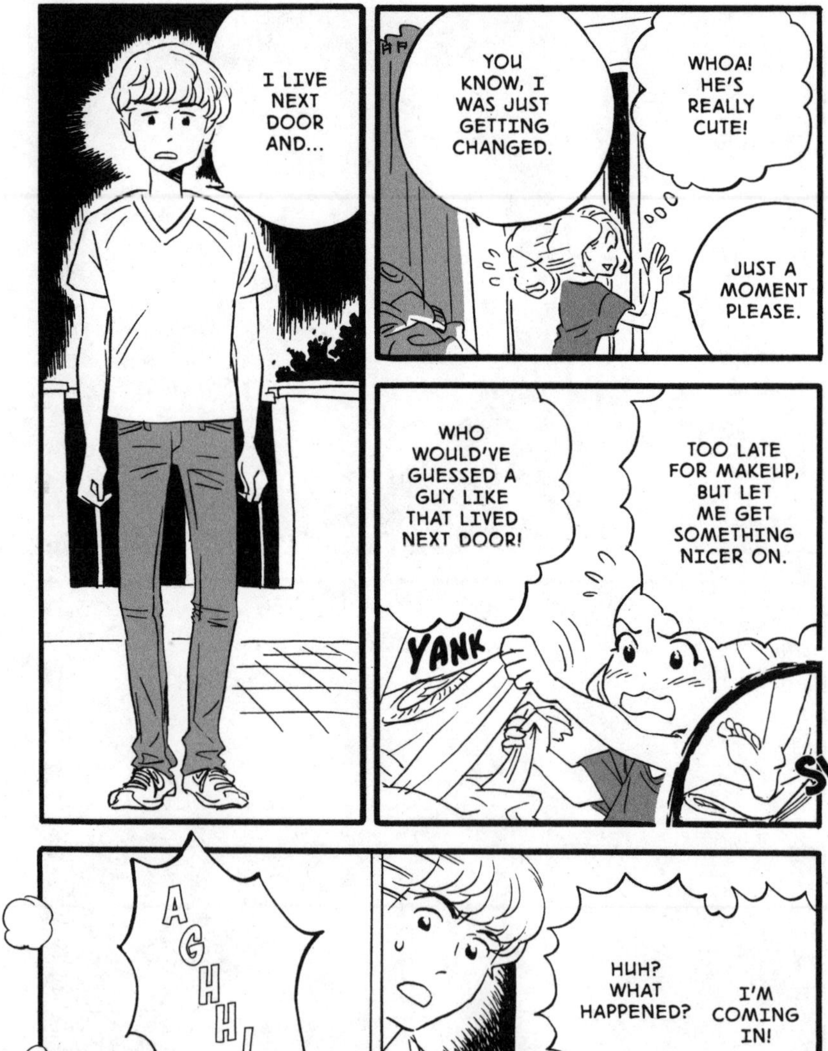
I LIVE NEXT DOOR AND...
YOU KNOW, I WAS JUST GETTING CHANGED.
WHOA! HE'S REALLY CUTE!
JUST A MOMENT PLEASE.
WHO WOULD'VE GUESSED A GUY LIKE THAT LIVED NEXT DOOR!
TOO LATE FOR MAKEUP, BUT LET ME GET SOMETHING NICER ON.
YANK
SLIP
AGHH!
BUMP-BUMP
THUD!
HUH? WHAT HAPPENED?
I'M COMING IN!

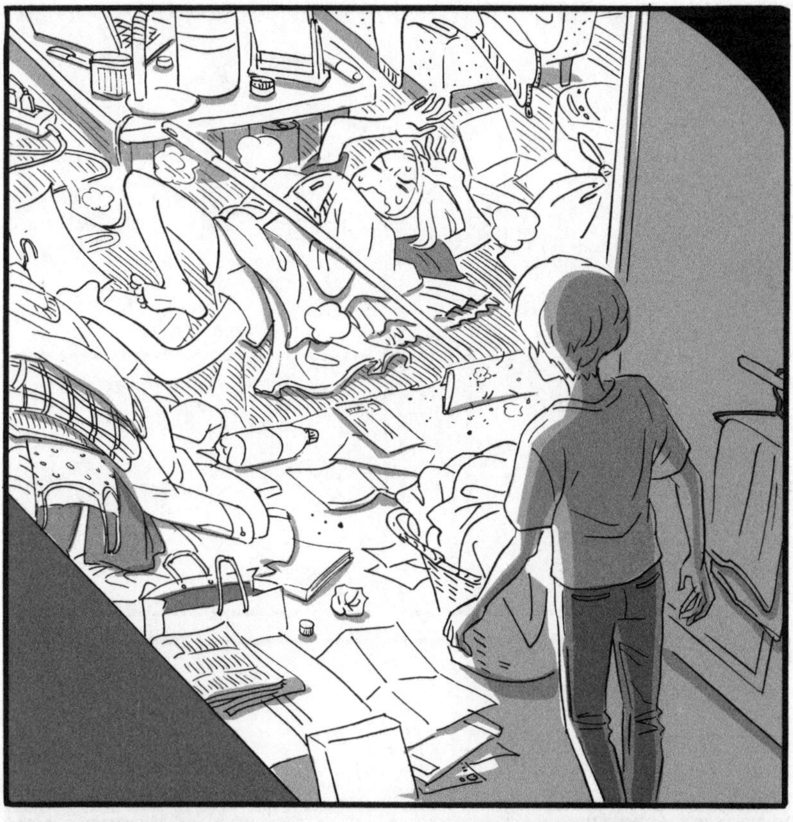

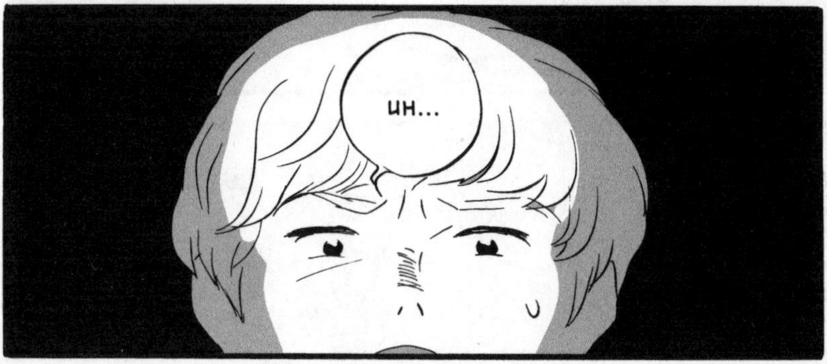
UH...

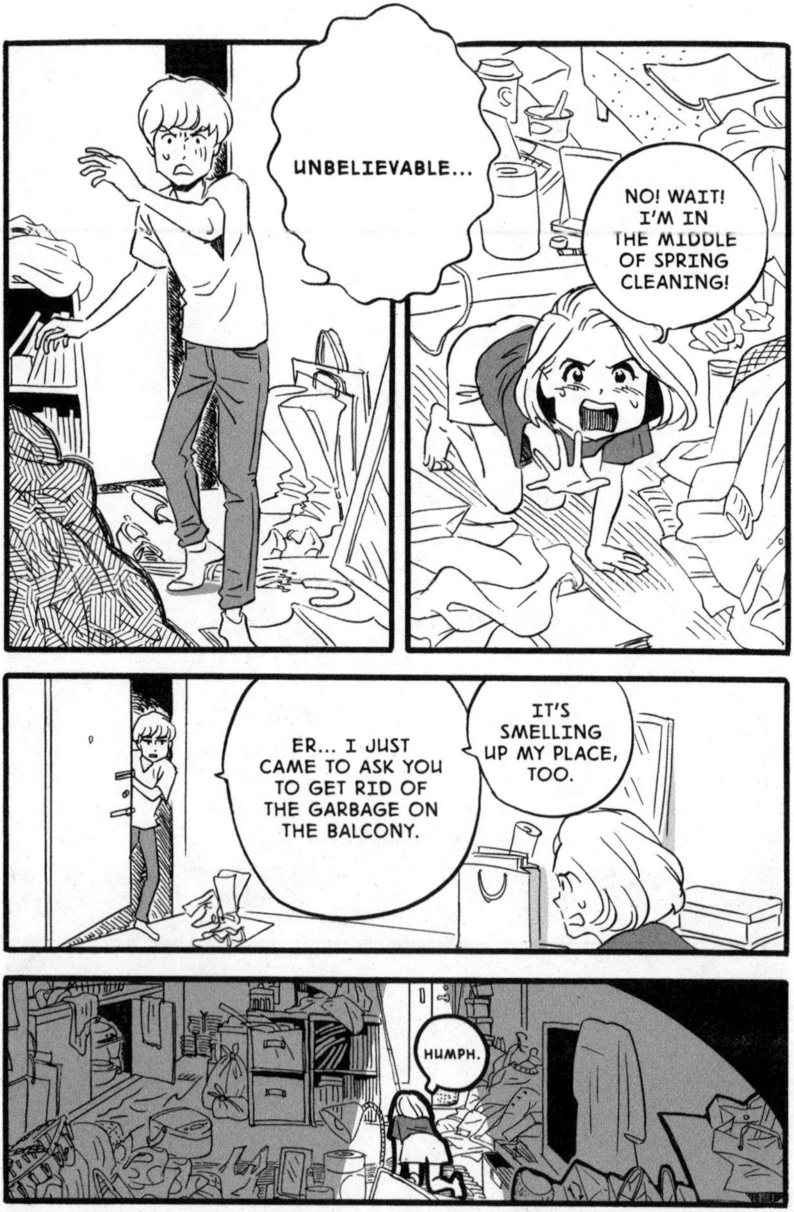
UNBELIEVABLE...
NO! WAIT! I'M IN THE MIDDLE OF SPRING CLEANING!
ER... I JUST CAME TO ASK YOU TO GET RID OF THE GARBAGE ON THE BALCONY.
IT'S SMELLING UP MY PLACE, TOO.
HUMPH.

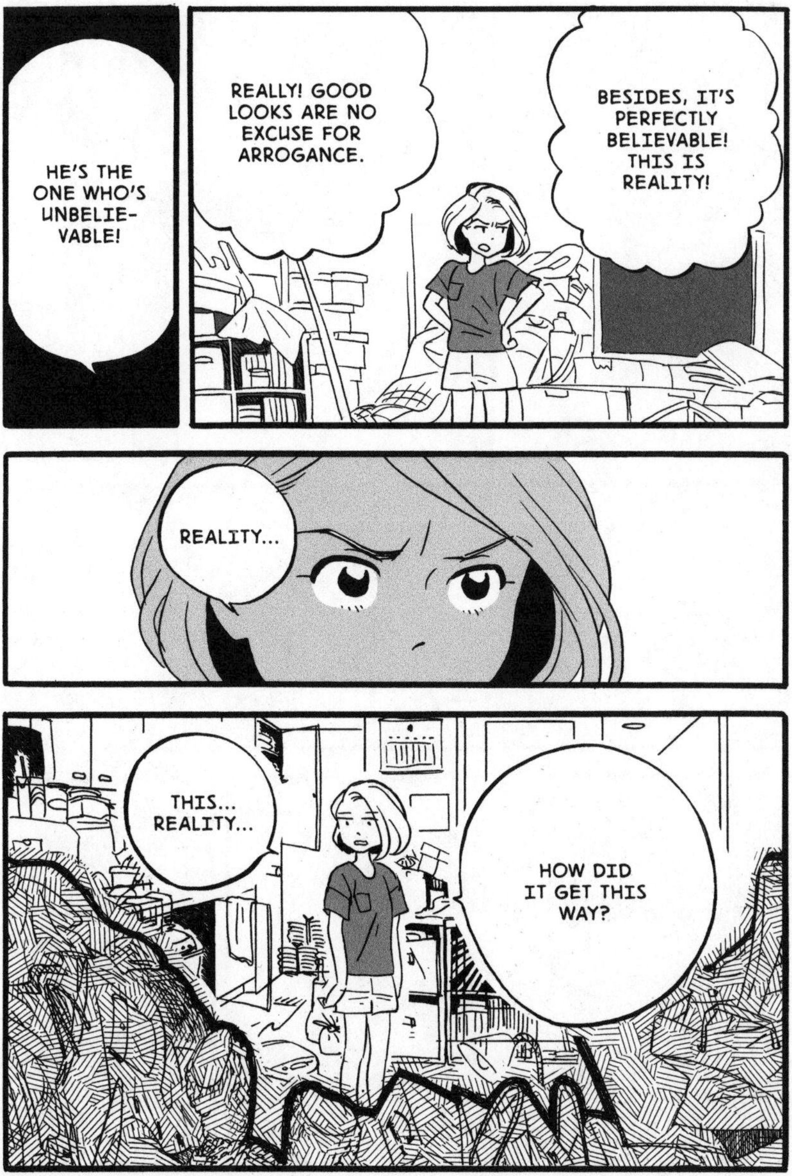
HE'S THE ONE WHO'S UNBELIE-VABLE!
REALLY! GOOD LOOKS ARE NO EXCUSE FOR ARROGANCE.
BESIDES, IT'S PERFECTLY BELIEVABLE! THIS IS REALITY!
REALITY...
THIS... REALITY...
HOW DID IT GET THIS WAY?

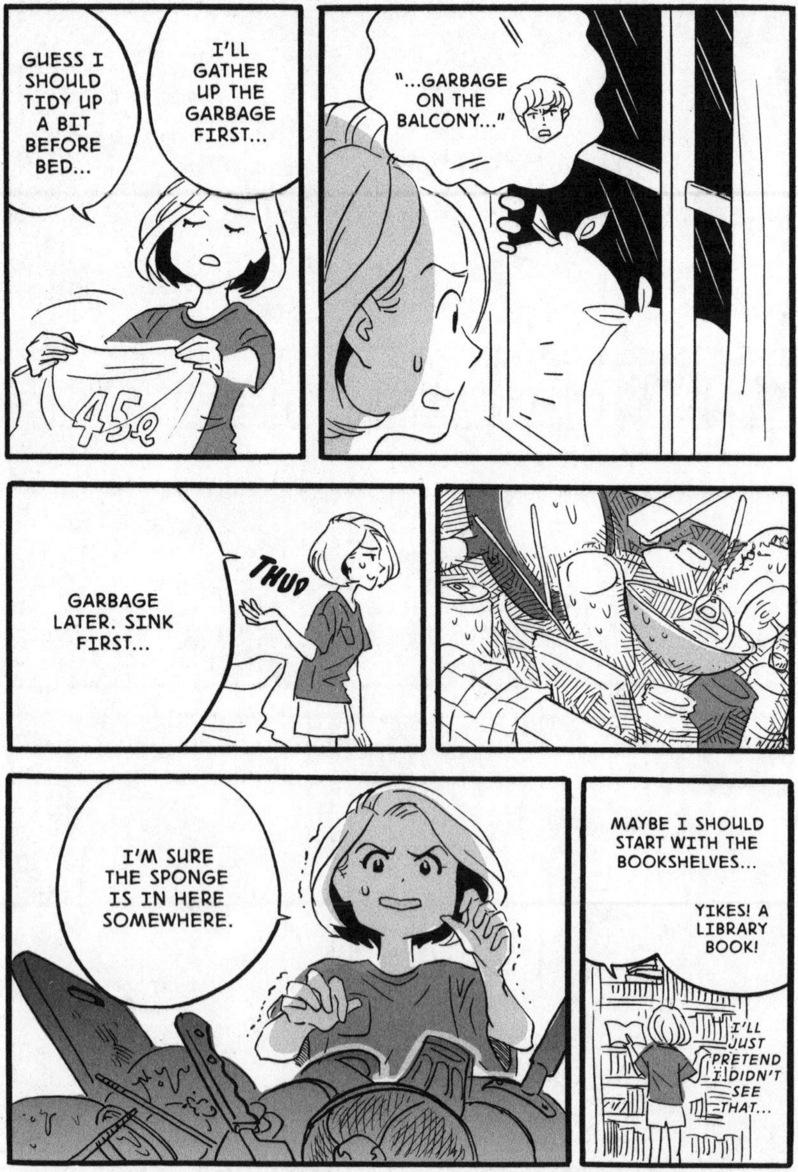
GUESS I SHOULD TIDY UP A BIT BEFORE BED...
I'LL GATHER UP THE GARBAGE FIRST...
45ℓ
"...GARBAGE ON THE BALCONY..."
GARBAGE LATER. SINK FIRST...
THUD
I'M SURE THE SPONGE IS IN HERE SOMEWHERE.
MAYBE I SHOULD START WITH THE BOOKSHELVES...
YIKES! A LIBRARY BOOK!
I'LL JUST PRETEND I DIDN'T SEE THAT...

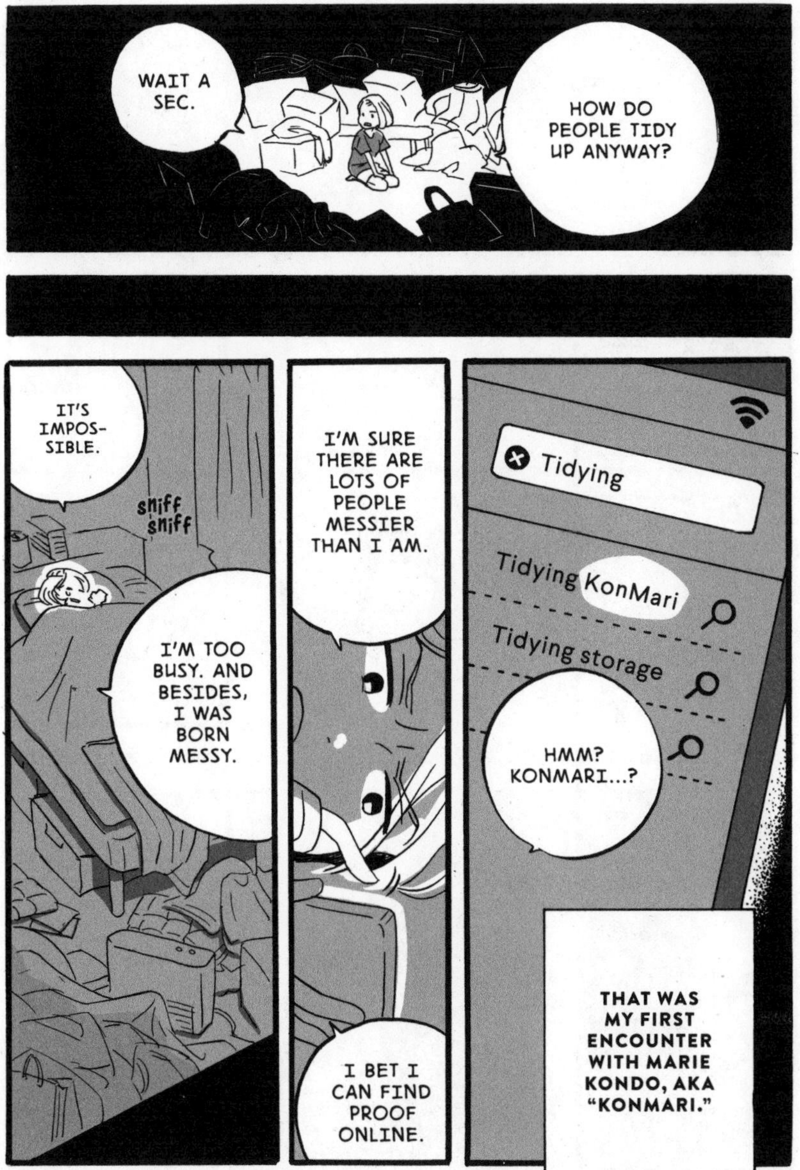
WAIT A SEC.
HOW DO PEOPLE TIDY UP ANYWAY?
IT'S IMPOS-SIBLE.
sniff sniff
I'M TOO BUSY. AND BESIDES, I WAS BORN MESSY.
I'M SURE THERE ARE LOTS OF PEOPLE MESSIER THAN I AM.
I BET I CAN FIND PROOF ONLINE.
Tidying
Tidying KonMari
Tidying storage
HMM? KONMARI...?
THAT WAS MY FIRST ENCOUNTER WITH MARIE KONDO, AKA "KONMARI."

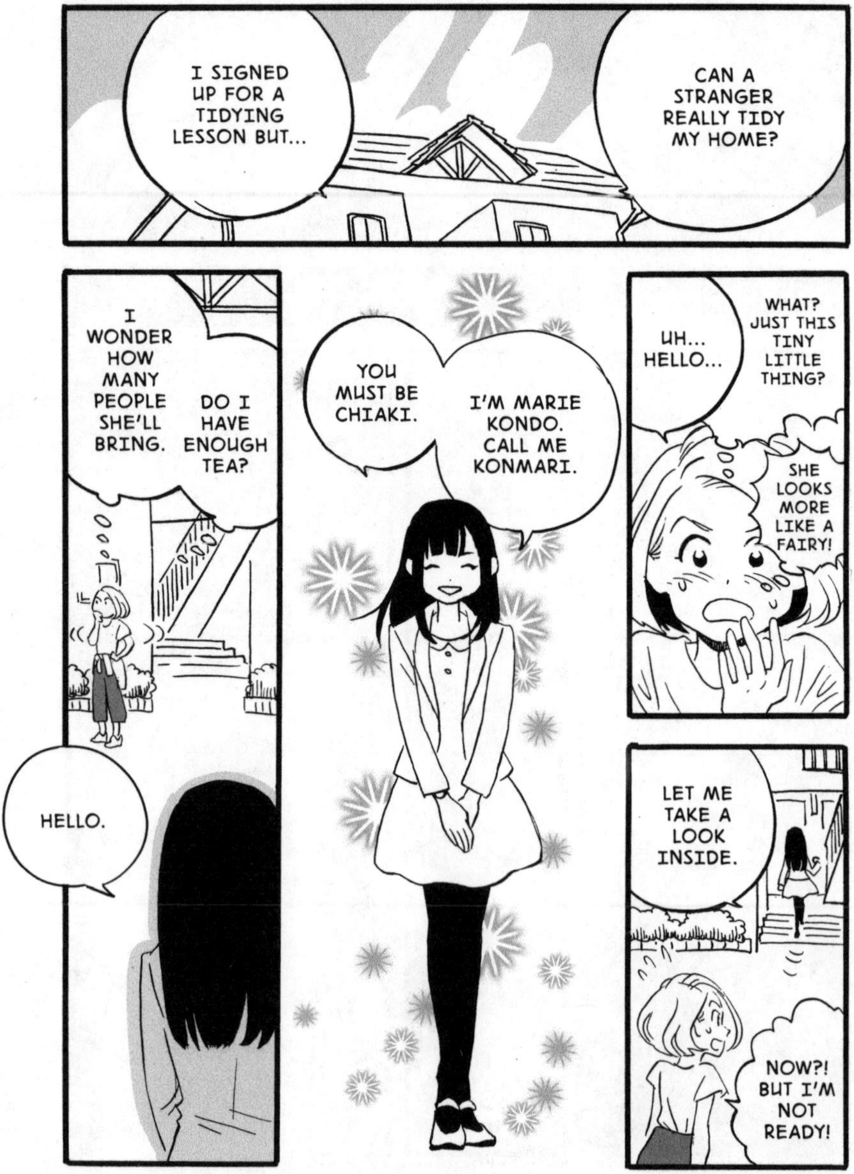
I SIGNED UP FOR A TIDYING LESSON BUT...
CAN A STRANGER REALLY TIDY MY HOME?
I WONDER HOW MANY PEOPLE SHE'LL BRING.
DO I HAVE ENOUGH TEA?
HELLO.
YOU MUST BE CHIAKI.
I'M MARIE KONDO. CALL ME KONMARI.
UH... HELLO...
WHAT? JUST THIS TINY LITTLE THING?
SHE LOOKS MORE LIKE A FAIRY!
LET ME TAKE A LOOK INSIDE.
NOW?! BUT I'M NOT READY!

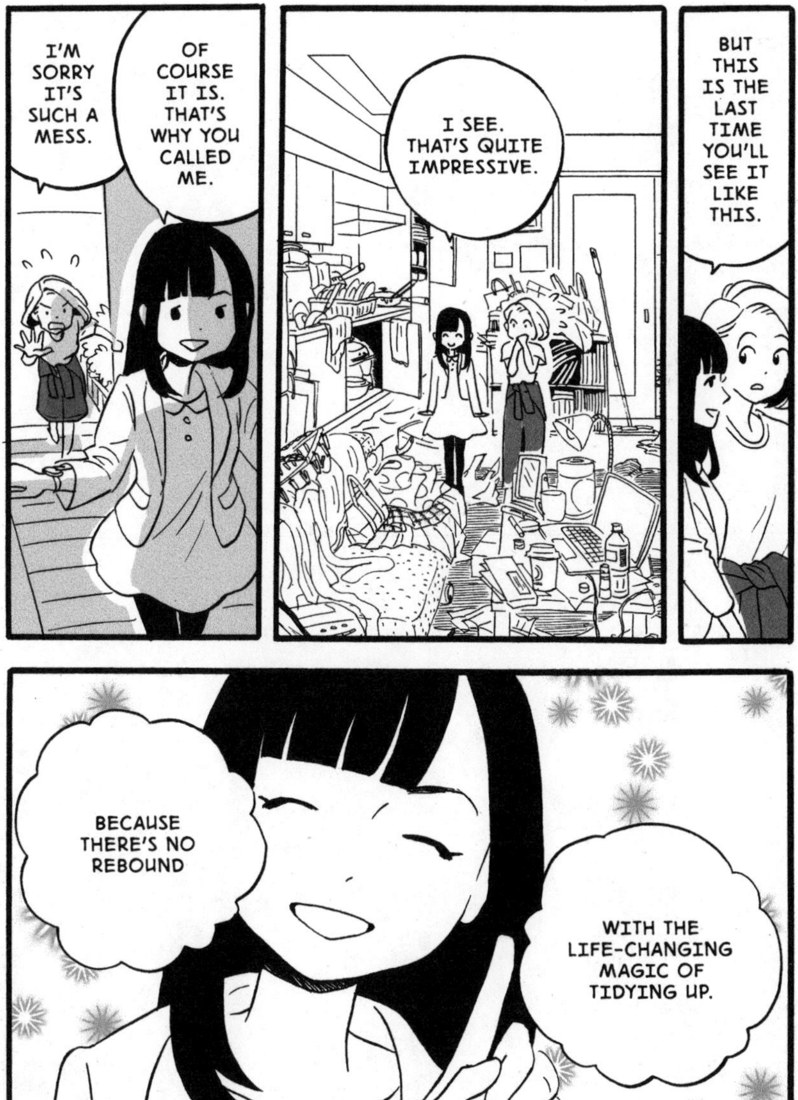
I'M SORRY IT'S SUCH A MESS.
OF COURSE IT IS. THAT'S WHY YOU CALLED ME.
I SEE. THAT'S QUITE IMPRESSIVE.
BUT THIS IS THE LAST TIME YOU'LL SEE IT LIKE THIS.
BECAUSE THERE'S NO REBOUND
WITH THE LIFE-CHANGING MAGIC OF TIDYING UP.

Think you can't do it? If so, you're
wrong. Everyone can learn how to
tidy up.

———

Success in tidying depends
90 percent on your mind-set. Of
course, know-how is important,
too, but the chances of a rebound
are higher if you only learn the
"how-to's" of tidying.

The approach that you are about
to start is not simply about
decluttering your home or making
it look neat when visitors drop in.
Instead, it will change your whole
life and fill it with joy.

Start by believing with all your heart
that you can and will be tidy.

2

visualize
your ideal
lifestyle

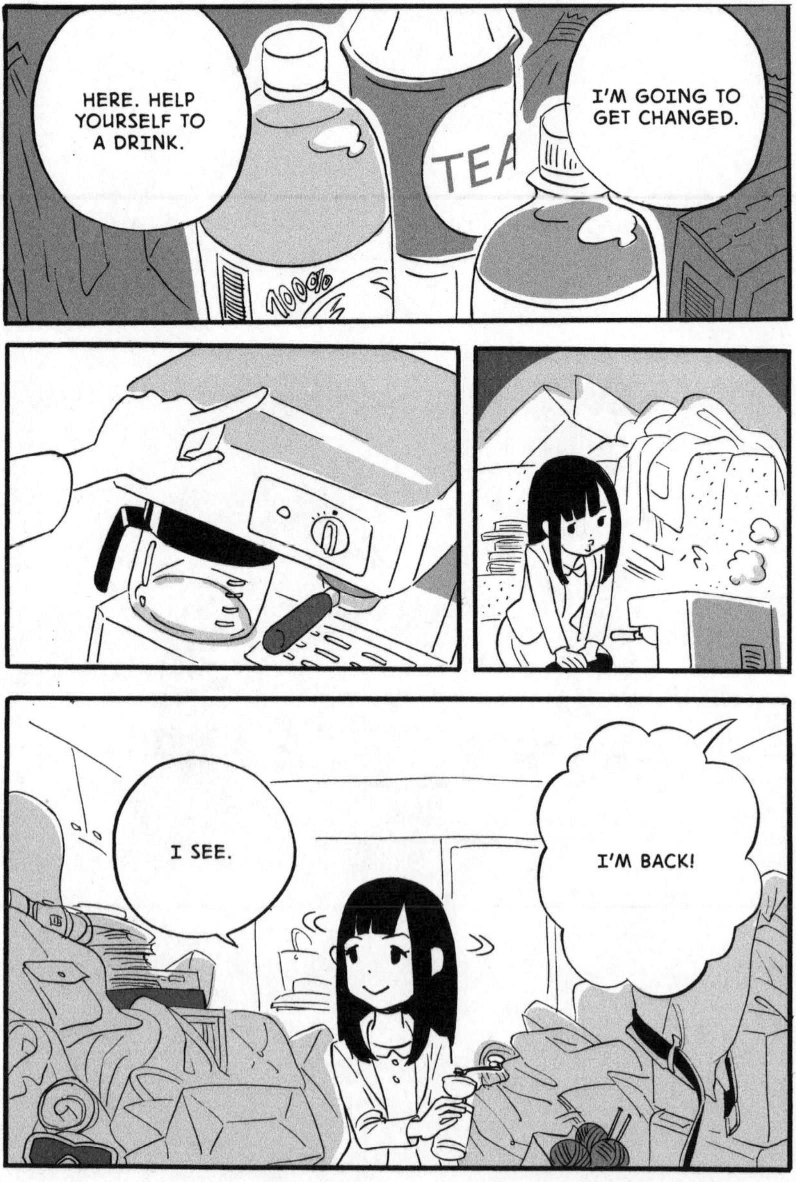
HERE. HELP YOURSELF TO A DRINK.
I'M GOING TO GET CHANGED.
TEA
100%
I SEE.
I'M BACK!

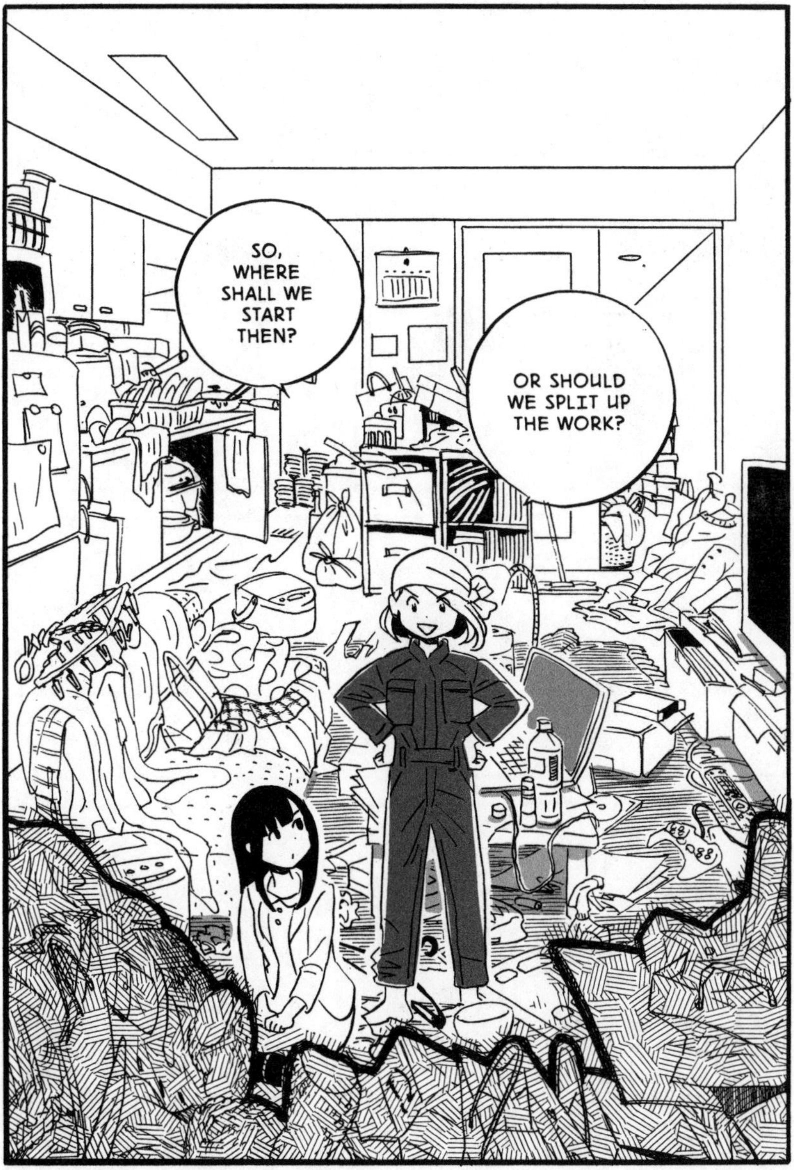
SO, WHERE SHALL WE START THEN?
OR SHOULD WE SPLIT UP THE WORK?

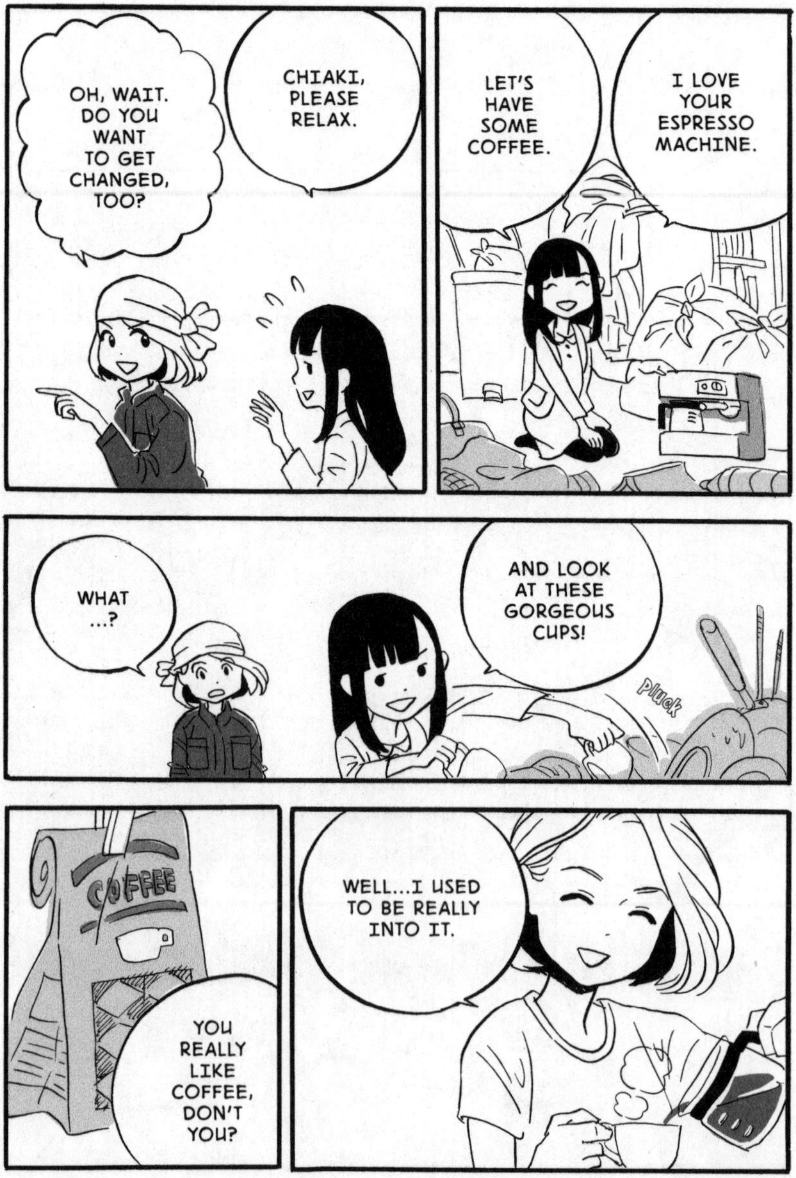
OH, WAIT. DO YOU WANT TO GET CHANGED, TOO?
CHIAKI, PLEASE RELAX.
LET'S HAVE SOME COFFEE.
I LOVE YOUR ESPRESSO MACHINE.
WHAT ...?
AND LOOK AT THESE GORGEOUS CUPS!
Pluck
COFFEE
YOU REALLY LIKE COFFEE, DON'T YOU?
WELL...I USED TO BE REALLY INTO IT.

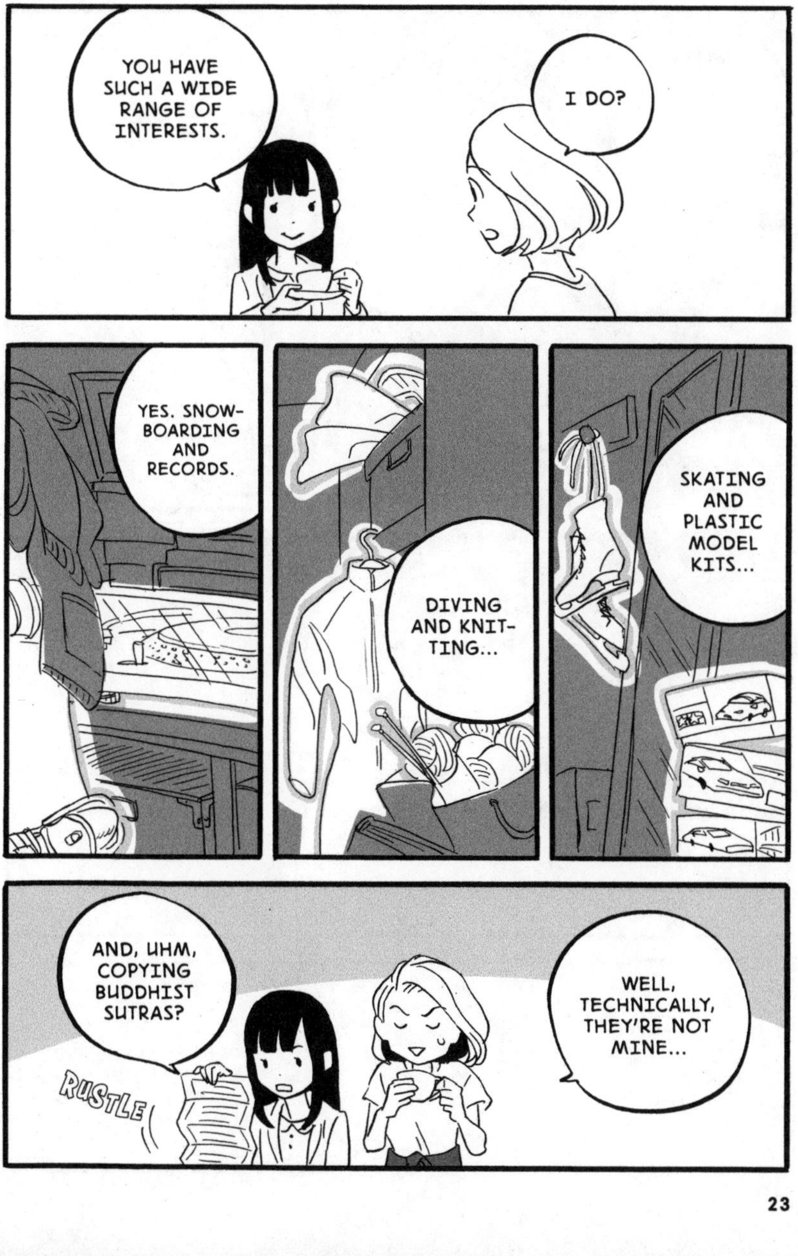
YOU HAVE SUCH A WIDE RANGE OF INTERESTS.
I DO?
YES. SNOW-BOARDING AND RECORDS.
DIVING AND KNIT-TING...
SKATING AND PLASTIC MODEL KITS...
AND, UHM, COPYING BUDDHIST SUTRAS?
RUSTLE
WELL, TECHNICALLY, THEY'RE NOT MINE...

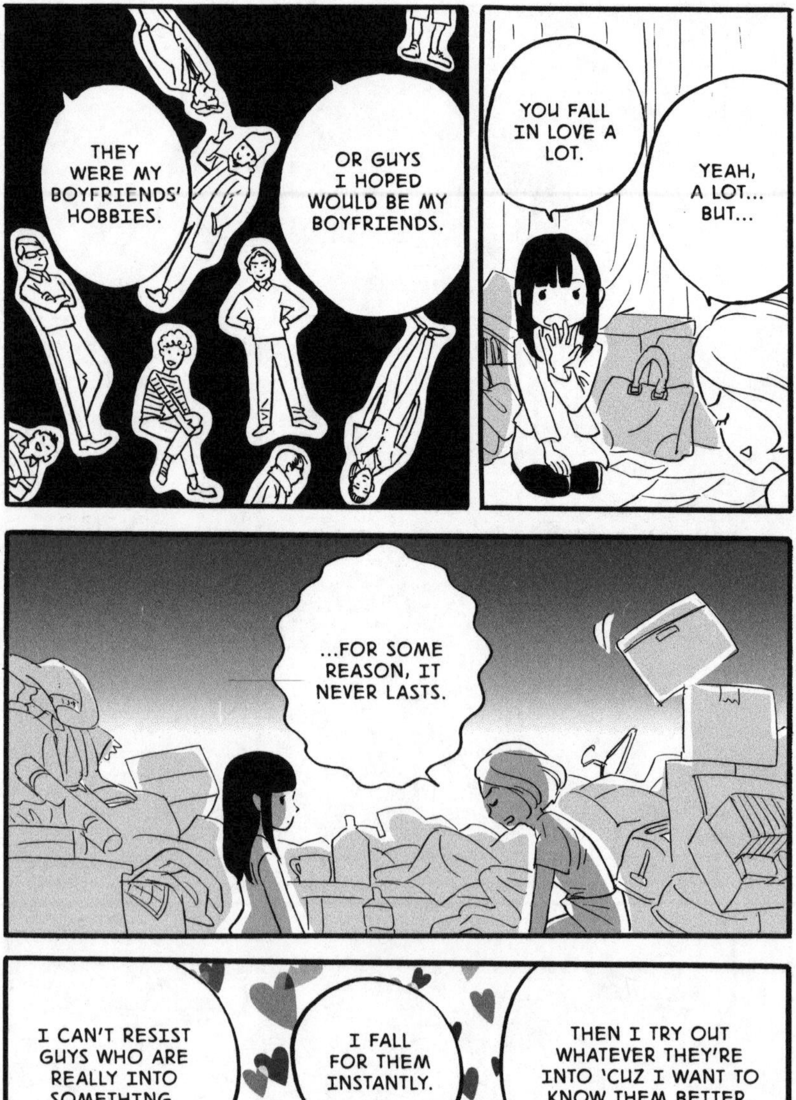
THEY WERE MY BOYFRIENDS' HOBBIES.
OR GUYS I HOPED WOULD BE MY BOYFRIENDS.
YOU FALL IN LOVE A LOT.
YEAH, A LOT... BUT...
...FOR SOME REASON, IT NEVER LASTS.
I CAN'T RESIST GUYS WHO ARE REALLY INTO SOMETHING.
I FALL FOR THEM INSTANTLY.
THEN I TRY OUT WHATEVER THEY'RE INTO 'CUZ I WANT TO KNOW THEM BETTER.

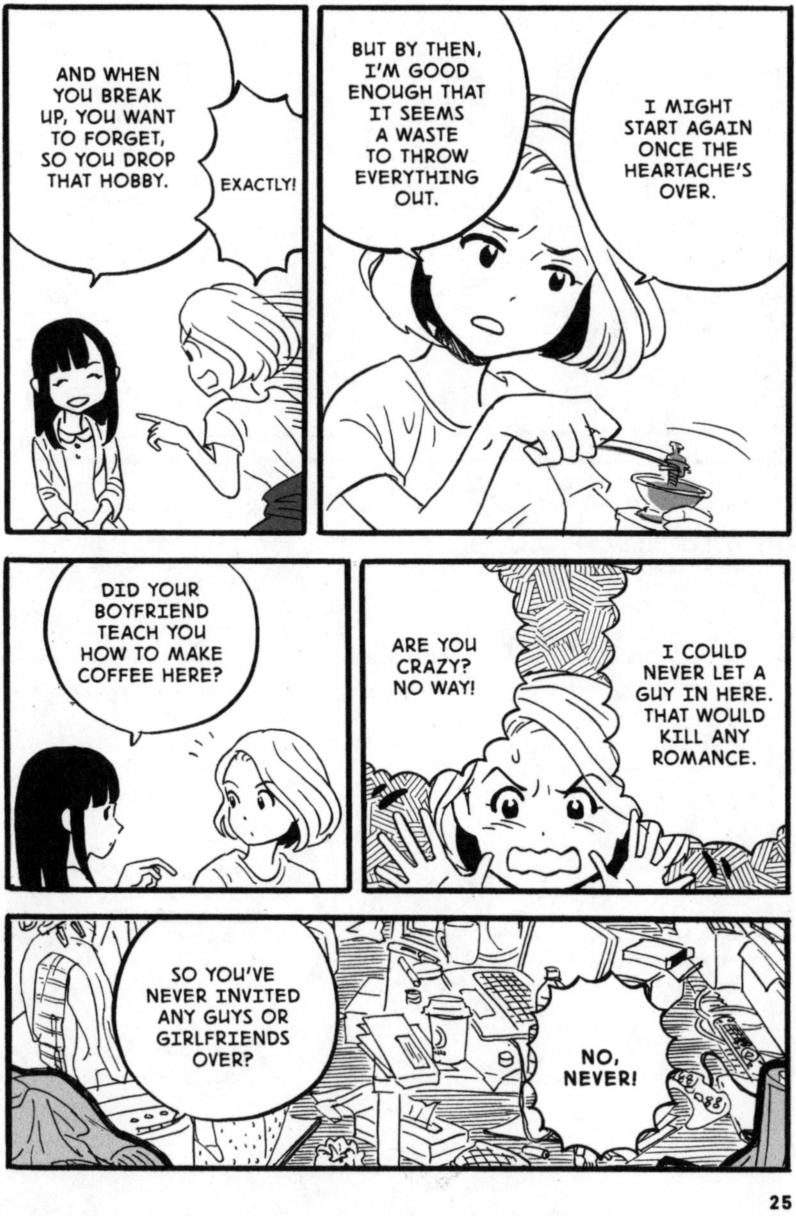
AND WHEN YOU BREAK UP, YOU WANT TO FORGET, SO YOU DROP THAT HOBBY.
EXACTLY!
BUT BY THEN, I'M GOOD ENOUGH THAT IT SEEMS A WASTE TO THROW EVERYTHING OUT.
I MIGHT START AGAIN ONCE THE HEARTACHE'S OVER.
DID YOUR BOYFRIEND TEACH YOU HOW TO MAKE COFFEE HERE?
ARE YOU CRAZY? NO WAY!
I COULD NEVER LET A GUY IN HERE. THAT WOULD KILL ANY ROMANCE.
SO YOU'VE NEVER INVITED ANY GUYS OR GIRLFRIENDS OVER?
NO, NEVER!

THIS PLACE MAY BE A MESS

BUT WHEN I GO OUT, I TRY TO ACT LIKE I'VE GOT IT ALL TOGETHER.

YOU'RE IN SALES, RIGHT?

I WORK FOR A BEVERAGE COMPANY. I OFTEN WORK LATE, DOING RESEARCH OR MEETING CUSTOMERS.

YES!

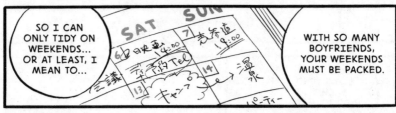

SO I CAN ONLY TIDY ON WEEKENDS... OR AT LEAST, I MEAN TO...

WITH SO MANY BOYFRIENDS, YOUR WEEKENDS MUST BE PACKED.

MAYBE I'M GREEDY TO WANT BOTH A CAREER AND A LOVE LIFE.

SIGH

26

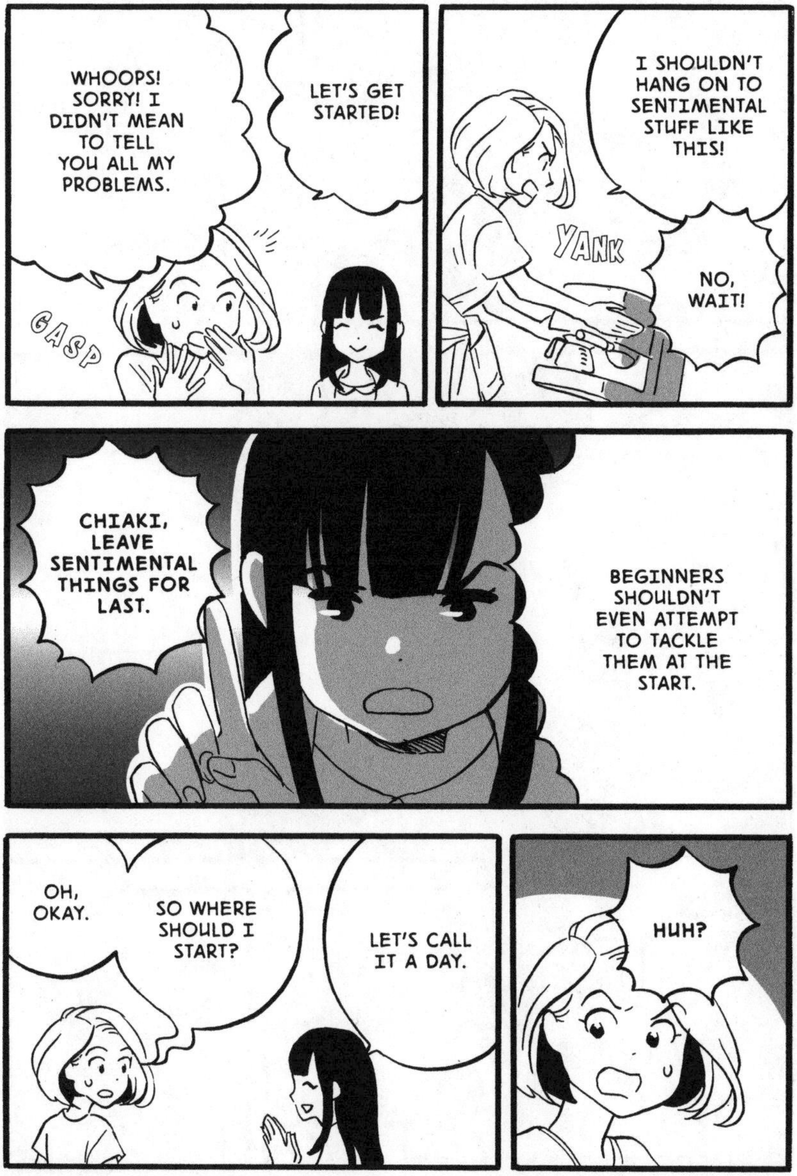
WHOOPS! SORRY! I DIDN'T MEAN TO TELL YOU ALL MY PROBLEMS.
LET'S GET STARTED!
GASP
I SHOULDN'T HANG ON TO SENTIMENTAL STUFF LIKE THIS!
YANK
NO, WAIT!
CHIAKI, LEAVE SENTIMENTAL THINGS FOR LAST.
BEGINNERS SHOULDN'T EVEN ATTEMPT TO TACKLE THEM AT THE START.
OH, OKAY.
SO WHERE SHOULD I START?
LET'S CALL IT A DAY.
HUH?

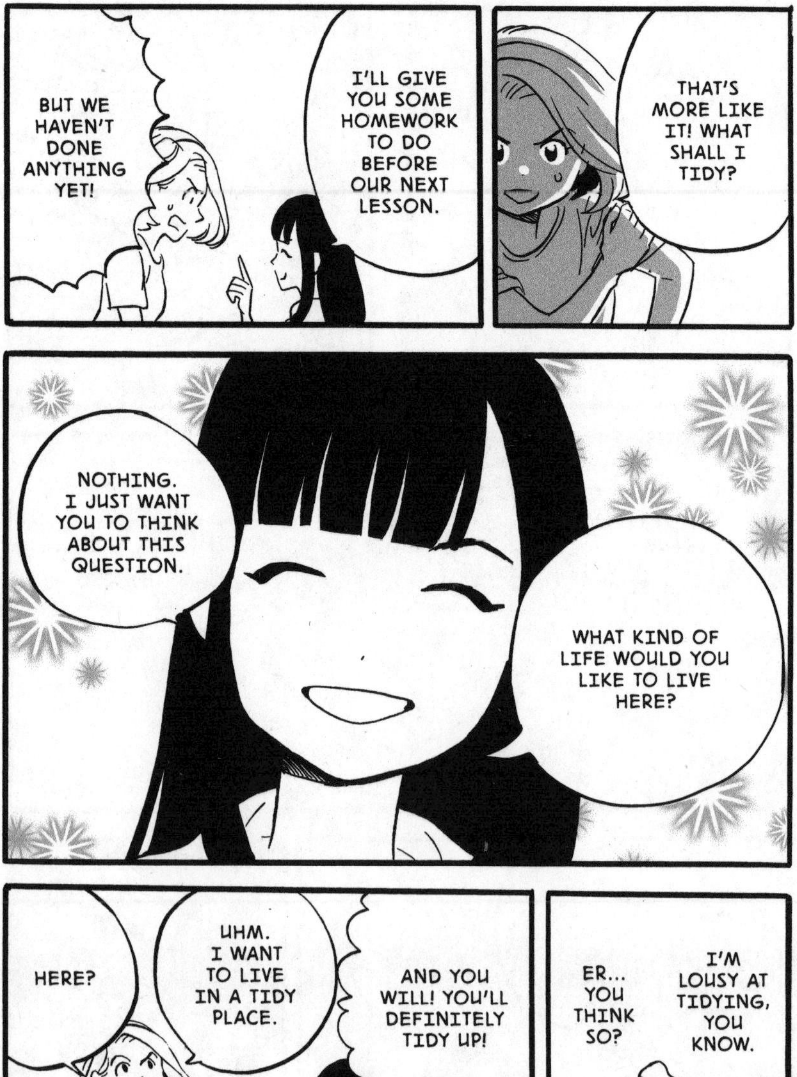
BUT WE HAVEN'T DONE ANYTHING YET!
I'LL GIVE YOU SOME HOMEWORK TO DO BEFORE OUR NEXT LESSON.
THAT'S MORE LIKE IT! WHAT SHALL I TIDY?
NOTHING. I JUST WANT YOU TO THINK ABOUT THIS QUESTION.
WHAT KIND OF LIFE WOULD YOU LIKE TO LIVE HERE?
HERE?
UHM. I WANT TO LIVE IN A TIDY PLACE.
AND YOU WILL! YOU'LL DEFINITELY TIDY UP!
ER... YOU THINK SO?
I'M LOUSY AT TIDYING, YOU KNOW.

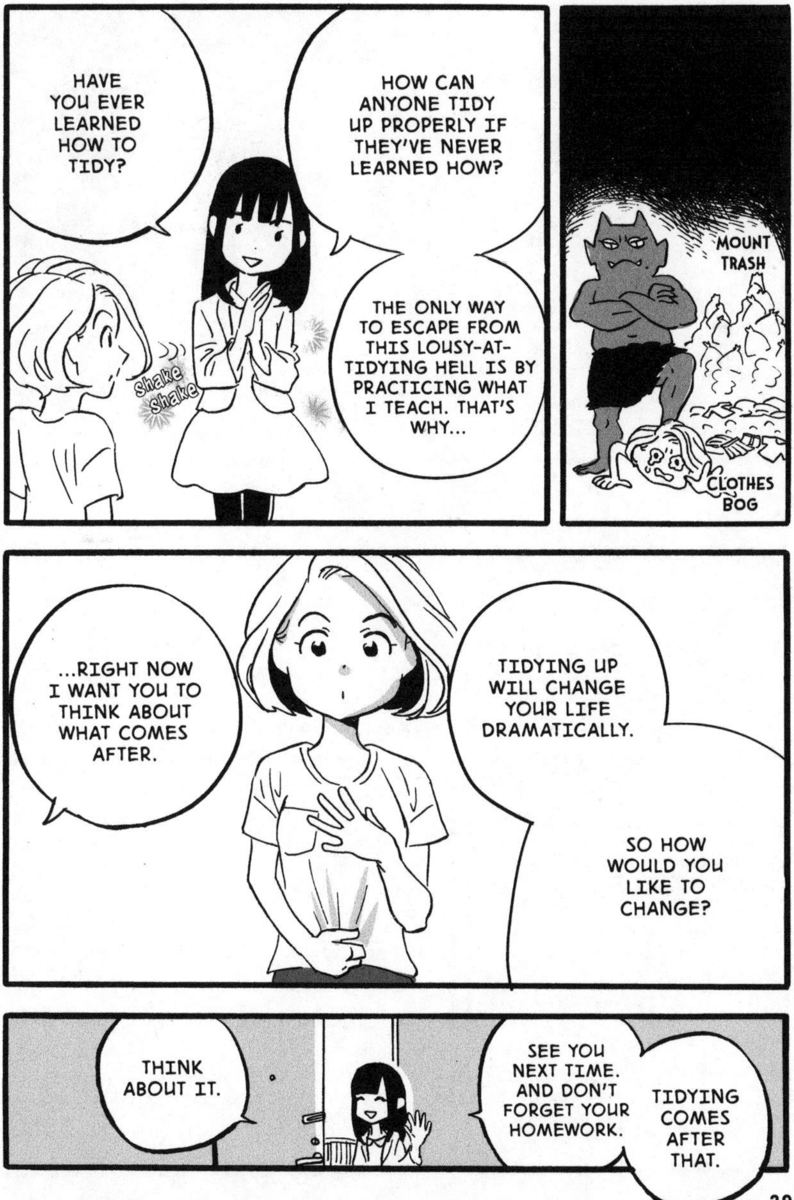
HAVE YOU EVER LEARNED HOW TO TIDY?
HOW CAN ANYONE TIDY UP PROPERLY IF THEY'VE NEVER LEARNED HOW?
Shake Shake
THE ONLY WAY TO ESCAPE FROM THIS LOUSY-AT-TIDYING HELL IS BY PRACTICING WHAT I TEACH. THAT'S WHY...
MOUNT TRASH
CLOTHES BOG
...RIGHT NOW I WANT YOU TO THINK ABOUT WHAT COMES AFTER.
TIDYING UP WILL CHANGE YOUR LIFE DRAMATICALLY.
SO HOW WOULD YOU LIKE TO CHANGE?
THINK ABOUT IT.
SEE YOU NEXT TIME. AND DON'T FORGET YOUR HOMEWORK.
TIDYING COMES AFTER THAT.

HMMMMM...
HOMEWORK, SHE SAYS...
OH.
OH.
JUST SO YOU KNOW, I THREW OUT THE GARBAGE.
MAYBE IT'S NONE OF MY BUSINESS, BUT WHY DON'T YOU TIDY UP—

NO NEED TO TELL ME THAT! I HAD MY FIRST TIDYING LESSON TODAY!

HA!

TIDYING LESSON...?

NO, DON'T LOOK! I'VE ONLY JUST STARTED!

ACTUALLY...

I WAS EXPECTING THE TEACHER TO BE BIG AND BRAWNY, LIKE A PROFESSIONAL MOVER,

BUT SHE LOOKED MORE LIKE A LITTLE FAIRY.

TODAY WE JUST TALKED. I'M SUPPOSED TO THINK ABOUT MY IDEAL LIFESTYLE BY NEXT TIME.

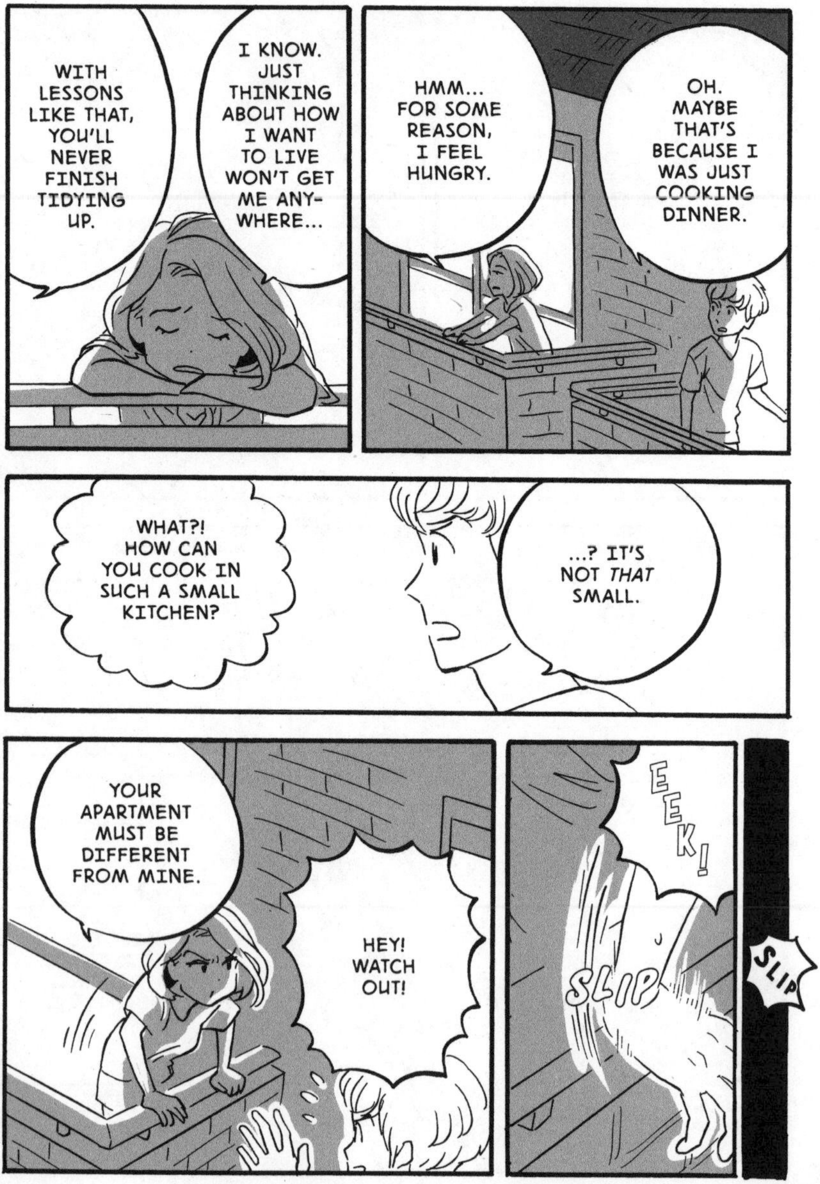
WITH LESSONS LIKE THAT, YOU'LL NEVER FINISH TIDYING UP.
I KNOW. JUST THINKING ABOUT HOW I WANT TO LIVE WON'T GET ME ANY-WHERE...
HMM... FOR SOME REASON, I FEEL HUNGRY.
OH. MAYBE THAT'S BECAUSE I WAS JUST COOKING DINNER.
WHAT?! HOW CAN YOU COOK IN SUCH A SMALL KITCHEN?
...? IT'S NOT *THAT* SMALL.
YOUR APARTMENT MUST BE DIFFERENT FROM MINE.
HEY! WATCH OUT!
EEK!
SLIP
SLIP

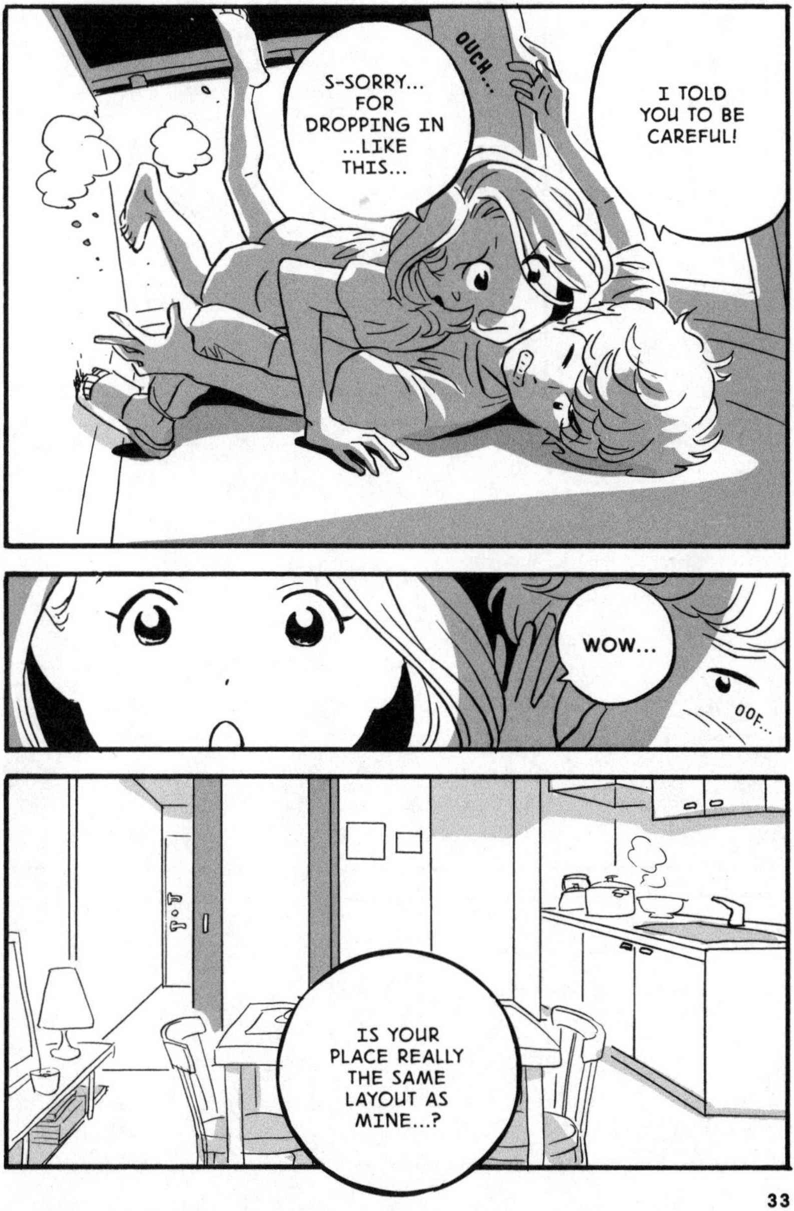
S-SORRY... FOR DROPPING IN ...LIKE THIS...
OUCH...
I TOLD YOU TO BE CAREFUL!
WOW...
OOF...
IS YOUR PLACE REALLY THE SAME LAYOUT AS MINE...?

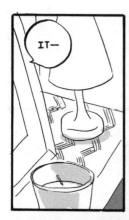

IT—

IT LOOKS LIKE A LOVELY CAFÉ.

EVEN THE FOOD LOOKS GOOD!

WHAT THE HECK ARE YOU!?

WELL, ACTUALLY, I WORK IN THE KITCHEN AT A CAFÉ.

LUCKY YOU...

I EAT ONIGIRI IN THE COMPANY CAR

AND BUY A PACKED LUNCH FROM THE CONVENIENCE STORE ON MY WAY HOME.

I WISH I COULD EAT A PROPER MEAL AT HOME LIKE YOU.

THAT SOUNDS ROUGH...

SNICKER

BUT YOU'VE GOT SUCH AN IDEAL PLACE...

GASP!

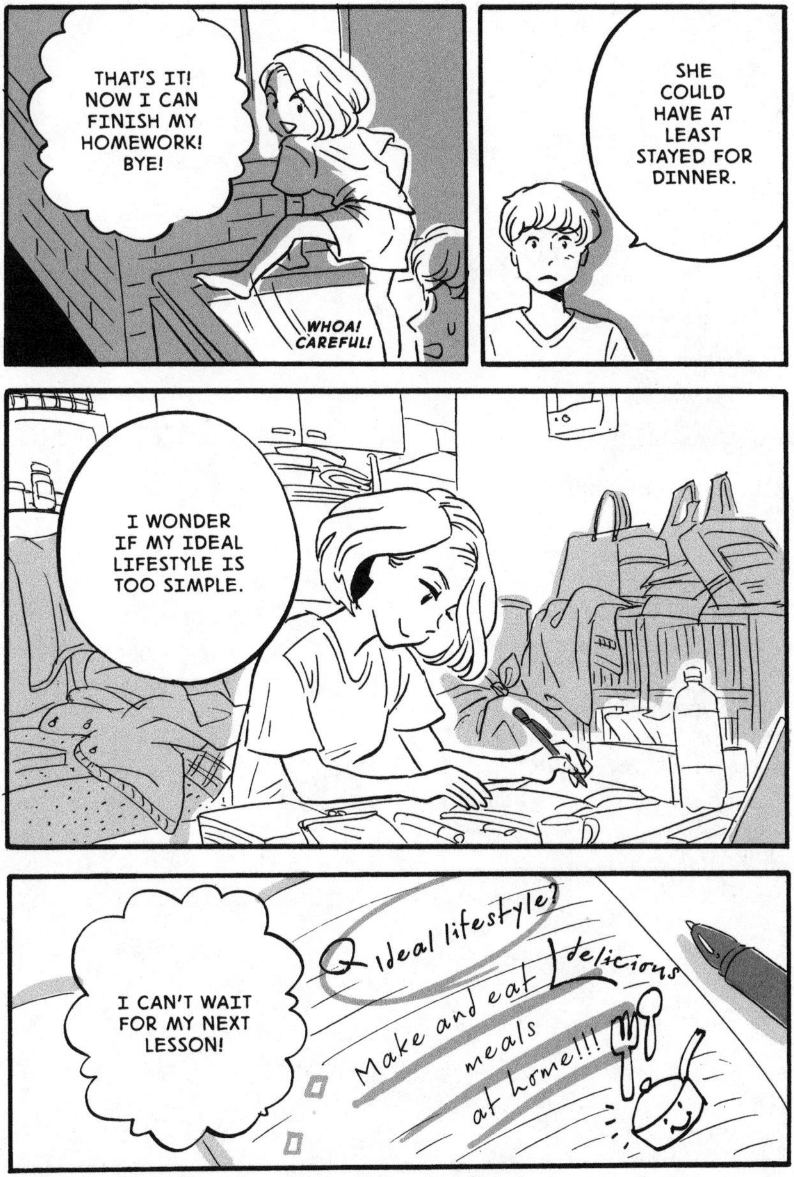
THAT'S IT! NOW I CAN FINISH MY HOMEWORK! BYE!
WHOA! CAREFUL!
SHE COULD HAVE AT LEAST STAYED FOR DINNER.
I WONDER IF MY IDEAL LIFESTYLE IS TOO SIMPLE.
I CAN'T WAIT FOR MY NEXT LESSON!
Q Ideal lifestyle?
Make and eat delicious meals at home!!!

It all starts with visualizing your ideal lifestyle.

———

Start by thinking about how you really want to live. What kind of house would you like and what kind of life would you like to lead in it?

If you feel artistic, draw a picture. If you like writing, jot down your thoughts on paper. I also recommend cutting out photos of homes you like from interior decorating magazines.

By thinking about your ideal lifestyle, you will begin identifying why you really want to tidy and the kind of life you want once you have finished. That is how life-changing tidying can be.

finish
discarding
first

3

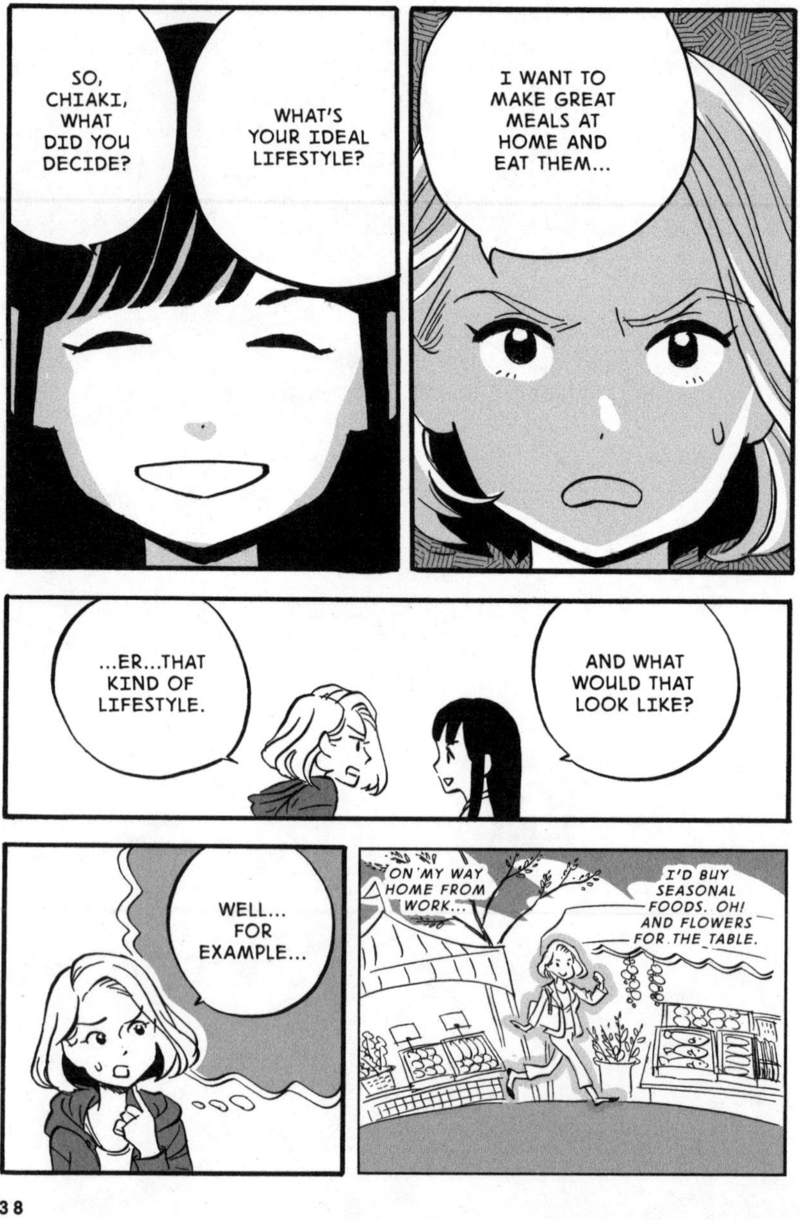
SO, CHIAKI, WHAT DID YOU DECIDE?
WHAT'S YOUR IDEAL LIFESTYLE?
I WANT TO MAKE GREAT MEALS AT HOME AND EAT THEM...
...ER...THAT KIND OF LIFESTYLE.
AND WHAT WOULD THAT LOOK LIKE?
WELL... FOR EXAMPLE...
ON MY WAY HOME FROM WORK...
I'D BUY SEASONAL FOODS. OH! AND FLOWERS FOR THE TABLE.

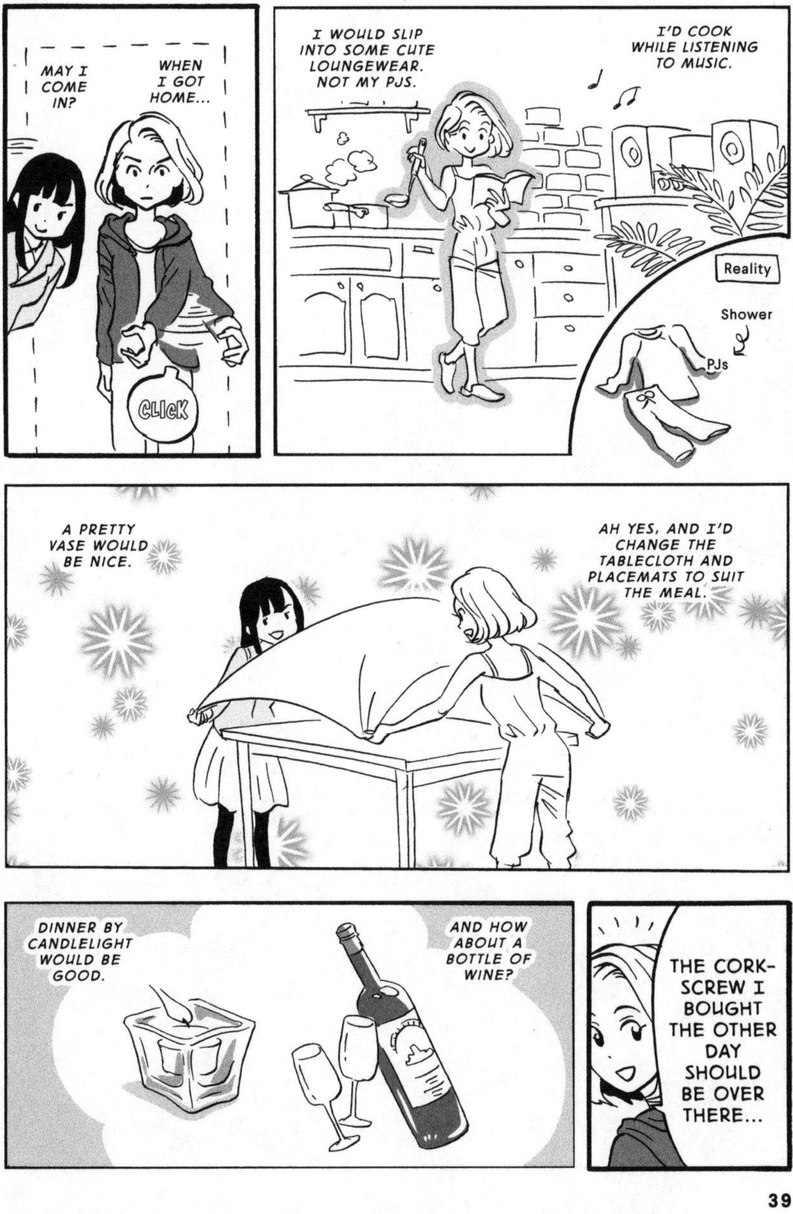
MAY I COME IN?
WHEN I GOT HOME...
CLICK
I WOULD SLIP INTO SOME CUTE LOUNGEWEAR. NOT MY PJS.
I'D COOK WHILE LISTENING TO MUSIC.
Reality
Shower
PJs
A PRETTY VASE WOULD BE NICE.
AH YES, AND I'D CHANGE THE TABLECLOTH AND PLACEMATS TO SUIT THE MEAL.
DINNER BY CANDLELIGHT WOULD BE GOOD.
AND HOW ABOUT A BOTTLE OF WINE?
THE CORK-SCREW I BOUGHT THE OTHER DAY SHOULD BE OVER THERE...

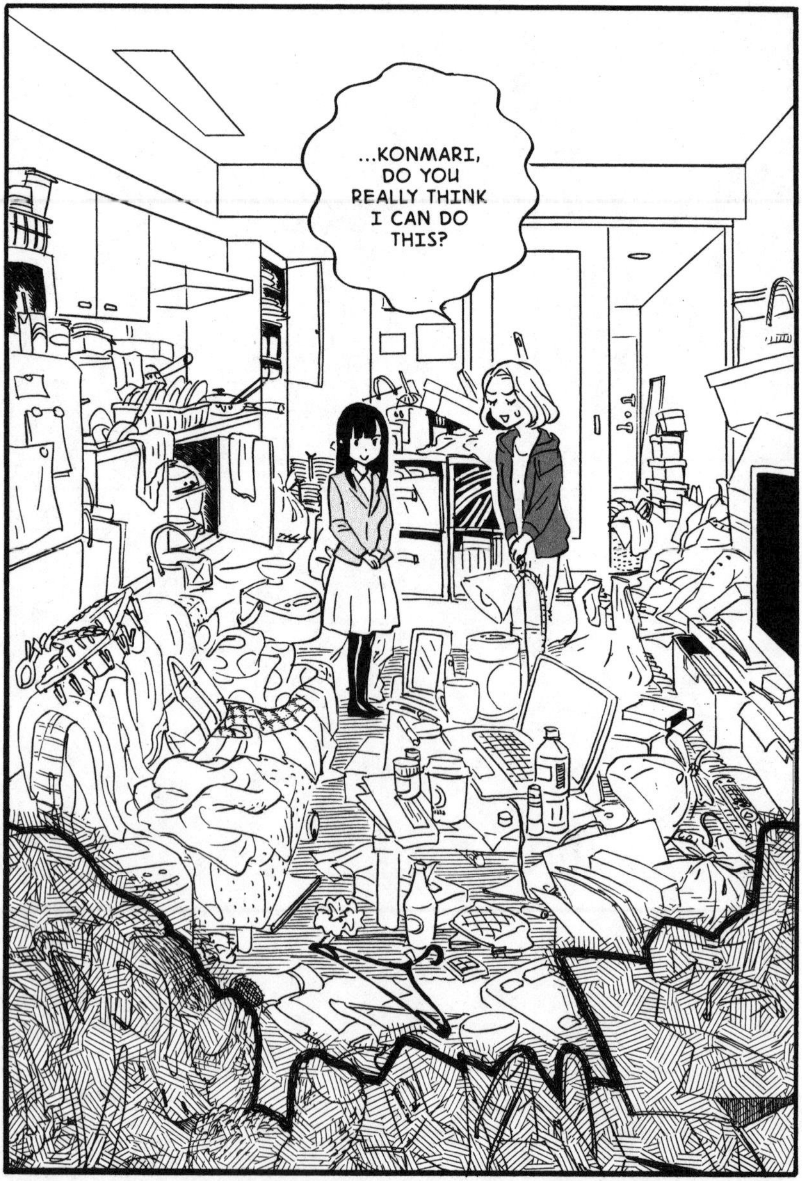
...KONMARI, DO YOU REALLY THINK I CAN DO THIS?

ABSOLUTELY!
ANYONE CAN DO IT, IF THEY LEARN HOW TO TIDY UP PROPERLY.
IF YOU SAY SO, IT MUST BE TRUE.
PHEW!
SO LET'S GET TO WORK!
WAIT!
I KNOW HOW YOU FEEL, BUT LET'S TAKE A LITTLE MORE TIME.
CHIAKI,
WHY
DO YOU WANT THAT KIND OF LIFESTYLE?
Ideal lifestyle?
Make and eat meals at home!!!
delicious
HUH?
"WHY"??
UHM... BECAUSE IT'S HEALTHY TO EAT PROPERLY...
WHY?

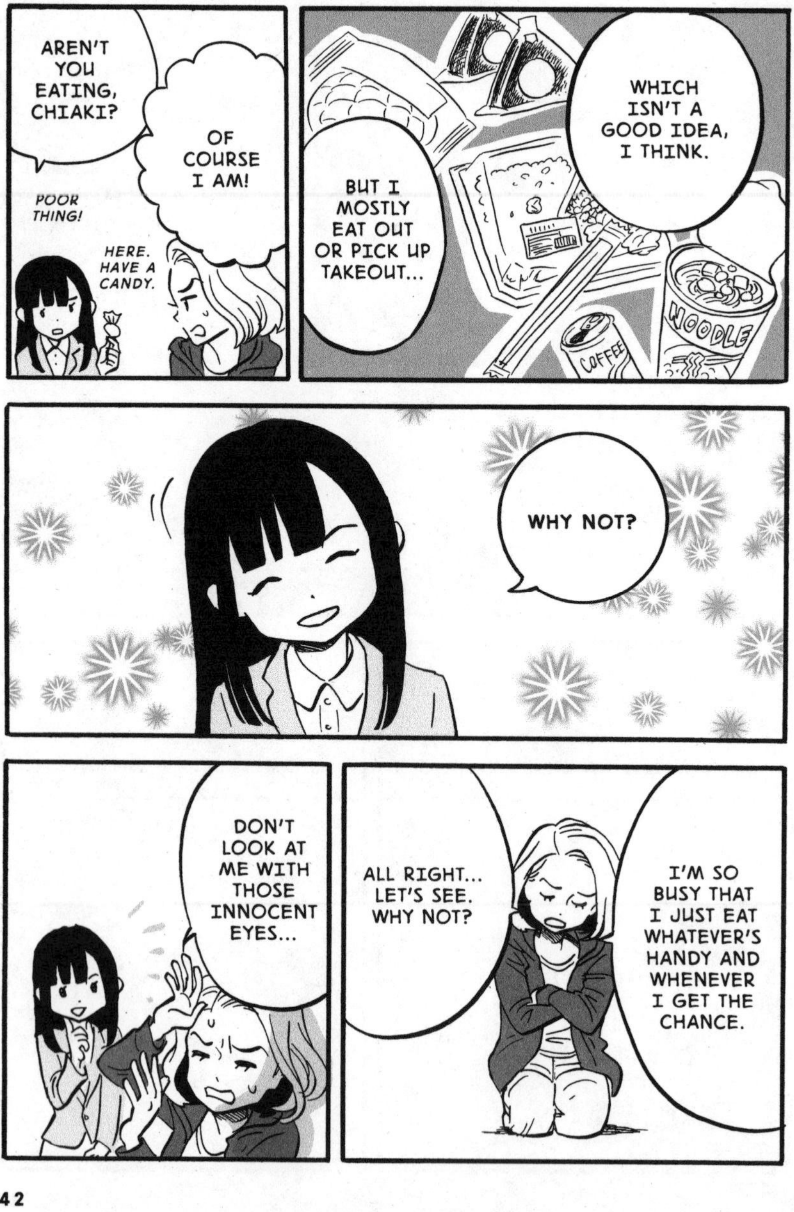
AREN'T YOU EATING, CHIAKI?
OF COURSE I AM!
POOR THING!
HERE. HAVE A CANDY.
BUT I MOSTLY EAT OUT OR PICK UP TAKEOUT...
WHICH ISN'T A GOOD IDEA, I THINK.
COFFEE
NOODLE
WHY NOT?
DON'T LOOK AT ME WITH THOSE INNOCENT EYES...
ALL RIGHT... LET'S SEE. WHY NOT?
I'M SO BUSY THAT I JUST EAT WHATEVER'S HANDY AND WHENEVER I GET THE CHANCE.

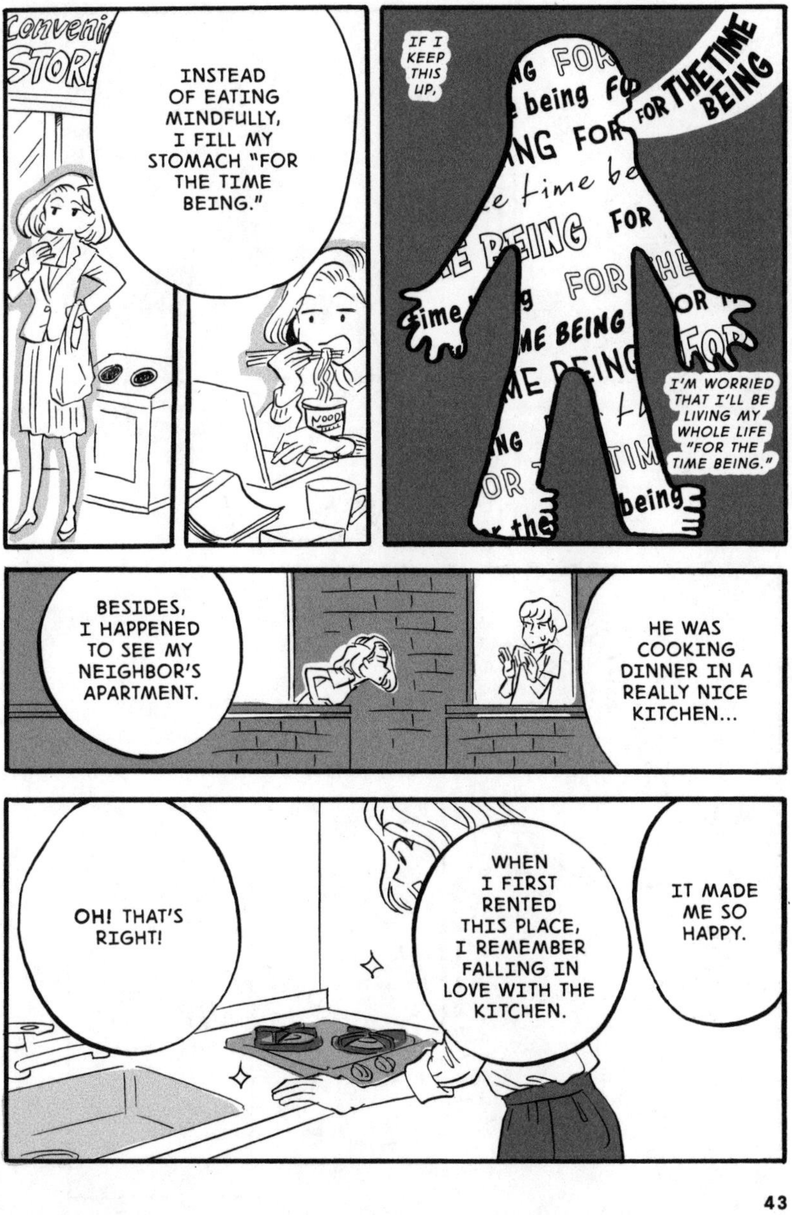
INSTEAD OF EATING MINDFULLY, I FILL MY STOMACH "FOR THE TIME BEING."
IF I KEEP THIS UP,
FOR THE TIME BEING
I'M WORRIED THAT I'LL BE LIVING MY WHOLE LIFE "FOR THE TIME BEING."
BESIDES, I HAPPENED TO SEE MY NEIGHBOR'S APARTMENT.
HE WAS COOKING DINNER IN A REALLY NICE KITCHEN...
OH! THAT'S RIGHT!
WHEN I FIRST RENTED THIS PLACE, I REMEMBER FALLING IN LOVE WITH THE KITCHEN.
IT MADE ME SO HAPPY.

UHM... KONMARI, DOES THIS HAVE ANYTHING TO DO WITH TIDYING?

OH YES!

FINDING OUT WHY YOU WANT TO TIDY UP IS A CRUCIAL STEP.

BY ASKING "WHY?" I CAN SEE CLEARLY WHAT HAPPINESS LOOKS LIKE FOR YOU.

WHAT HAPPINESS LOOKS LIKE FOR ME...

HAPPINESS... WHAT I LIKE... OH! I KNOW!

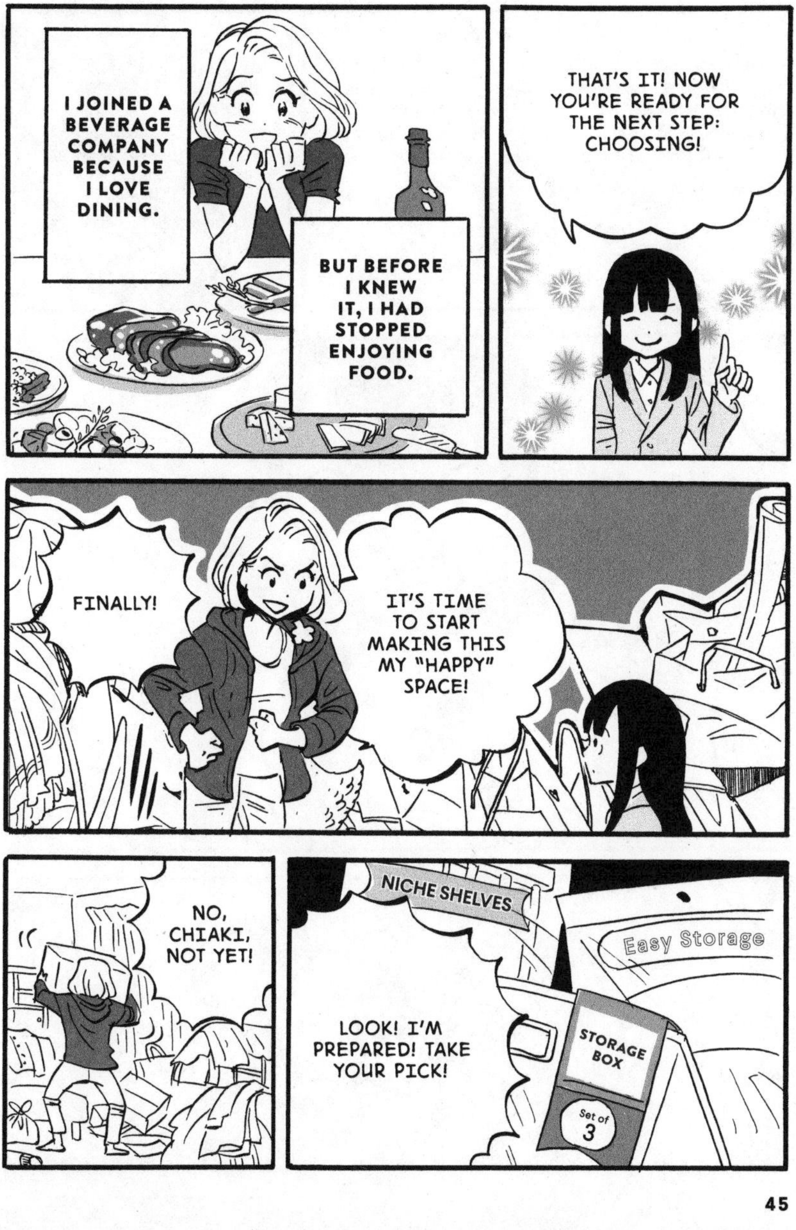
I JOINED A BEVERAGE COMPANY BECAUSE I LOVE DINING.
BUT BEFORE I KNEW IT, I HAD STOPPED ENJOYING FOOD.
THAT'S IT! NOW YOU'RE READY FOR THE NEXT STEP: CHOOSING!
FINALLY!
IT'S TIME TO START MAKING THIS MY "HAPPY" SPACE!
NO, CHIAKI, NOT YET!
NICHE SHELVES
Easy Storage
LOOK! I'M PREPARED! TAKE YOUR PICK!
STORAGE BOX
Set of 3

...SO THAT'S WHY YOU HAVE MORE THINGS THAN LAST TIME.
YOU BOUGHT THESE, DID YOU?
Easy Storage
STORAGE BOX
LET ME BE VERY CLEAR.
STORAGE IS NOT THE ANSWER TO CLUTTER!
YOU MUST BEGIN BY DISCARDING!
STORAGE! IT'S NOTHING BUT A COSMETIC SOLUTION!
UH... OKAY...

AND BY THE WAY, I SEE YOU BOUGHT TWO OF EACH CLEANING SUPPLY.

BUT I WON'T BE DOING ANY TIDYING. I JUST TEACH YOU HOW.

WHAT?!

I WAS KIND OF HOPING...

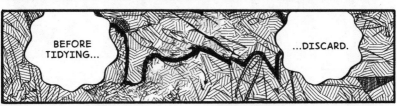

BEFORE TIDYING...

...DISCARD.

UHM, OKAY...BUT WHAT SHOULD I GET RID OF?

SIMPLE. WHATEVER DOESN'T SPARK JOY.

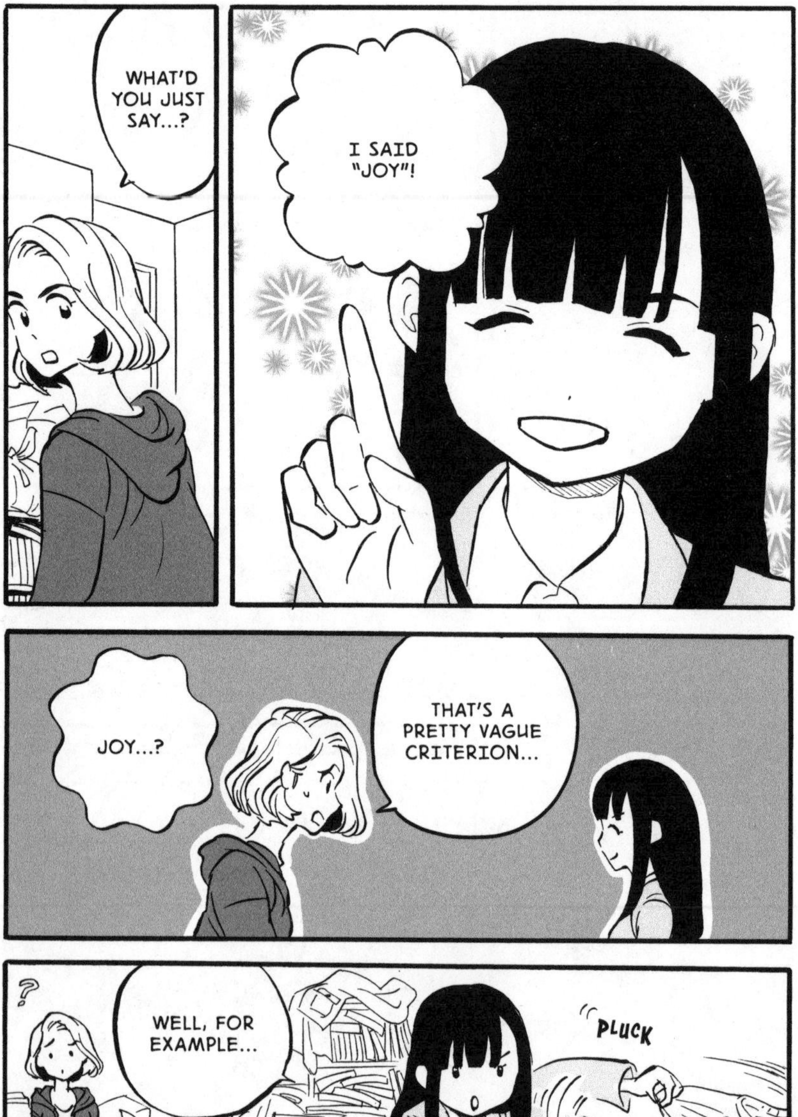
WHAT'D YOU JUST SAY...?
I SAID "JOY"!
JOY...?
THAT'S A PRETTY VAGUE CRITERION...
?
WELL, FOR EXAMPLE...
PLUCK
PLUCK

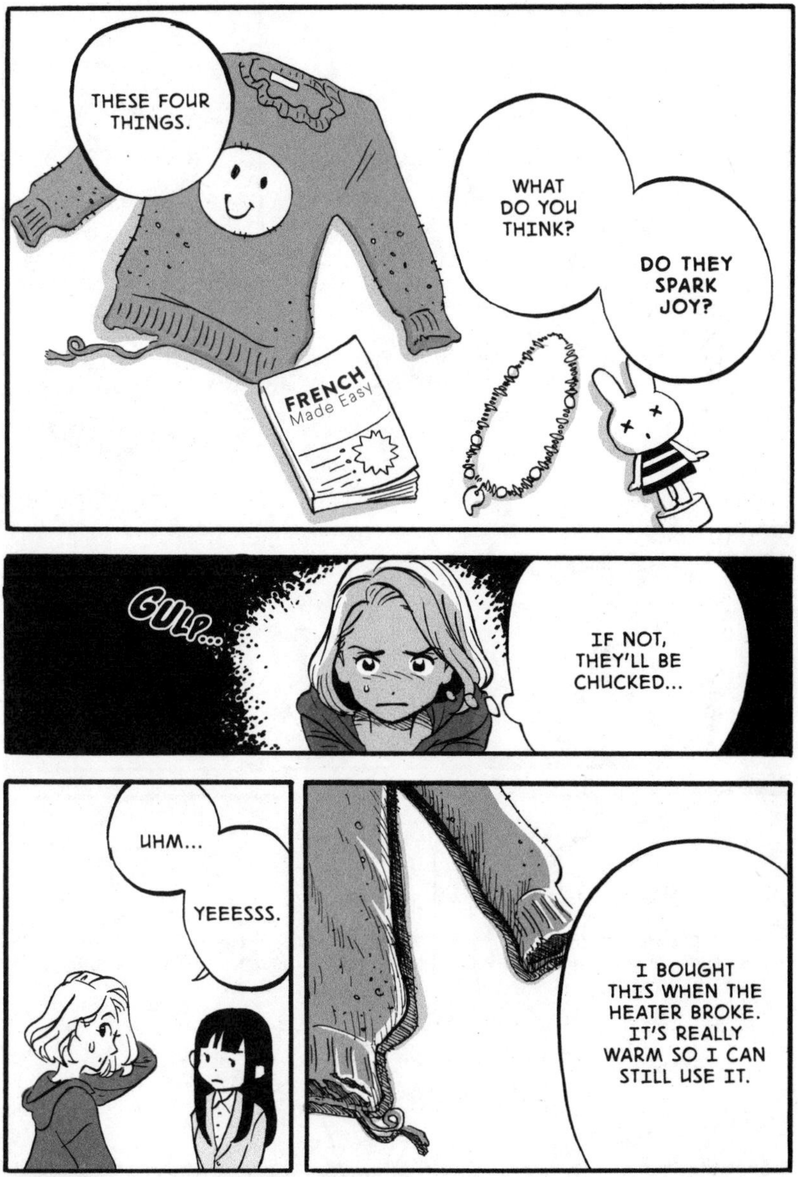
THESE FOUR THINGS.
WHAT DO YOU THINK?
DO THEY SPARK JOY?
FRENCH Made Easy
GULP...
IF NOT, THEY'LL BE CHUCKED...
UHM...
YEEESSS.
I BOUGHT THIS WHEN THE HEATER BROKE. IT'S REALLY WARM SO I CAN STILL USE IT.

I GOT THIS TO STUDY FRENCH.

ENCH
de Easy

AND MY UNCLE GAVE ME THIS NECKLACE.

THIS IS FROM A BAND I USED TO LOVE. I PAID A LOT FOR IT ONLINE.

I SEE.

BUT THAT'S

NOT QUITE THE SAME AS JOY.

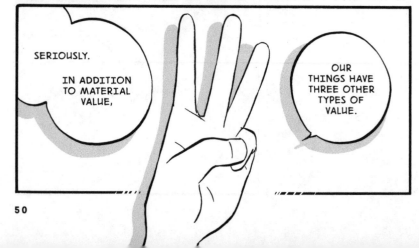

SERIOUSLY.

IN ADDITION TO MATERIAL VALUE,

OUR THINGS HAVE THREE OTHER TYPES OF VALUE.

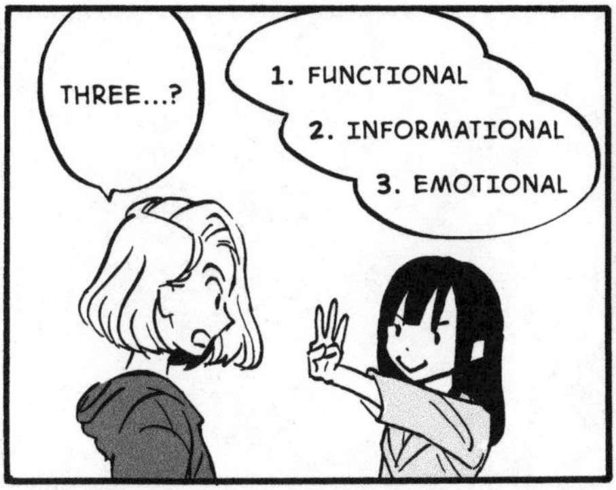
THREE...?
1. FUNCTIONAL
2. INFORMATIONAL
3. EMOTIONAL
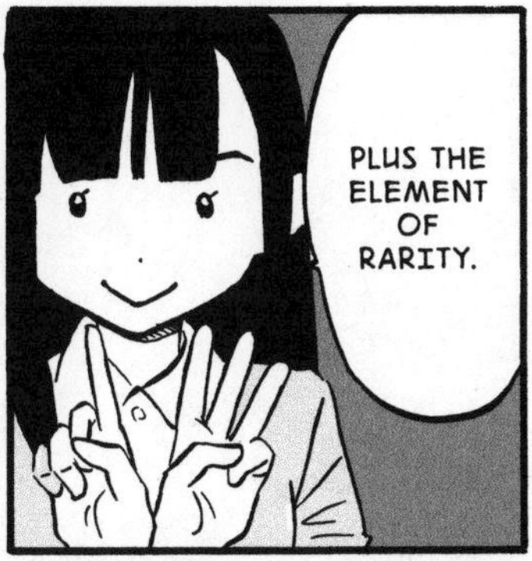
PLUS THE ELEMENT OF RARITY.
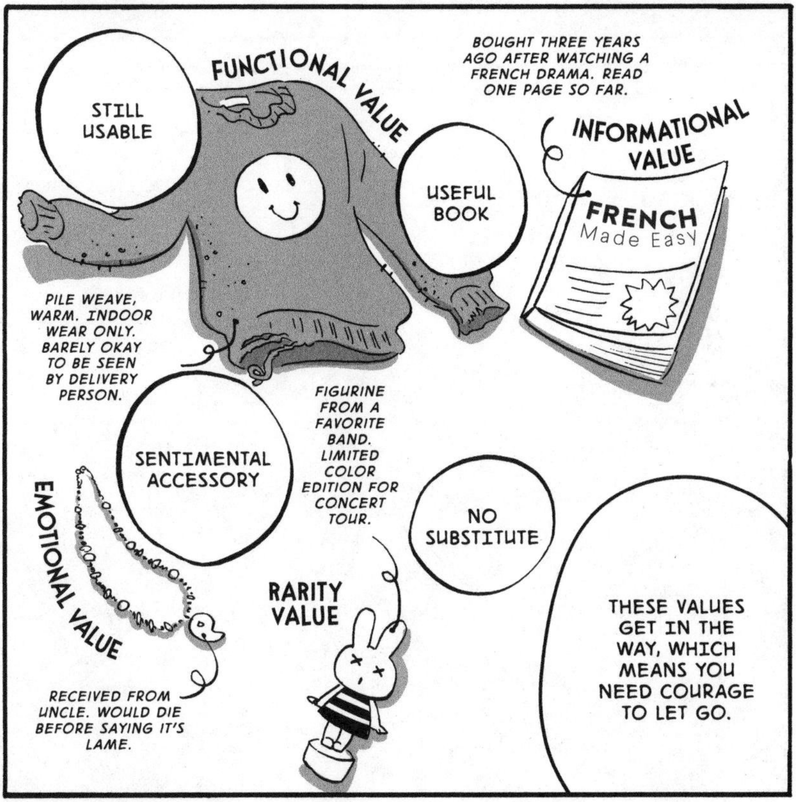
FUNCTIONAL VALUE
STILL USABLE
PILE WEAVE, WARM. INDOOR WEAR ONLY. BARELY OKAY TO BE SEEN BY DELIVERY PERSON.
BOUGHT THREE YEARS AGO AFTER WATCHING A FRENCH DRAMA. READ ONE PAGE SO FAR.
INFORMATIONAL VALUE
USEFUL BOOK
FRENCH
Made Easy
EMOTIONAL VALUE
SENTIMENTAL ACCESSORY
RECEIVED FROM UNCLE. WOULD DIE BEFORE SAYING IT'S LAME.
FIGURINE FROM A FAVORITE BAND. LIMITED COLOR EDITION FOR CONCERT TOUR.
RARITY VALUE
NO SUBSTITUTE
THESE VALUES GET IN THE WAY, WHICH MEANS YOU NEED COURAGE TO LET GO.

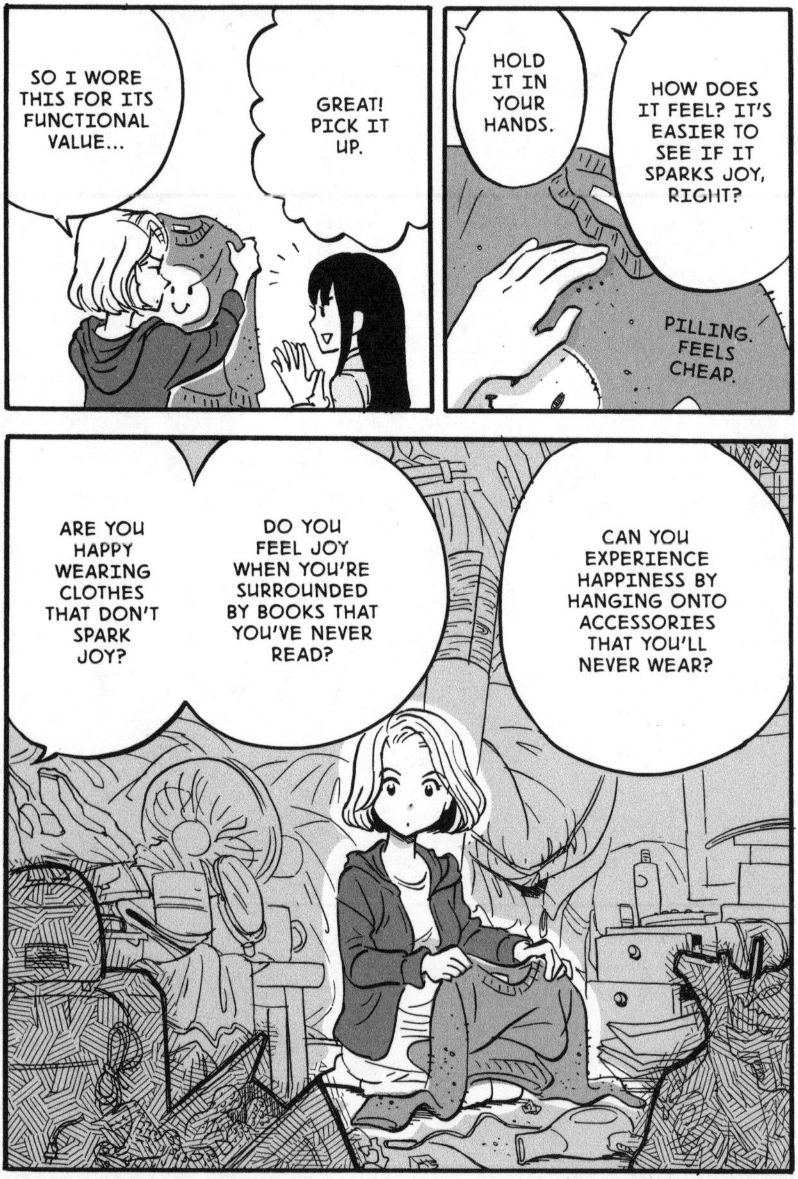
SO I WORE THIS FOR ITS FUNCTIONAL VALUE...
GREAT! PICK IT UP.
HOLD IT IN YOUR HANDS.
HOW DOES IT FEEL? IT'S EASIER TO SEE IF IT SPARKS JOY, RIGHT?
PILLING. FEELS CHEAP.
ARE YOU HAPPY WEARING CLOTHES THAT DON'T SPARK JOY?
DO YOU FEEL JOY WHEN YOU'RE SURROUNDED BY BOOKS THAT YOU'VE NEVER READ?
CAN YOU EXPERIENCE HAPPINESS BY HANGING ONTO ACCESSORIES THAT YOU'LL NEVER WEAR?

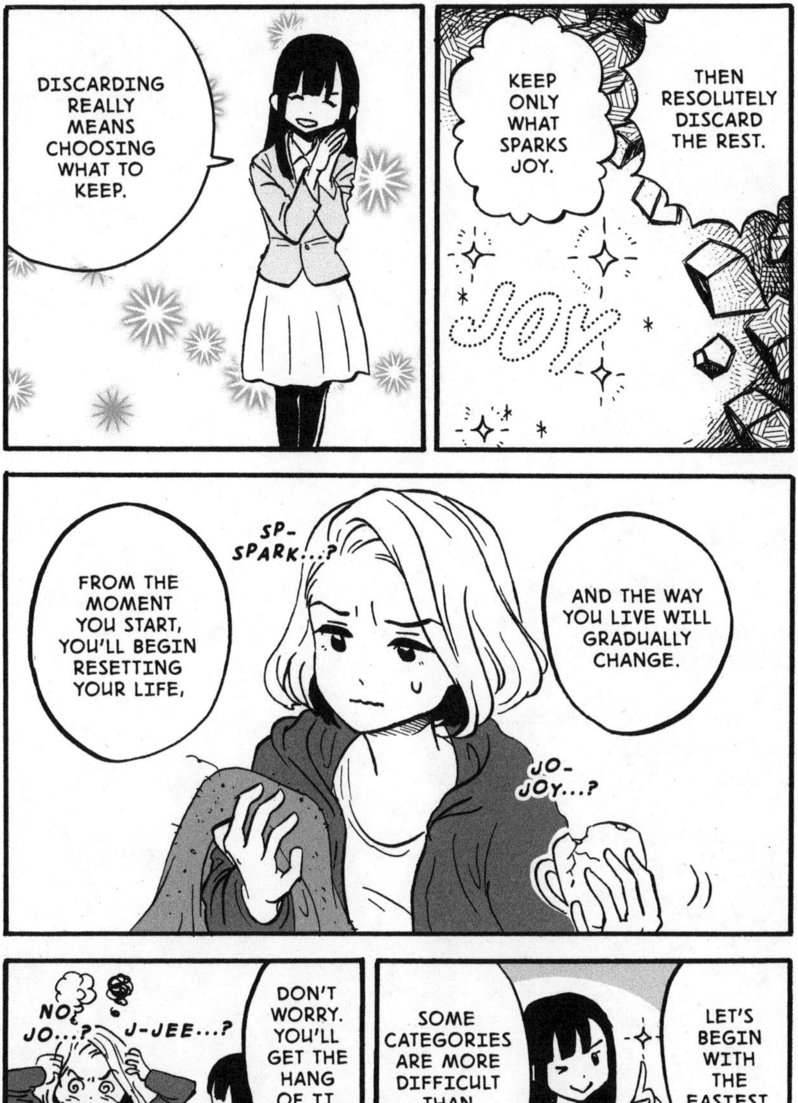
DISCARDING REALLY MEANS CHOOSING WHAT TO KEEP.
KEEP ONLY WHAT SPARKS JOY.
THEN RESOLUTELY DISCARD THE REST.
JOY
FROM THE MOMENT YOU START, YOU'LL BEGIN RESETTING YOUR LIFE,
SP- SPARK...?
AND THE WAY YOU LIVE WILL GRADUALLY CHANGE.
JO- JOY...?
NO, JO...?
J-JEE...?
EEHEEHEE
DON'T WORRY. YOU'LL GET THE HANG OF IT.
SOME CATEGORIES ARE MORE DIFFICULT THAN OTHERS.
LET'S BEGIN WITH THE EASIEST.

Finish discarding first. But don't choose what to discard. Choose what to keep.

———

If you focus on what to throw away, you will lose sight of the real purpose of tidying.

The best criterion for choosing what to keep is this: Does it spark joy when you touch it?

Take each item in your hand. Keep those that spark joy and discard those that don't. This is the simplest and most accurate way to figure out what you should keep.

The true purpose of your home and your things is to bring you happiness. So, naturally, the criterion for choosing should be whether keeping something will make you happy—whether it will bring you joy.

4

tidy by
category

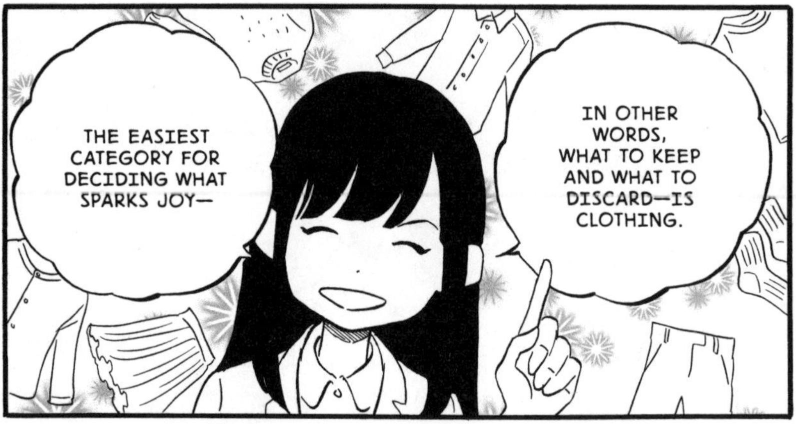
THE EASIEST CATEGORY FOR DECIDING WHAT SPARKS JOY—
IN OTHER WORDS, WHAT TO KEEP AND WHAT TO DISCARD—IS CLOTHING.

CLOTHING IS EASIEST BECAUSE IT'S A CLEARLY DEFINED CATEGORY WITHOUT MUCH "RARITY."

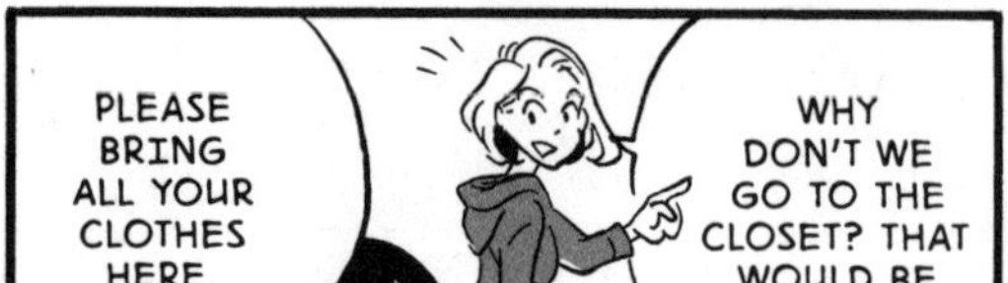
PLEASE BRING ALL YOUR CLOTHES HERE.
WHY DON'T WE GO TO THE CLOSET? THAT WOULD BE FASTER.

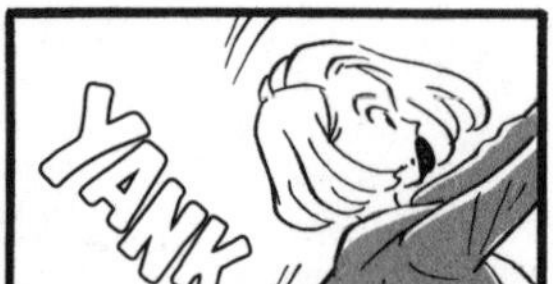
YANK

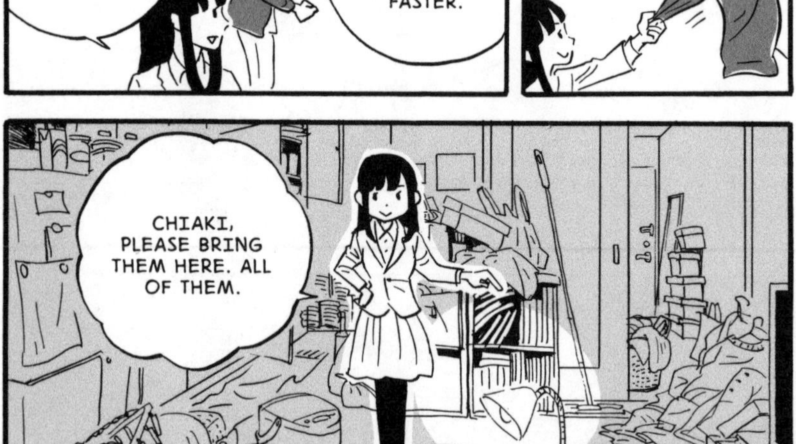
CHIAKI, PLEASE BRING THEM HERE. ALL OF THEM.

REALLY? HERE?

DO I HAVE TO?

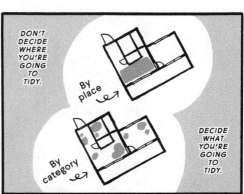

DON'T DECIDE WHERE YOU'RE GOING TO TIDY.

By place

By category

DECIDE WHAT YOU'RE GOING TO TIDY.

THIS IS THE KEY TO MY METHOD OF TIDYING UP!

NOT BY PLACE, BY CATEGORY!!!

NOT BY PLACE, BY CATEGORY...?

YOU MEAN TIDYING JUST CLOTHES OR JUST BOOKS ALL AT ONCE?

THAT'S RIGHT!

CHIAKI, YOU'VE GOT TIDYING TALENT!

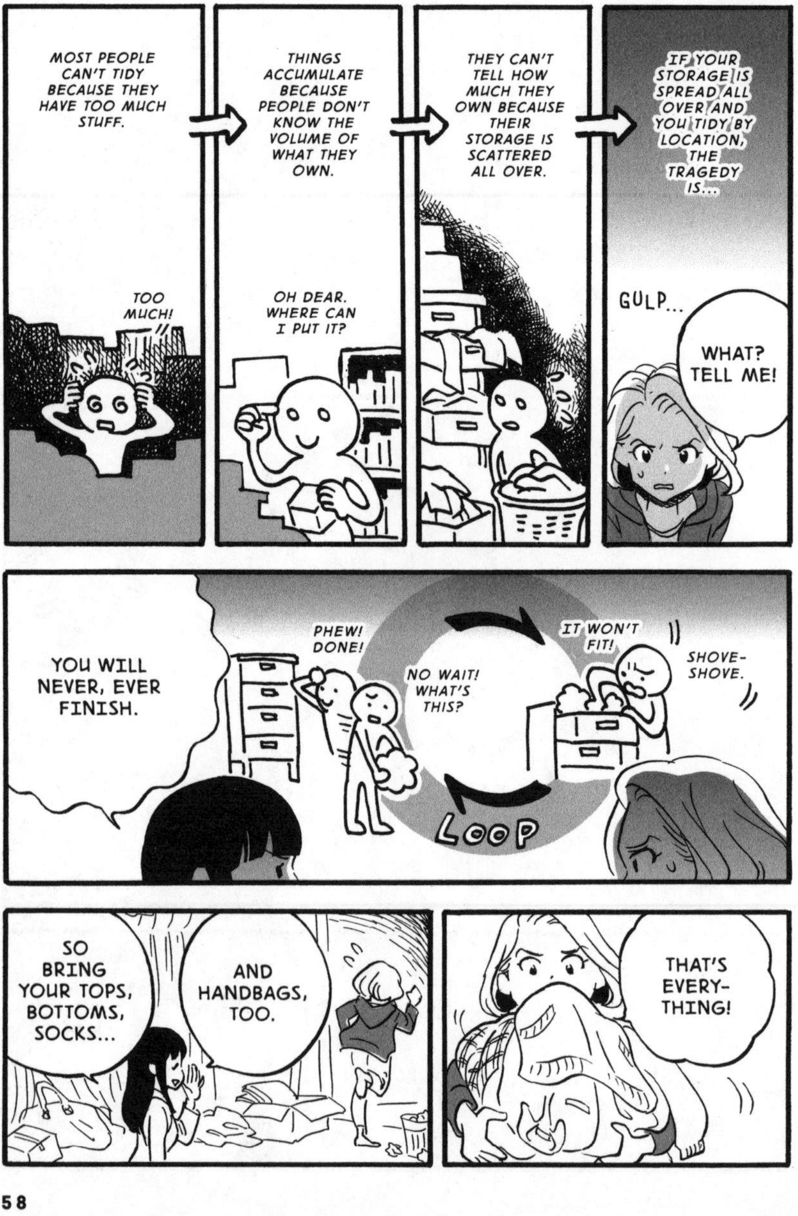
MOST PEOPLE CAN'T TIDY BECAUSE THEY HAVE TOO MUCH STUFF.
TOO MUCH!
THINGS ACCUMULATE BECAUSE PEOPLE DON'T KNOW THE VOLUME OF WHAT THEY OWN.
OH DEAR. WHERE CAN I PUT IT?
THEY CAN'T TELL HOW MUCH THEY OWN BECAUSE THEIR STORAGE IS SCATTERED ALL OVER.
IF YOUR STORAGE IS SPREAD ALL OVER AND YOU TIDY BY LOCATION, THE TRAGEDY IS...
GULP...
WHAT? TELL ME!
YOU WILL NEVER, EVER FINISH.
PHEW! DONE!
NO WAIT! WHAT'S THIS?
IT WON'T FIT!
SHOVE-SHOVE.
LOOP
SO BRING YOUR TOPS, BOTTOMS, SOCKS...
AND HANDBAGS, TOO.
THAT'S EVERY-THING!

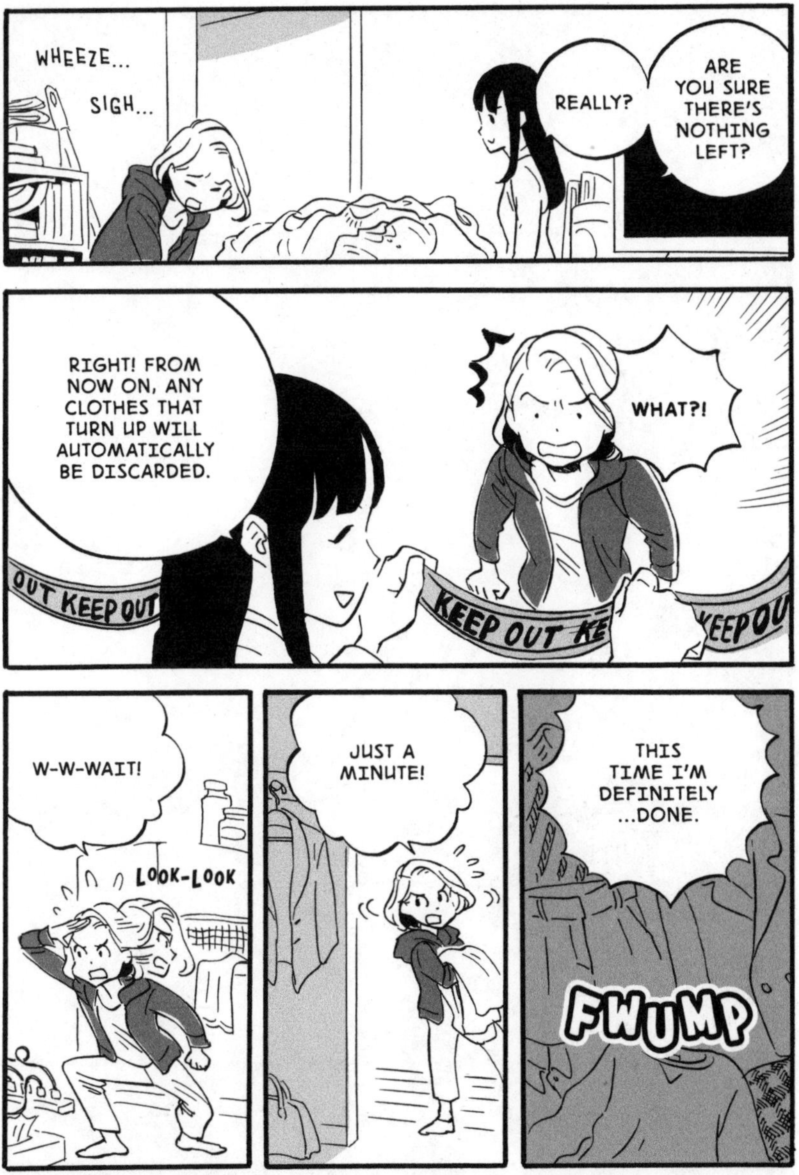
WHEEZE...
SIGH...
REALLY?
ARE YOU SURE THERE'S NOTHING LEFT?
RIGHT! FROM NOW ON, ANY CLOTHES THAT TURN UP WILL AUTOMATICALLY BE DISCARDED.
WHAT?!
OUT KEEP OUT
KEEP OUT KE
KEEP OU
W-W-WAIT!
LOOK-LOOK
JUST A MINUTE!
THIS TIME I'M DEFINITELY ...DONE.
FWUMP

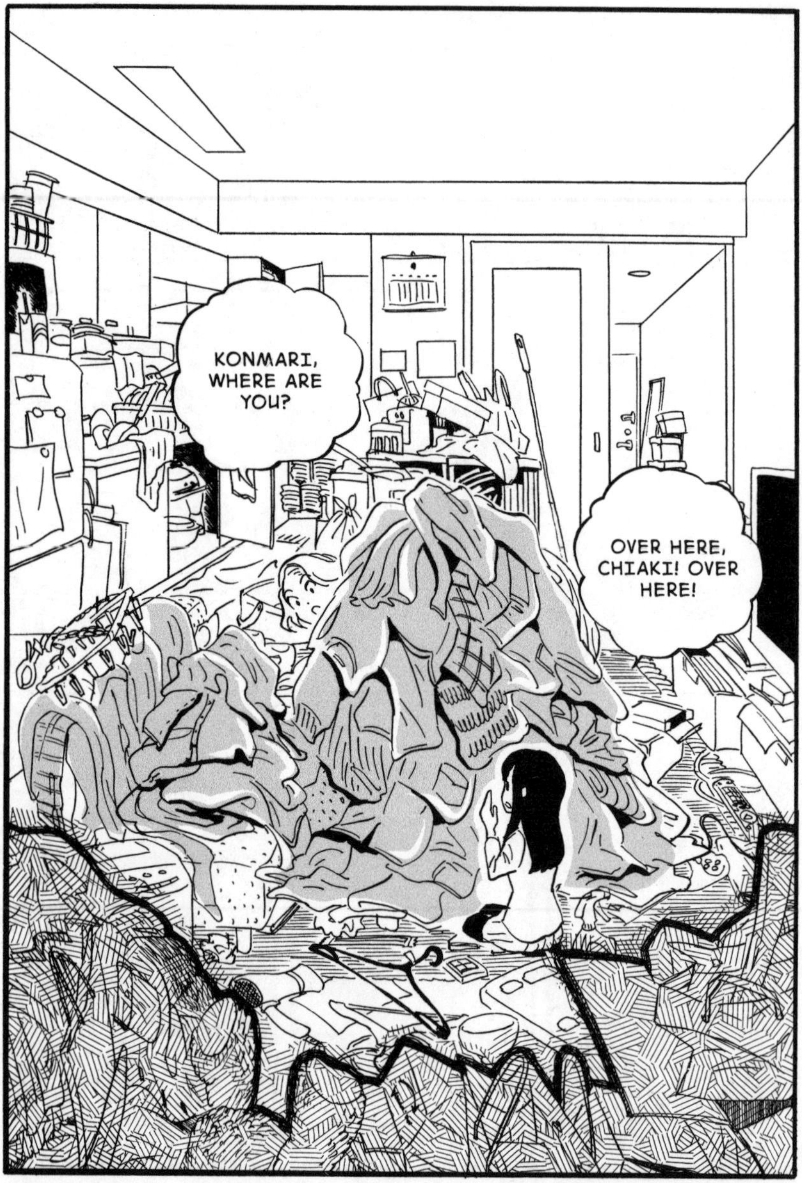
KONMARI, WHERE ARE YOU?
OVER HERE, CHIAKI! OVER HERE!

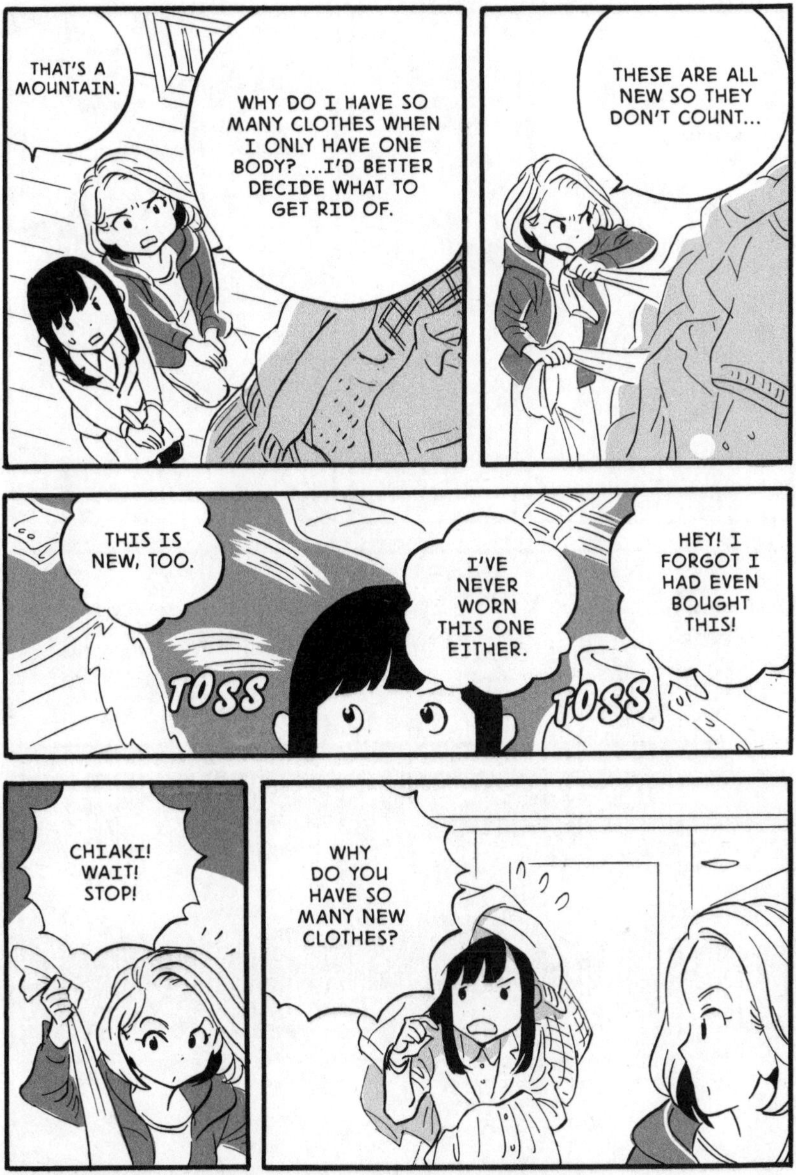
THAT'S A MOUNTAIN.
WHY DO I HAVE SO MANY CLOTHES WHEN I ONLY HAVE ONE BODY? ...I'D BETTER DECIDE WHAT TO GET RID OF.
THESE ARE ALL NEW SO THEY DON'T COUNT...
THIS IS NEW, TOO.
I'VE NEVER WORN THIS ONE EITHER.
HEY! I FORGOT I HAD EVEN BOUGHT THIS!
TOSS
TOSS
CHIAKI! WAIT! STOP!
WHY DO YOU HAVE SO MANY NEW CLOTHES?

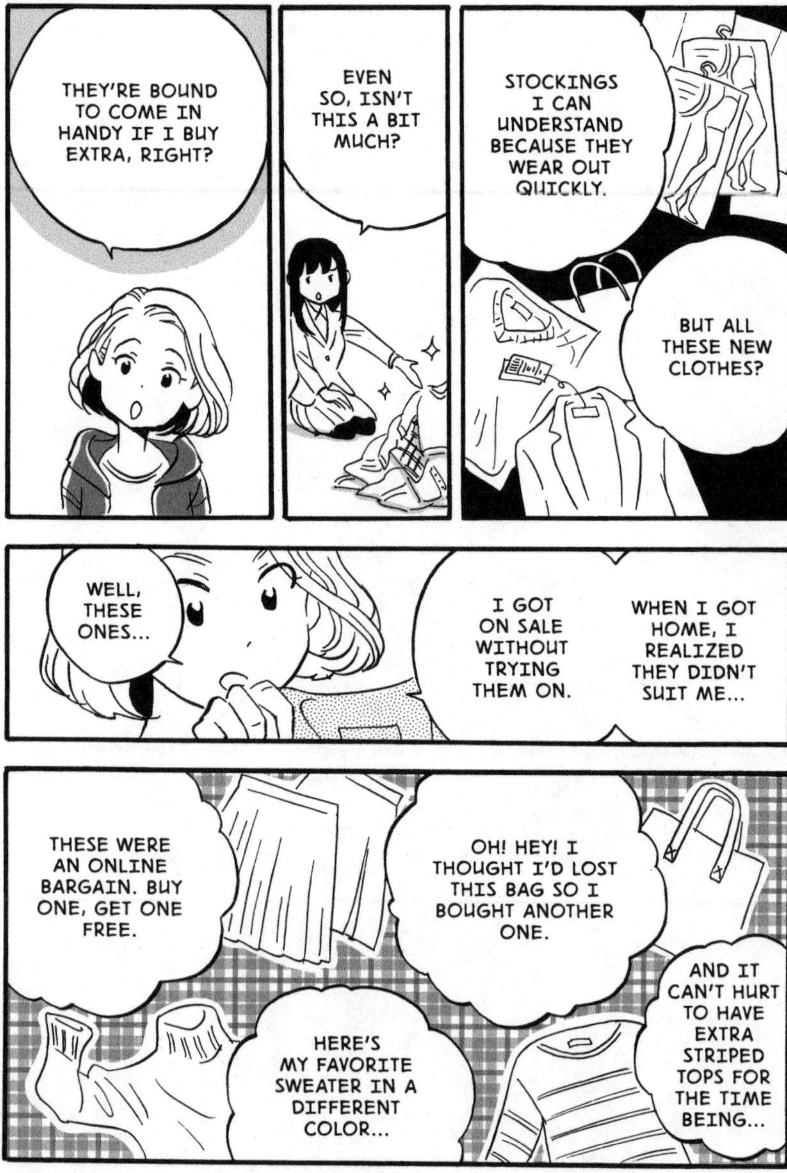
THEY'RE BOUND TO COME IN HANDY IF I BUY EXTRA, RIGHT?
EVEN SO, ISN'T THIS A BIT MUCH?
STOCKINGS I CAN UNDERSTAND BECAUSE THEY WEAR OUT QUICKLY.
BUT ALL THESE NEW CLOTHES?
WELL, THESE ONES...
I GOT ON SALE WITHOUT TRYING THEM ON.
WHEN I GOT HOME, I REALIZED THEY DIDN'T SUIT ME...
THESE WERE AN ONLINE BARGAIN. BUY ONE, GET ONE FREE.
OH! HEY! I THOUGHT I'D LOST THIS BAG SO I BOUGHT ANOTHER ONE.
AND IT CAN'T HURT TO HAVE EXTRA STRIPED TOPS FOR THE TIME BEING...
HERE'S MY FAVORITE SWEATER IN A DIFFERENT COLOR...

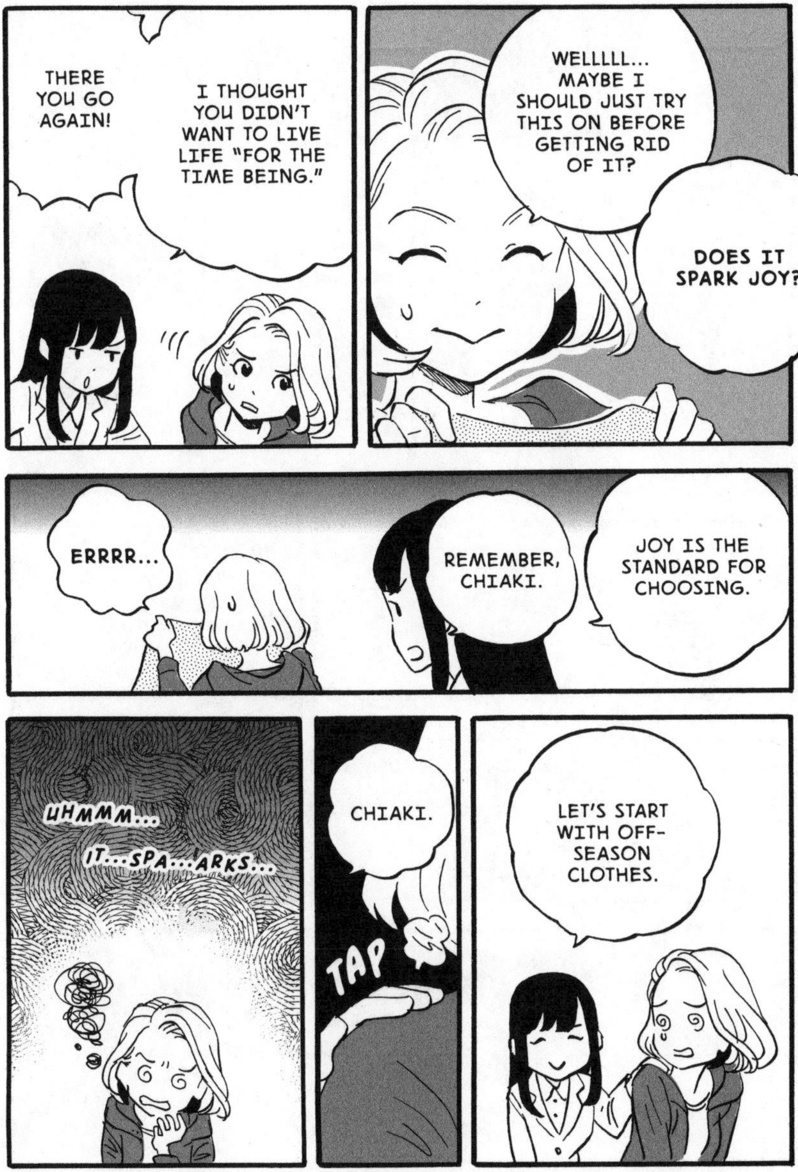
THERE YOU GO AGAIN!
I THOUGHT YOU DIDN'T WANT TO LIVE LIFE "FOR THE TIME BEING."
WELLLLL... MAYBE I SHOULD JUST TRY THIS ON BEFORE GETTING RID OF IT?
DOES IT SPARK JOY?
ERRRR...
REMEMBER, CHIAKI.
JOY IS THE STANDARD FOR CHOOSING.
UHMMM...
IT...SPA...ARKS...
CHIAKI.
TAP
LET'S START WITH OFF-SEASON CLOTHES.

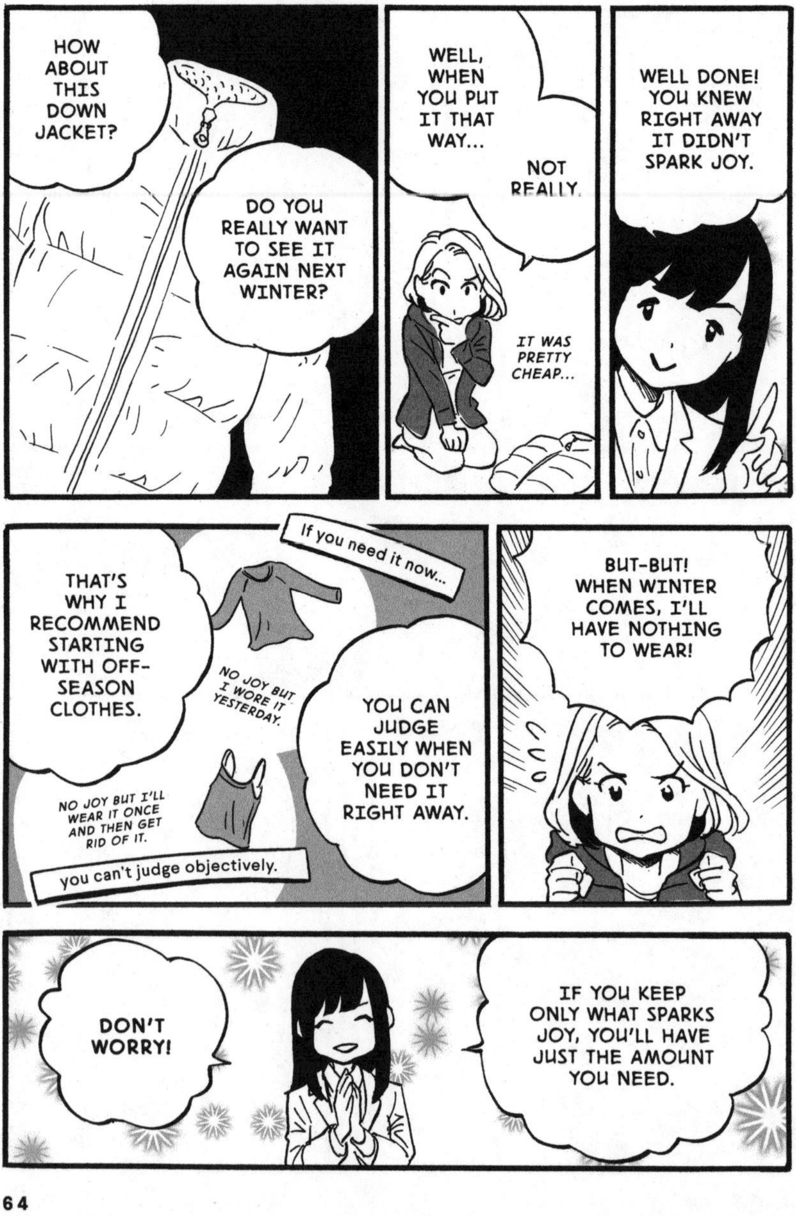
HOW ABOUT THIS DOWN JACKET?
DO YOU REALLY WANT TO SEE IT AGAIN NEXT WINTER?
WELL, WHEN YOU PUT IT THAT WAY...
NOT REALLY.
IT WAS PRETTY CHEAP...
WELL DONE! YOU KNEW RIGHT AWAY IT DIDN'T SPARK JOY.
THAT'S WHY I RECOMMEND STARTING WITH OFF-SEASON CLOTHES.
If you need it now...
NO JOY BUT I WORE IT YESTERDAY.
NO JOY BUT I'LL WEAR IT ONCE AND THEN GET RID OF IT.
you can't judge objectively.
YOU CAN JUDGE EASILY WHEN YOU DON'T NEED IT RIGHT AWAY.
BUT-BUT! WHEN WINTER COMES, I'LL HAVE NOTHING TO WEAR!
DON'T WORRY!
IF YOU KEEP ONLY WHAT SPARKS JOY, YOU'LL HAVE JUST THE AMOUNT YOU NEED.

ARE YOU SURE?

BELIEVE ME! LET'S GET TO WORK!

TOUCH EACH ONE AND ASK YOURSELF,

"DO I WANT TO SEE THIS NEXT SEASON?"

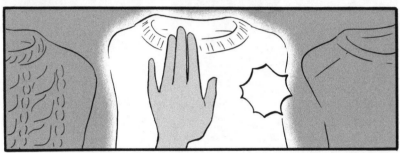

I HAVE SO MANY SWEATERS JUST LIKE THIS.

SO WHY DOES ONLY THIS ONE SPARK JOY?!

THIS IS IT!

IT COULD BE THE WAY IT FEELS OR THE SIZE...

ONLY THE OWNER KNOWS.

SEE YOU NEXT WINTER.

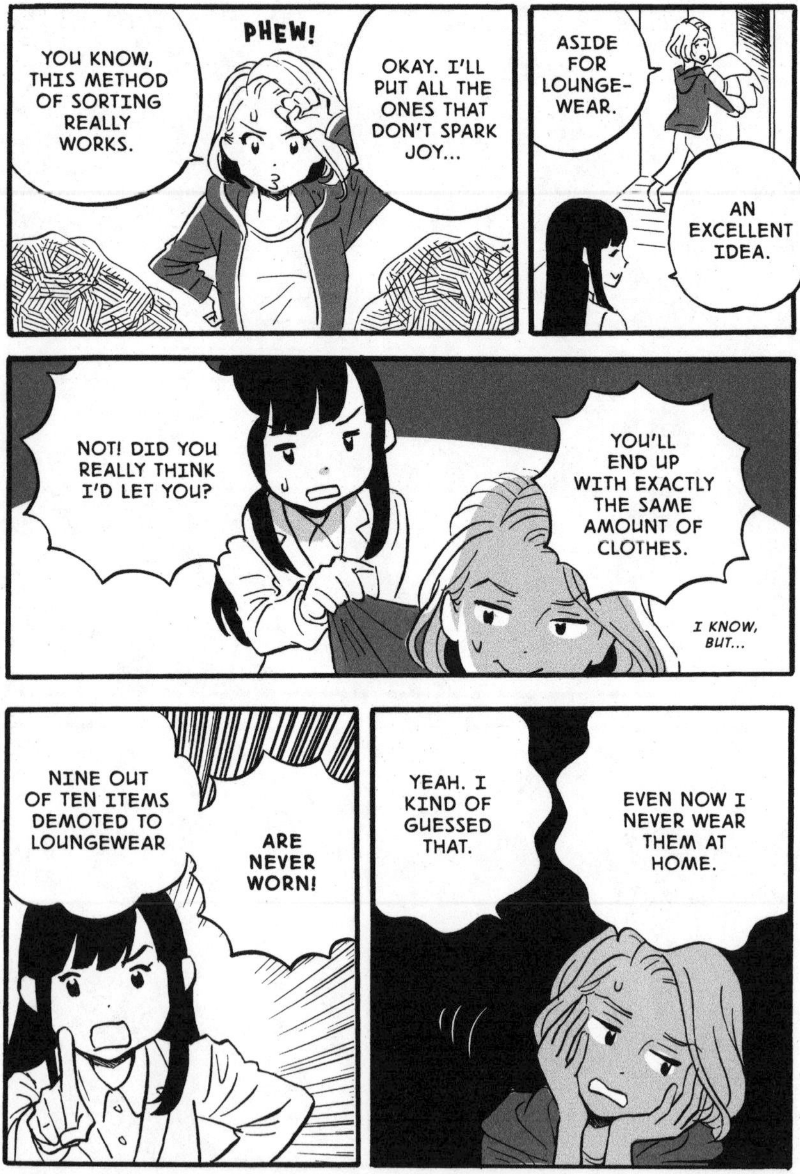
PHEW!
YOU KNOW, THIS METHOD OF SORTING REALLY WORKS.
OKAY. I'LL PUT ALL THE ONES THAT DON'T SPARK JOY...
ASIDE FOR LOUNGE-WEAR.
AN EXCELLENT IDEA.
NOT! DID YOU REALLY THINK I'D LET YOU?
YOU'LL END UP WITH EXACTLY THE SAME AMOUNT OF CLOTHES.
I KNOW, BUT...
NINE OUT OF TEN ITEMS DEMOTED TO LOUNGEWEAR
ARE NEVER WORN!
YEAH. I KIND OF GUESSED THAT.
EVEN NOW I NEVER WEAR THEM AT HOME.

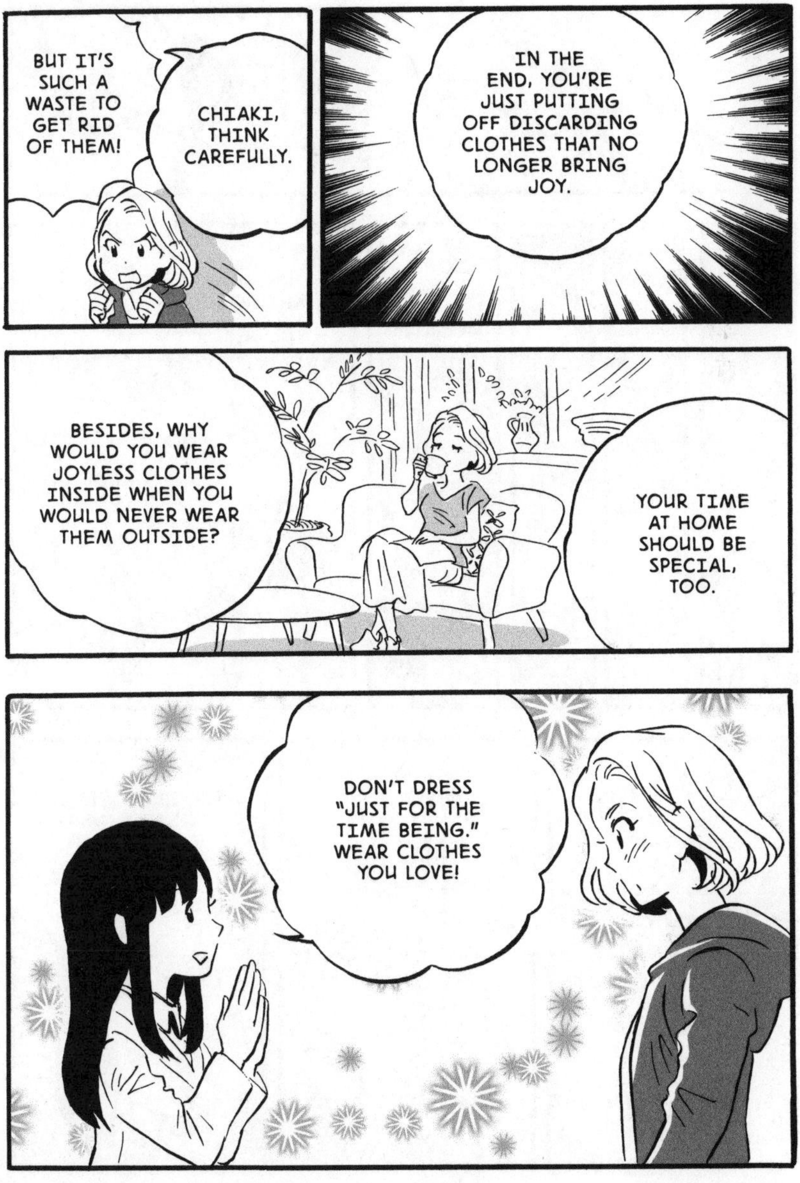
BUT IT'S SUCH A WASTE TO GET RID OF THEM!
CHIAKI, THINK CAREFULLY.
IN THE END, YOU'RE JUST PUTTING OFF DISCARDING CLOTHES THAT NO LONGER BRING JOY.
BESIDES, WHY WOULD YOU WEAR JOYLESS CLOTHES INSIDE WHEN YOU WOULD NEVER WEAR THEM OUTSIDE?
YOUR TIME AT HOME SHOULD BE SPECIAL, TOO.
DON'T DRESS "JUST FOR THE TIME BEING." WEAR CLOTHES YOU LOVE!

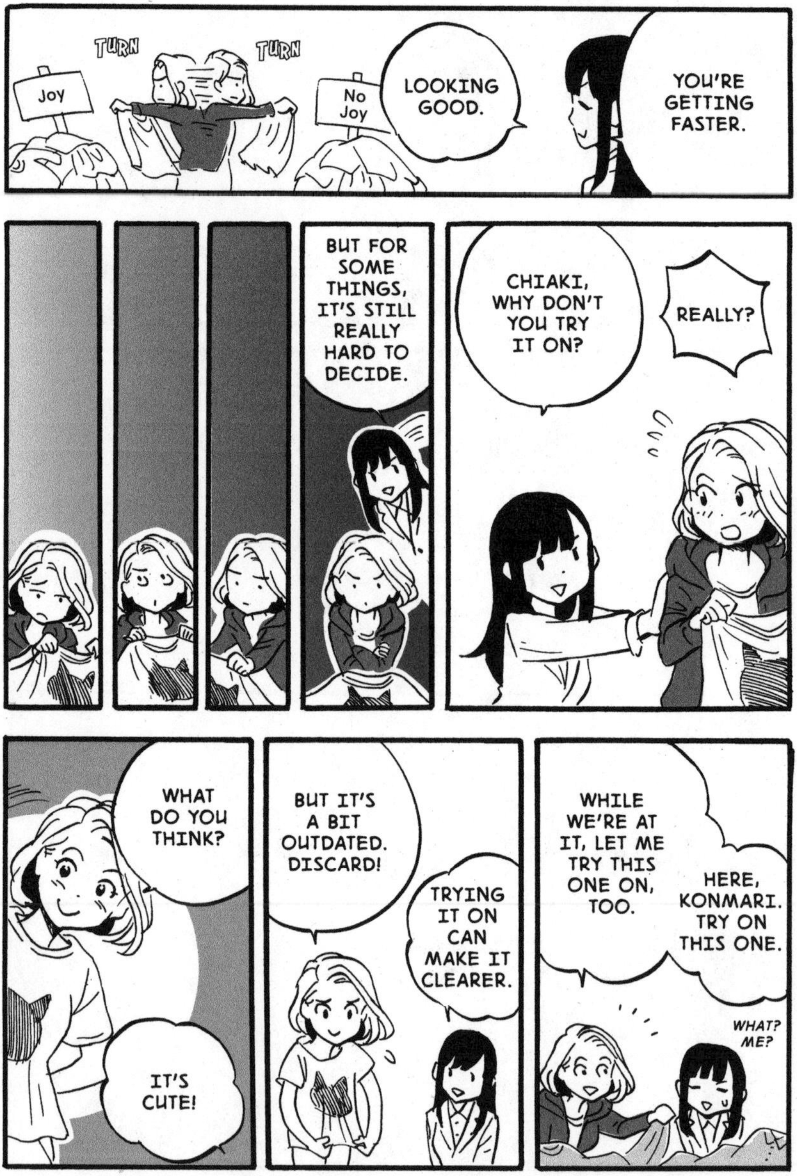
Joy
TURN
TURN
No Joy
LOOKING GOOD.
YOU'RE GETTING FASTER.
BUT FOR SOME THINGS, IT'S STILL REALLY HARD TO DECIDE.
CHIAKI, WHY DON'T YOU TRY IT ON?
REALLY?
WHAT DO YOU THINK?
IT'S CUTE!
BUT IT'S A BIT OUTDATED. DISCARD!
TRYING IT ON CAN MAKE IT CLEARER.
WHILE WE'RE AT IT, LET ME TRY THIS ONE ON, TOO.
HERE, KONMARI. TRY ON THIS ONE.
WHAT? ME?

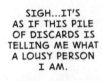

SIGH...IT'S AS IF THIS PILE OF DISCARDS IS TELLING ME WHAT A LOUSY PERSON I AM.

TOSS

I CAN'T BEAR TO LOOK AT IT...

?

WHAT ARE YOU DOING?

I'M THANKING YOUR CLOTHES.

YOU MUST HAVE FELT JOY AT LEAST WHEN YOU BOUGHT THEM. SO I'M SAYING, "THANKS FOR BRINGING JOY TO CHIAKI."

HMMM.

THANKS FOR TEACHING ME WHAT DOESN'T SUIT ME!

PHEW...

SLIP

THAT MAKES IT MUCH EASIER TO SAY "GOODBYE"!

DOESN'T IT!

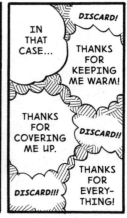

IN THAT CASE...

DISCARD!

THANKS FOR KEEPING ME WARM!

THANKS FOR COVERING ME UP.

DISCARD!!

DISCARD!!!

THANKS FOR EVERY-THING!

TUG

THIRTY BAGS!

WELL DONE! KEEP UP THE GOOD WORK!

YOU CAN DONATE THOSE IN GOOD CONDITION TO A CHARITY SHOP OR TAKE THEM TO A RECYCLE STATION.

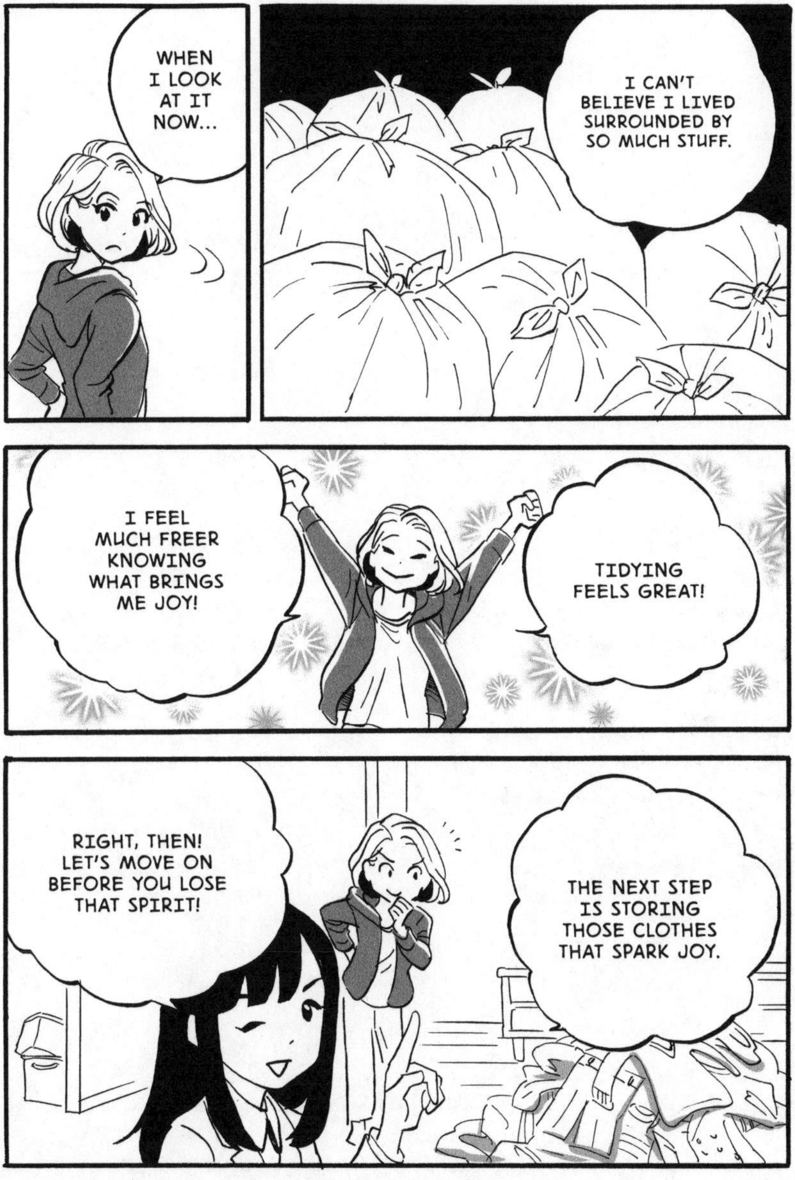
WHEN I LOOK AT IT NOW...
I CAN'T BELIEVE I LIVED SURROUNDED BY SO MUCH STUFF.
I FEEL MUCH FREER KNOWING WHAT BRINGS ME JOY!
TIDYING FEELS GREAT!
RIGHT, THEN! LET'S MOVE ON BEFORE YOU LOSE THAT SPIRIT!
THE NEXT STEP IS STORING THOSE CLOTHES THAT SPARK JOY.

Don't tidy by place or by room, but by category.

———

Most people can't tidy because they have too much stuff. They accumulate too much stuff because they don't know how much they actually own.

Gather every single item in the category from every corner of your home. Pile them all in one spot. This way, you can see exactly how much you have.

Things that have been put away in a drawer or a closet are basically dormant. Wake them up by taking them out and spreading them across the floor to expose them to the air. When you do, you will be amazed to find that your joy barometer becomes clear and focused.

Gathering everything in the same category in one spot is the best way to finish tidying up quickly.

5

just fold and
stand upright

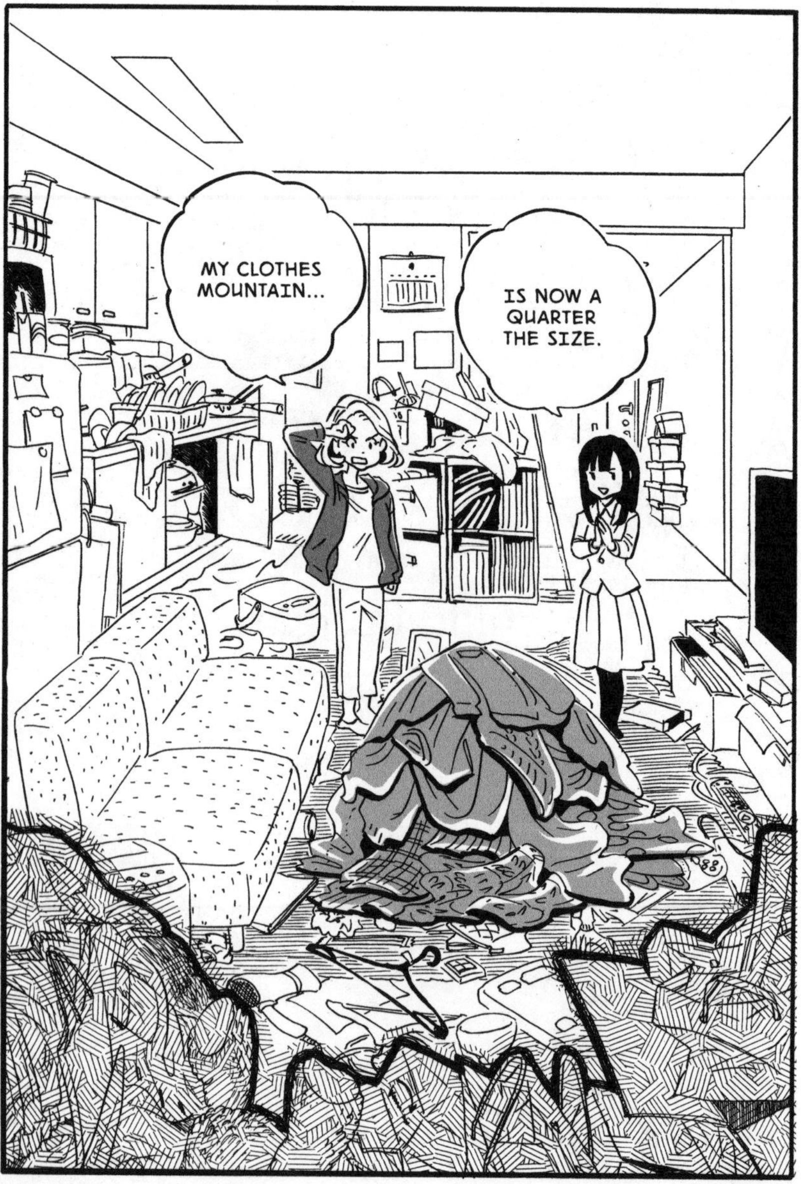
MY CLOTHES MOUNTAIN...
IS NOW A QUARTER THE SIZE.

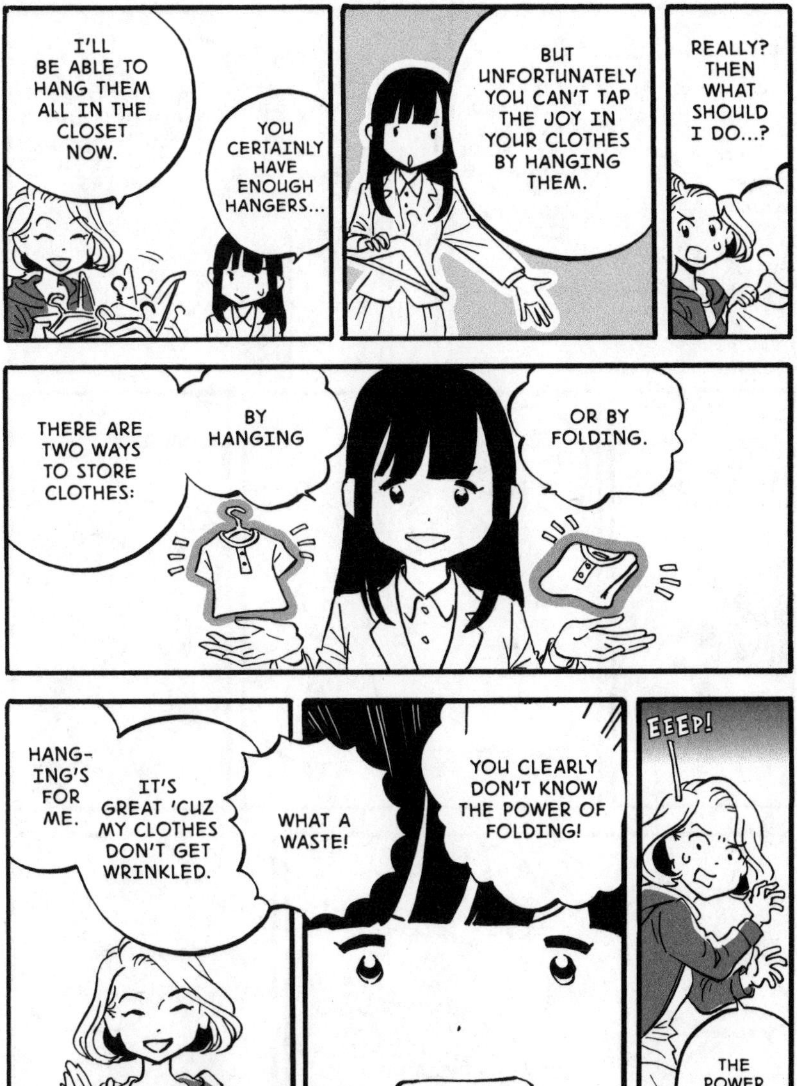
I'LL BE ABLE TO HANG THEM ALL IN THE CLOSET NOW.
YOU CERTAINLY HAVE ENOUGH HANGERS...
BUT UNFORTUNATELY YOU CAN'T TAP THE JOY IN YOUR CLOTHES BY HANGING THEM.
REALLY? THEN WHAT SHOULD I DO...?
THERE ARE TWO WAYS TO STORE CLOTHES:
BY HANGING
OR BY FOLDING.
HANG-ING'S FOR ME.
IT'S GREAT 'CUZ MY CLOTHES DON'T GET WRINKLED.
WHAT A WASTE!
YOU CLEARLY DON'T KNOW THE POWER OF FOLDING!
EEEP!
THE POWER OF FOLD-ING..?!

HANGING JUST CAN'T BEAT FOLDING FOR SAVING STORAGE SPACE!

IF YOU FOLD RIGHT, YOU CAN STORE TWO TO FOUR TIMES MORE THAN BY HANGING!

ALTHOUGH YOU HAVE FAR FEWER CLOTHES NOW,

THEY'LL NEVER FIT IN YOUR CLOSET IF YOU ONLY USE HANGERS.

AND THERE'S ANOTHER ADVANTAGE OF FOLDING.

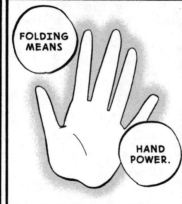

FOLDING MEANS

HAND POWER.

HAND...?

YOU KNOW THE JAPANESE EXPRESSION *TE-ATEH*, "APPLYING HANDS"?

YOU MEAN FOR TREATING INJURIES?

YES. AND I THINK HOLDING SOMEONE'S HAND OR GENTLY PATTING THEIR HEAD TO REASSURE THEM IS THE SAME IDEA.

JUST LIKE IT SOOTHES BODY AND SOUL, THE TOUCH OF THE PALM CAN ALSO AFFECT OUR CLOTHES.

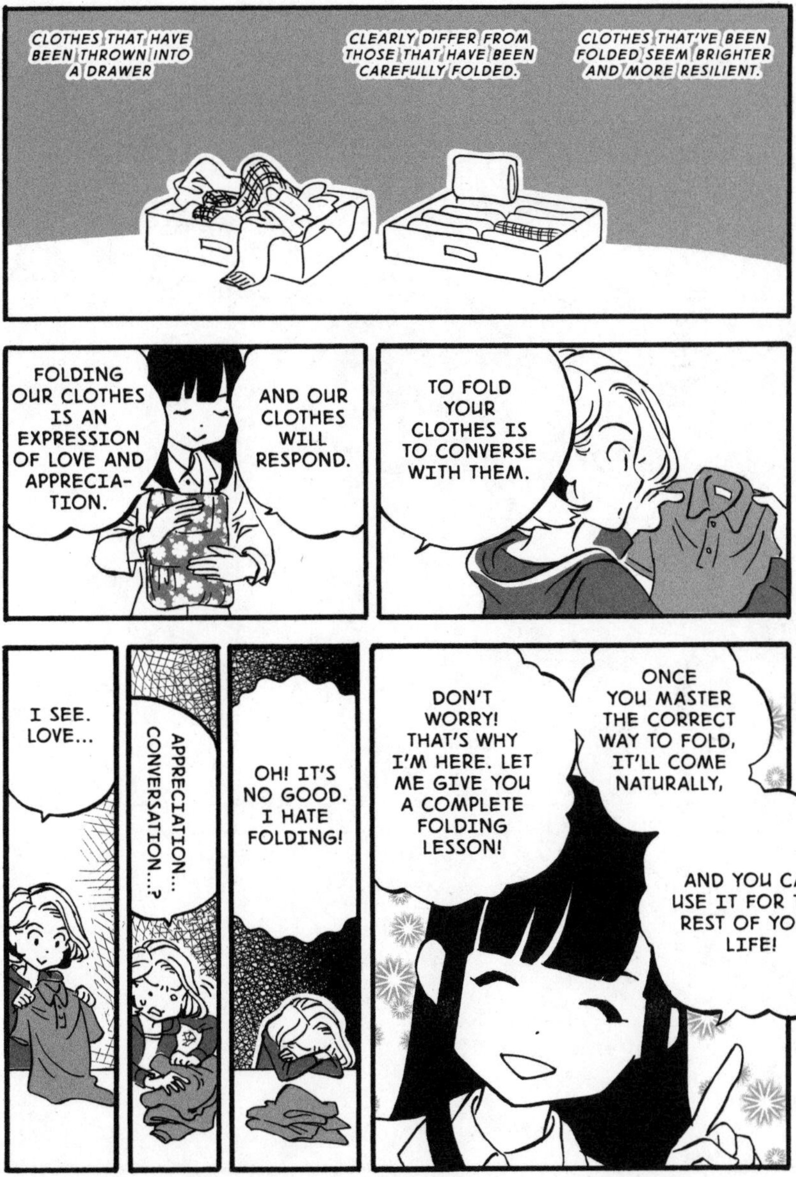
CLOTHES THAT HAVE BEEN THROWN INTO A DRAWER
CLEARLY DIFFER FROM THOSE THAT HAVE BEEN CAREFULLY FOLDED.
CLOTHES THAT'VE BEEN FOLDED SEEM BRIGHTER AND MORE RESILIENT.
FOLDING OUR CLOTHES IS AN EXPRESSION OF LOVE AND APPRECIATION.
AND OUR CLOTHES WILL RESPOND.
TO FOLD YOUR CLOTHES IS TO CONVERSE WITH THEM.
I SEE. LOVE...
APPRECIATION... CONVERSATION...?
OH! IT'S NO GOOD. I HATE FOLDING!
DON'T WORRY! THAT'S WHY I'M HERE. LET ME GIVE YOU A COMPLETE FOLDING LESSON!
ONCE YOU MASTER THE CORRECT WAY TO FOLD, IT'LL COME NATURALLY,
AND YOU CAN USE IT FOR THE REST OF YOUR LIFE!

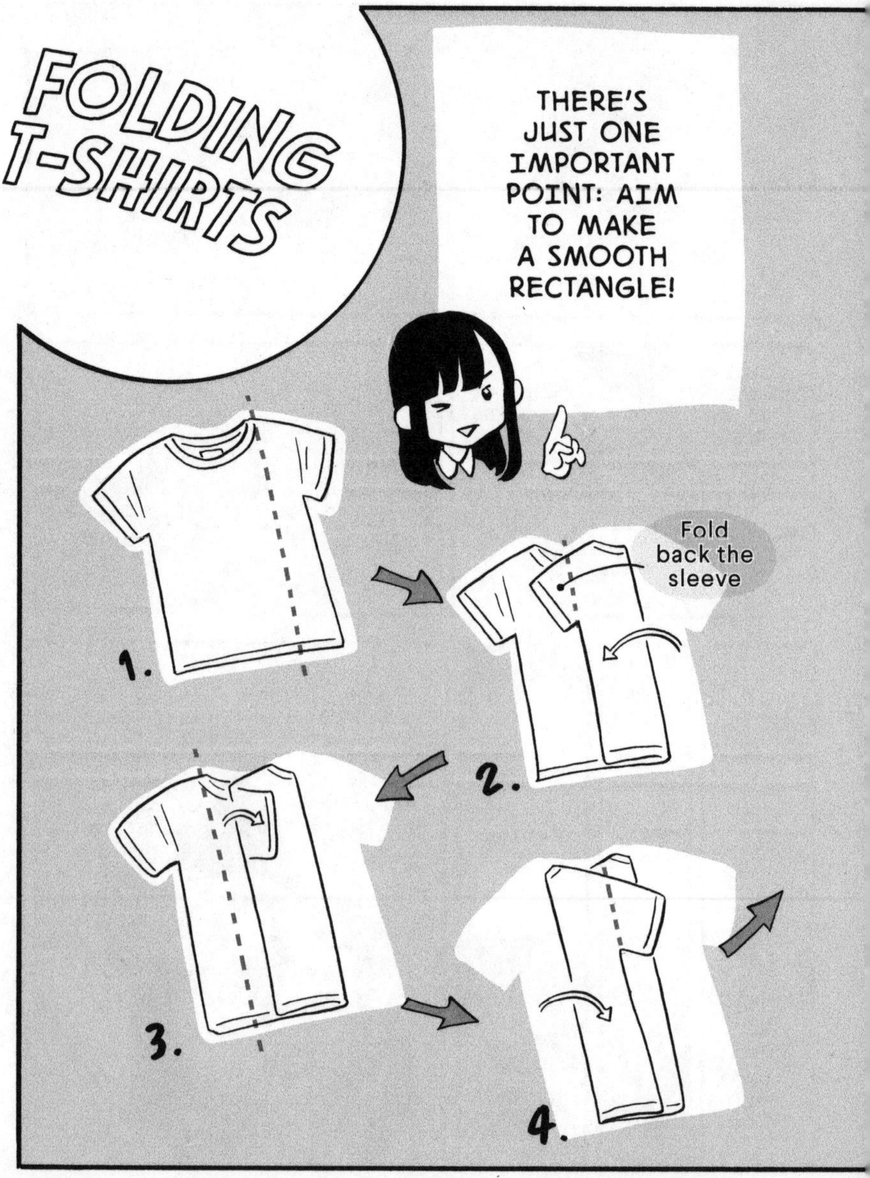
FOLDING T-SHIRTS
THERE'S JUST ONE IMPORTANT POINT: AIM TO MAKE A SMOOTH RECTANGLE!
1.
Fold back the sleeve
2.
3.
4.

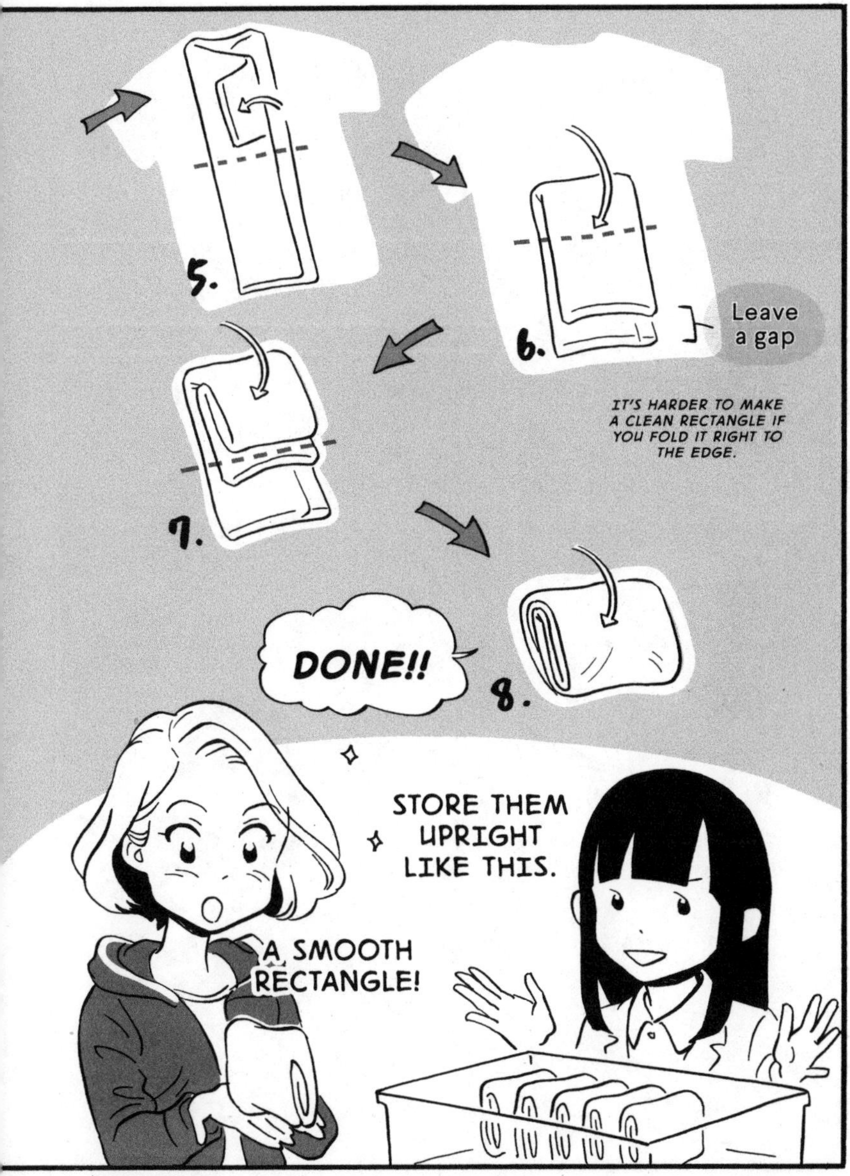
5.
6.
Leave a gap
IT'S HARDER TO MAKE A CLEAN RECTANGLE IF YOU FOLD IT RIGHT TO THE EDGE.
7.
8.
DONE!!
STORE THEM UPRIGHT LIKE THIS.
A SMOOTH RECTANGLE!

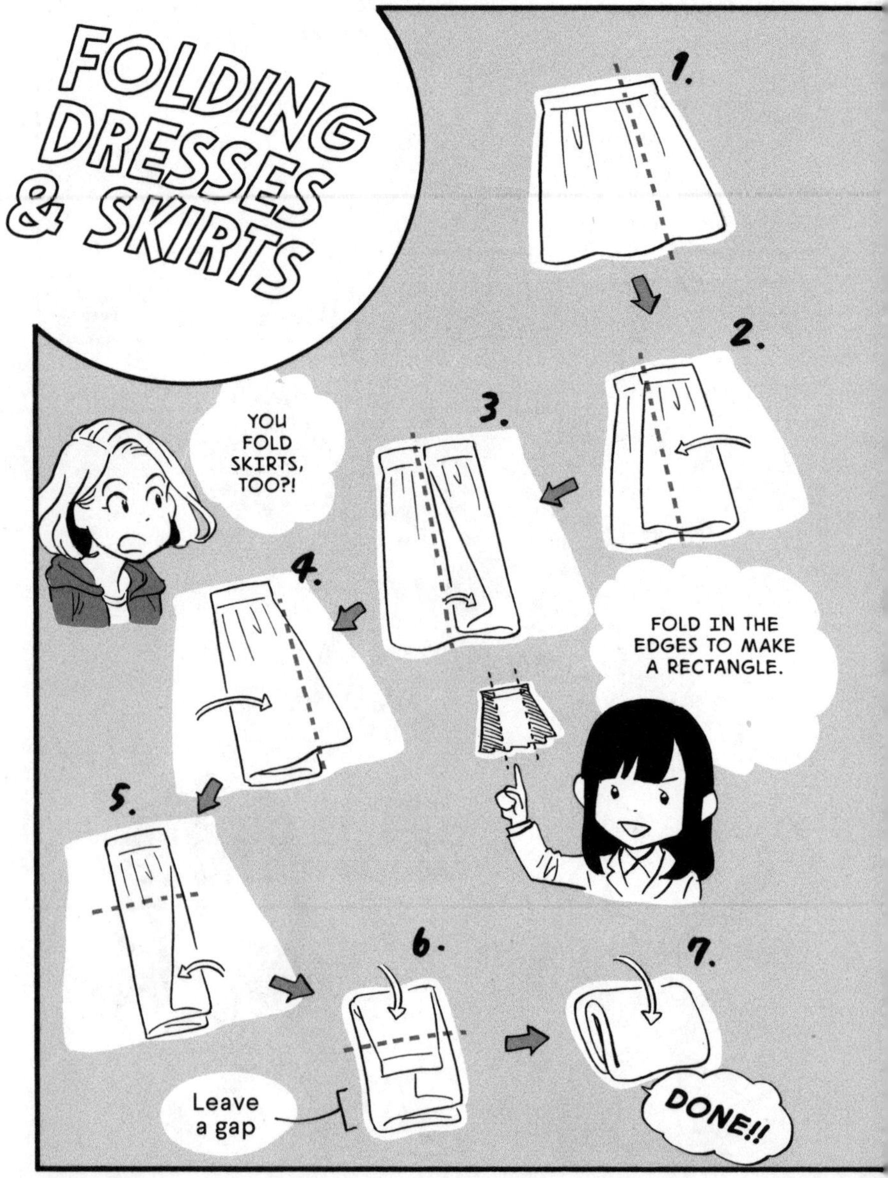
FOLDING DRESSES & SKIRTS
1.
2.
YOU FOLD SKIRTS, TOO?!
3.
4.
FOLD IN THE EDGES TO MAKE A RECTANGLE.
5.
6.
7.
Leave a gap
DONE!!

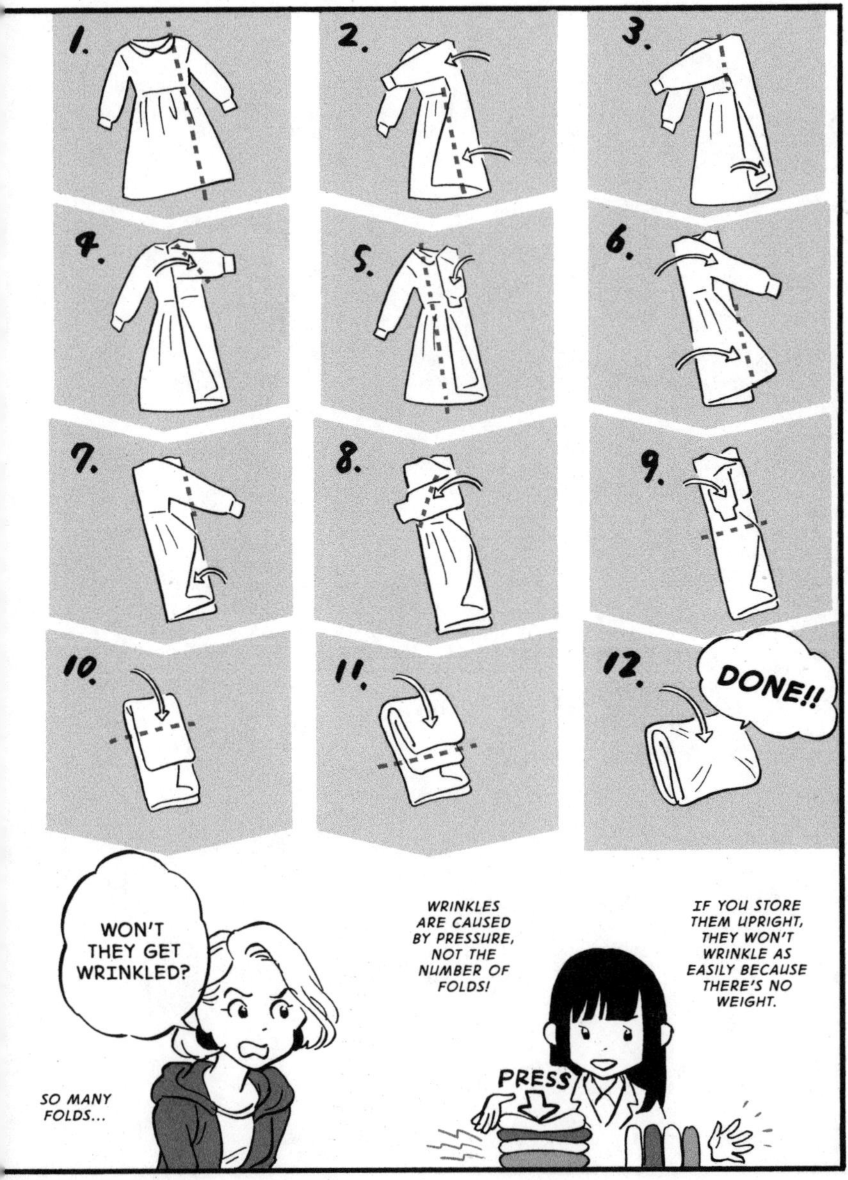

1.
2.
3.
4.
5.
6.
7.
8.
9.
10.
11.
12.
DONE!!
WON'T THEY GET WRINKLED?
SO MANY FOLDS...
WRINKLES ARE CAUSED BY PRESSURE, NOT THE NUMBER OF FOLDS!
IF YOU STORE THEM UPRIGHT, THEY WON'T WRINKLE AS EASILY BECAUSE THERE'S NO WEIGHT.
PRESS

FOLDING SOCKS & STOCKINGS

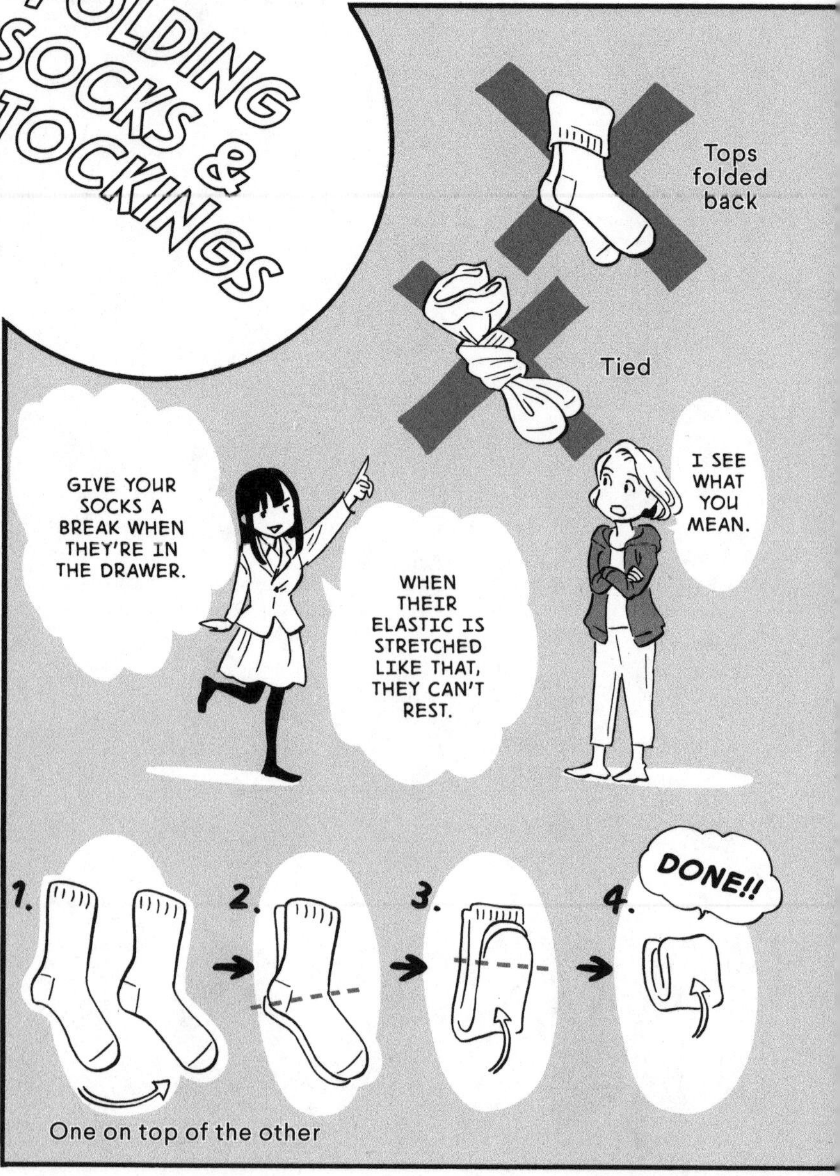

Tops folded back
Tied
GIVE YOUR SOCKS A BREAK WHEN THEY'RE IN THE DRAWER.
WHEN THEIR ELASTIC IS STRETCHED LIKE THAT, THEY CAN'T REST.
I SEE WHAT YOU MEAN.
1.
One on top of the other
2.
3.
4.
DONE!!

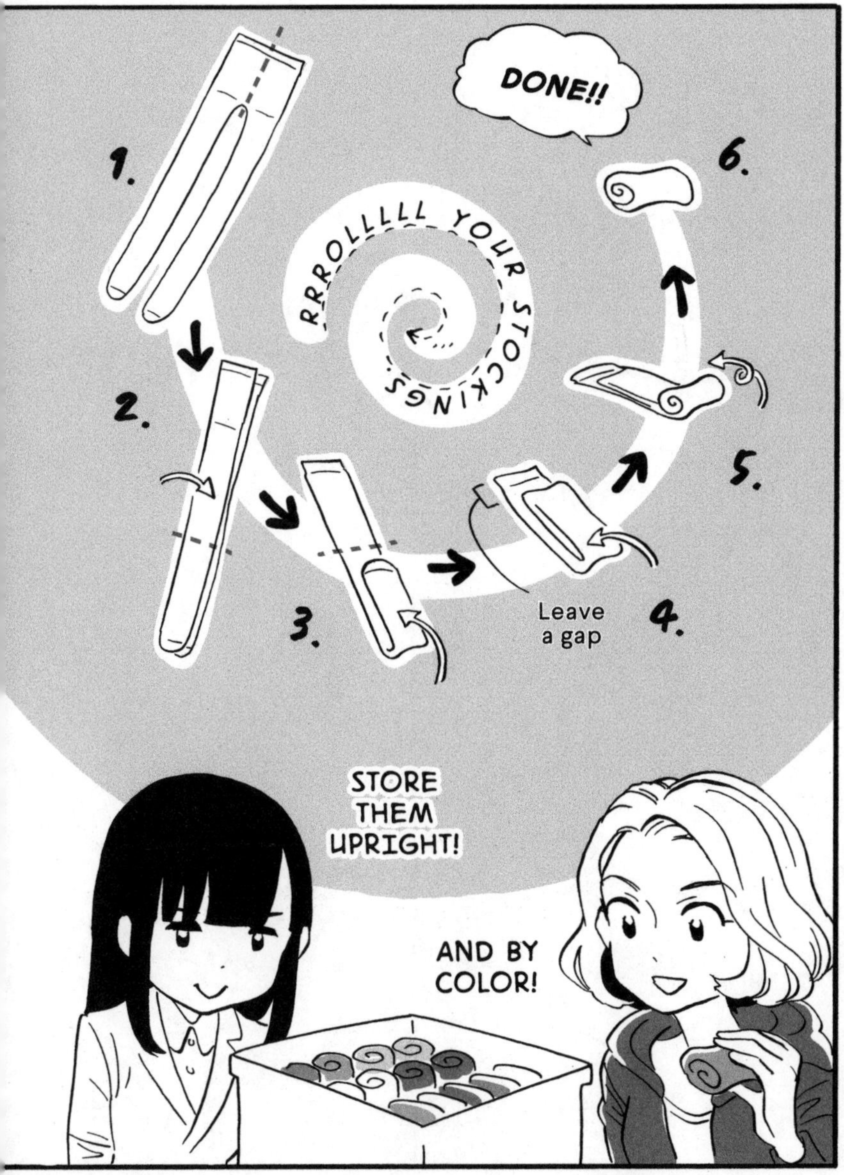
DONE!!
1.
RRROLLLLL YOUR STOCKINGS.
6.
2.
5.
3.
Leave a gap
4.
STORE THEM UPRIGHT!
AND BY COLOR!

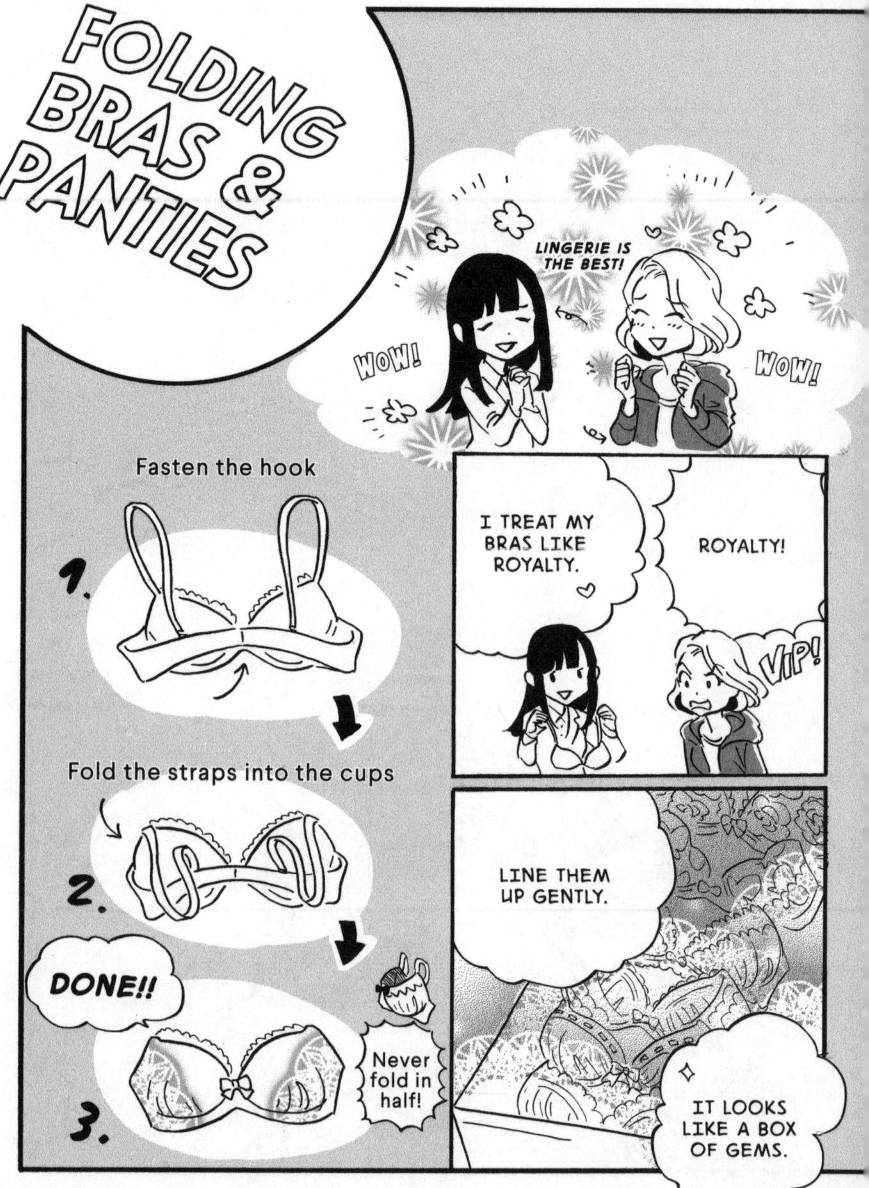
FOLDING BRAS & PANTIES
LINGERIE IS THE BEST!
WOW!
WOW!
Fasten the hook
1.
Fold the straps into the cups
2.
DONE!!
3.
Never fold in half!
I TREAT MY BRAS LIKE ROYALTY.
ROYALTY!
VIP!
LINE THEM UP GENTLY.
IT LOOKS LIKE A BOX OF GEMS.

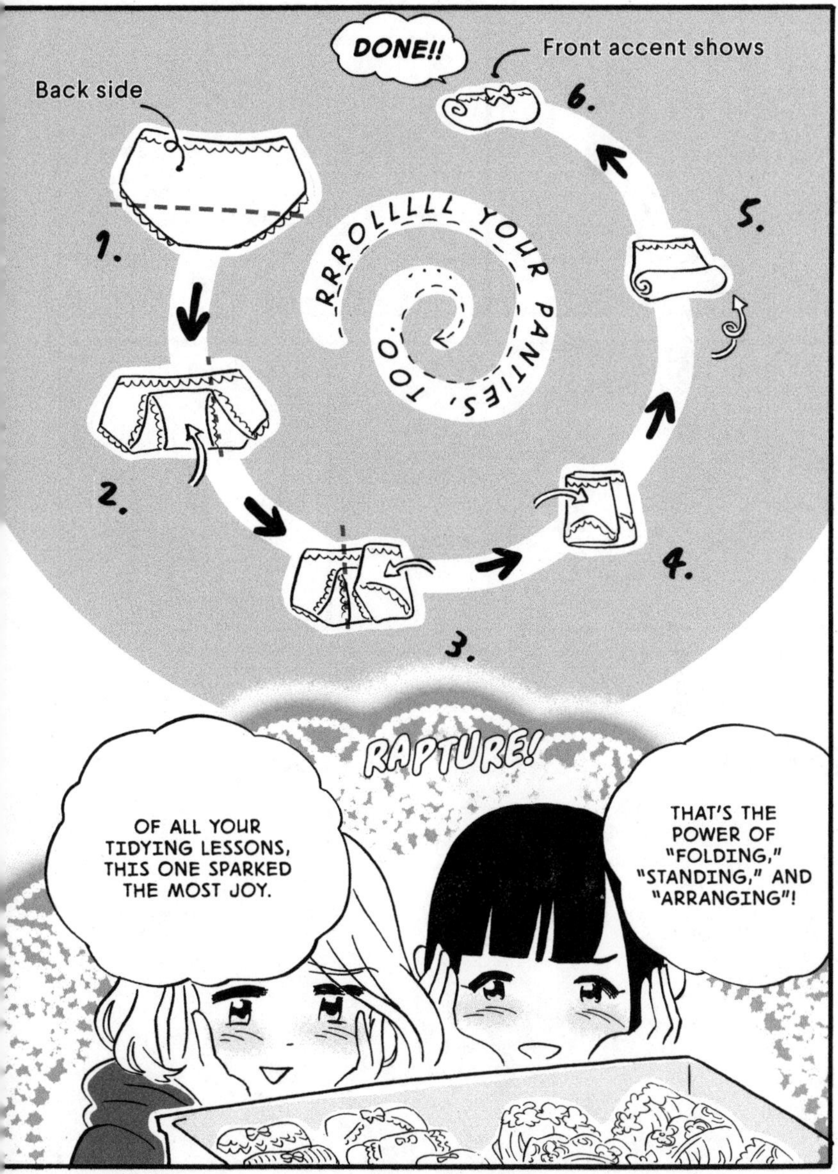

DONE!!
Front accent shows
Back side
1.
2.
3.
4.
5.
6.
RRROLLLLL YOUR PANTIES, TOO.
RAPTURE!
OF ALL YOUR TIDYING LESSONS, THIS ONE SPARKED THE MOST JOY.
THAT'S THE POWER OF "FOLDING," "STANDING," AND "ARRANGING"!

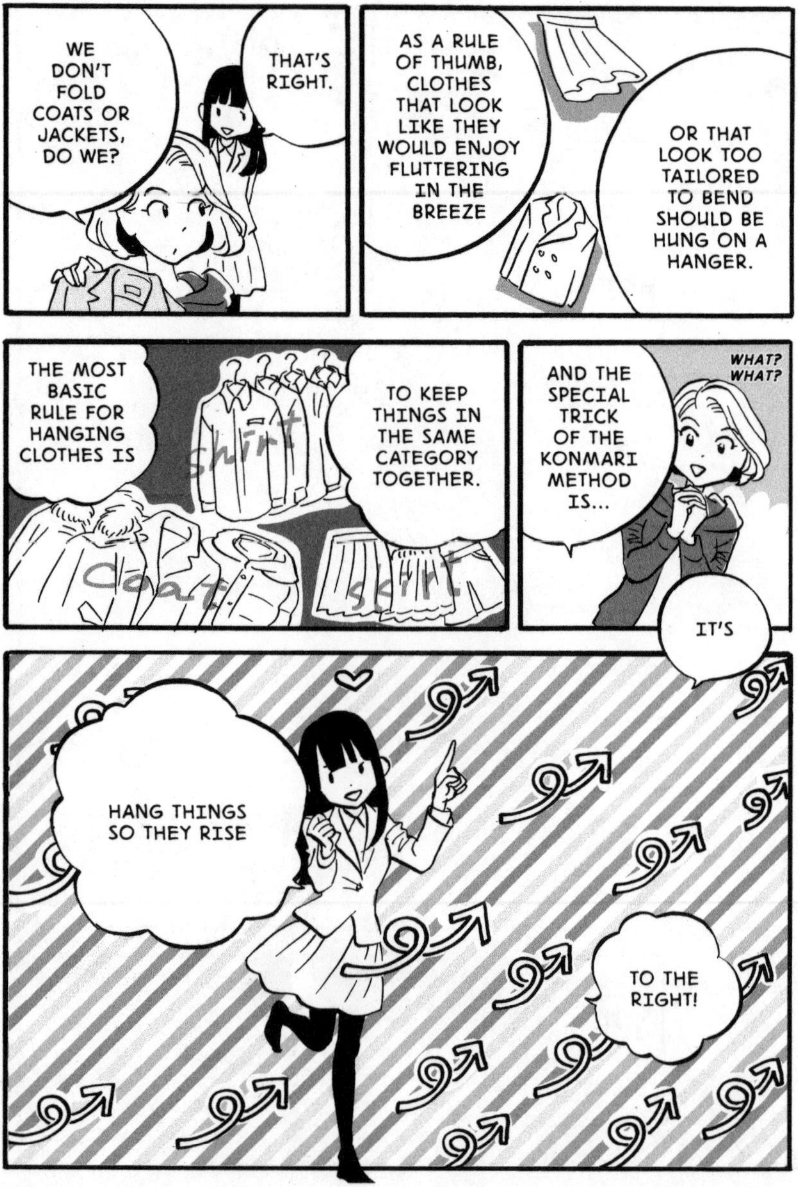
WE DON'T FOLD COATS OR JACKETS, DO WE?
THAT'S RIGHT.
AS A RULE OF THUMB, CLOTHES THAT LOOK LIKE THEY WOULD ENJOY FLUTTERING IN THE BREEZE
OR THAT LOOK TOO TAILORED TO BEND SHOULD BE HUNG ON A HANGER.
THE MOST BASIC RULE FOR HANGING CLOTHES IS
shirt
TO KEEP THINGS IN THE SAME CATEGORY TOGETHER.
coat
skirt
AND THE SPECIAL TRICK OF THE KONMARI METHOD IS...
WHAT? WHAT?
IT'S
HANG THINGS SO THEY RISE
TO THE RIGHT!

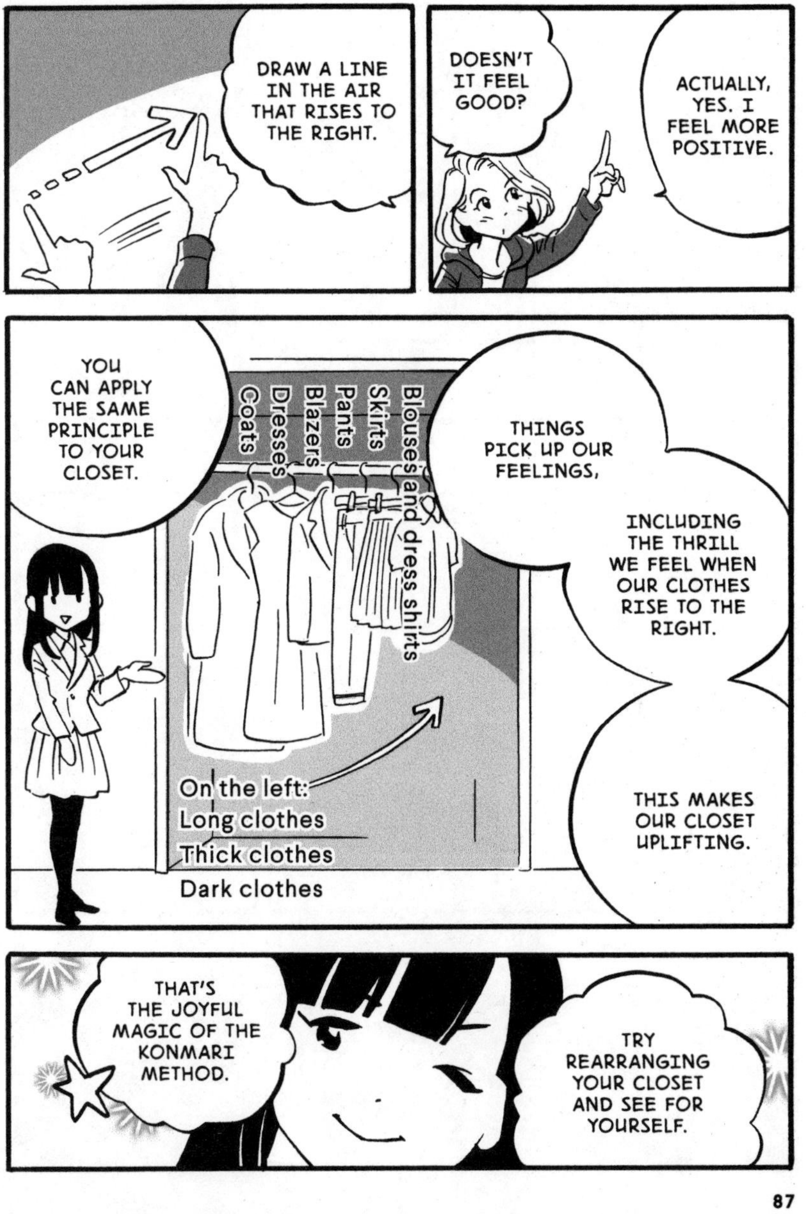
DRAW A LINE IN THE AIR THAT RISES TO THE RIGHT.
DOESN'T IT FEEL GOOD?
ACTUALLY, YES. I FEEL MORE POSITIVE.
YOU CAN APPLY THE SAME PRINCIPLE TO YOUR CLOSET.
Blouses and dress shirts
Skirts
Pants
Blazers
Dresses
Coats
On the left:
Long clothes
Thick clothes
Dark clothes
THINGS PICK UP OUR FEELINGS,
INCLUDING THE THRILL WE FEEL WHEN OUR CLOTHES RISE TO THE RIGHT.
THIS MAKES OUR CLOSET UPLIFTING.
THAT'S THE JOYFUL MAGIC OF THE KONMARI METHOD.
TRY REARRANGING YOUR CLOSET AND SEE FOR YOURSELF.

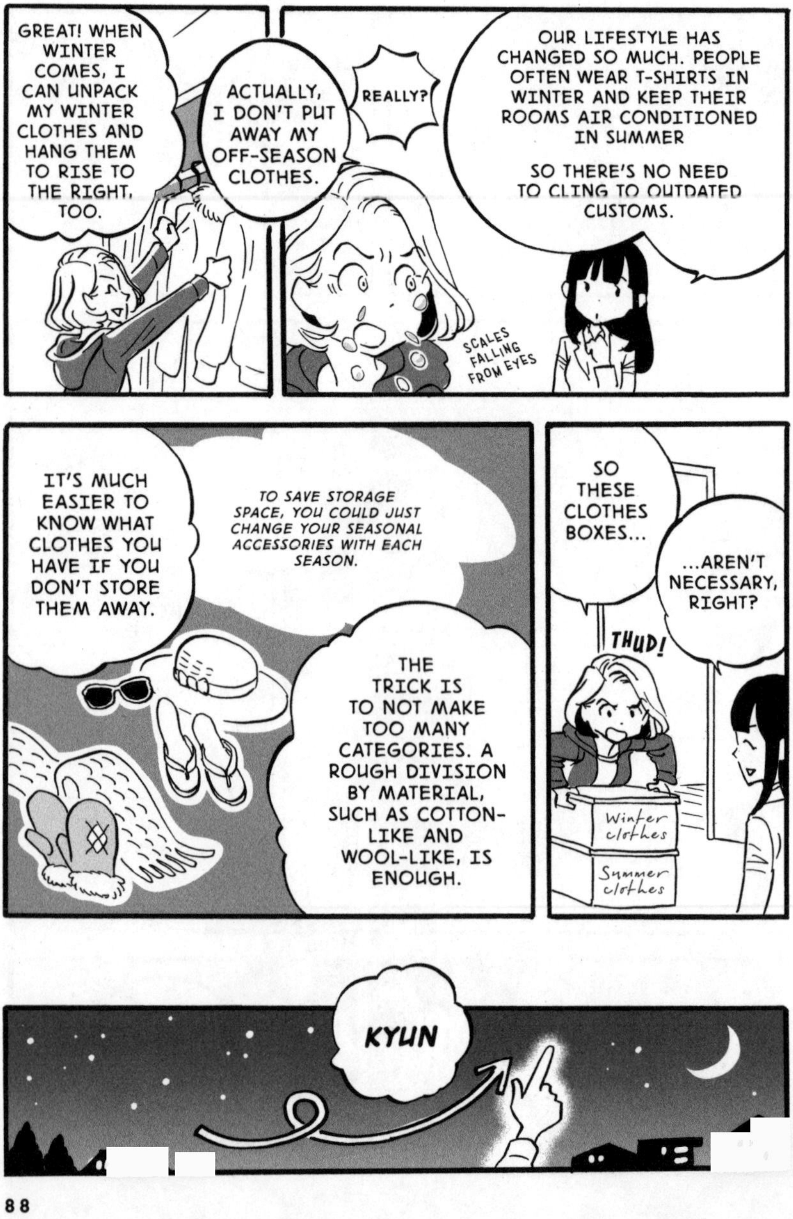
GREAT! WHEN WINTER COMES, I CAN UNPACK MY WINTER CLOTHES AND HANG THEM TO RISE TO THE RIGHT, TOO.
ACTUALLY, I DON'T PUT AWAY MY OFF-SEASON CLOTHES.
REALLY?
OUR LIFESTYLE HAS CHANGED SO MUCH. PEOPLE OFTEN WEAR T-SHIRTS IN WINTER AND KEEP THEIR ROOMS AIR CONDITIONED IN SUMMER
SO THERE'S NO NEED TO CLING TO OUTDATED CUSTOMS.
SCALES FALLING FROM EYES
IT'S MUCH EASIER TO KNOW WHAT CLOTHES YOU HAVE IF YOU DON'T STORE THEM AWAY.
TO SAVE STORAGE SPACE, YOU COULD JUST CHANGE YOUR SEASONAL ACCESSORIES WITH EACH SEASON.
THE TRICK IS TO NOT MAKE TOO MANY CATEGORIES. A ROUGH DIVISION BY MATERIAL, SUCH AS COTTON-LIKE AND WOOL-LIKE, IS ENOUGH.
SO THESE CLOTHES BOXES...
...AREN'T NECESSARY, RIGHT?
THUD!
Winter clothes
Summer clothes
KYUN

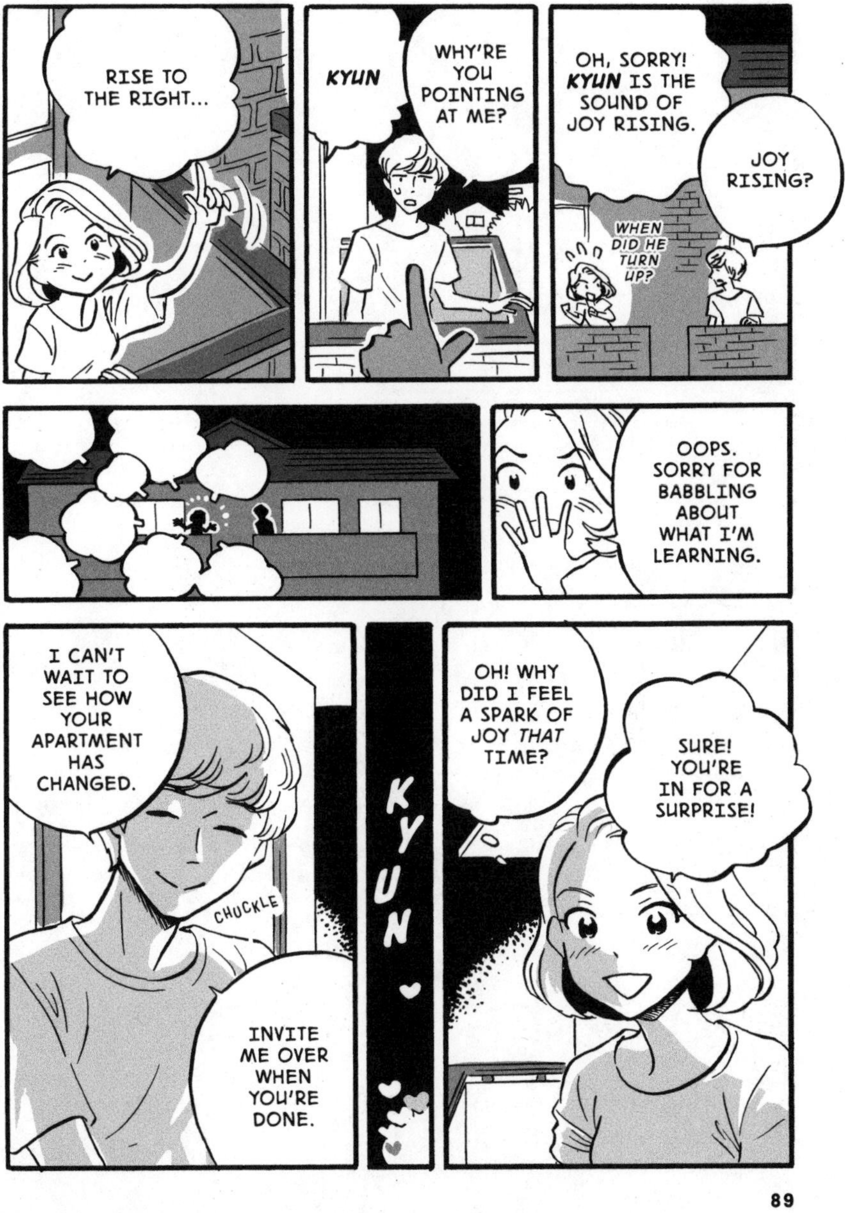
RISE TO THE RIGHT...
KYUN
WHY'RE YOU POINTING AT ME?
OH, SORRY! KYUN IS THE SOUND OF JOY RISING.
JOY RISING?
WHEN DID HE TURN UP?
OOPS. SORRY FOR BABBLING ABOUT WHAT I'M LEARNING.
I CAN'T WAIT TO SEE HOW YOUR APARTMENT HAS CHANGED.
CHUCKLE
INVITE ME OVER WHEN YOU'RE DONE.
KYUN
OH! WHY DID I FEEL A SPARK OF JOY THAT TIME?
SURE! YOU'RE IN FOR A SURPRISE!

Folding your clothes is an opportunity to show them your appreciation for all they do to support your life.

———

Do you think folding clothes and storing them in a drawer is a pain? Would you rather just hang them all in the closet? If so, you don't know the power of folding.

Folding can solve almost all your clothing storage problems. But the real value of folding is this:
By touching your clothes with your hands, you pass on your energy. Try folding your clothes with gratitude in your heart for the way they protect you.

6

choose
books
by feel

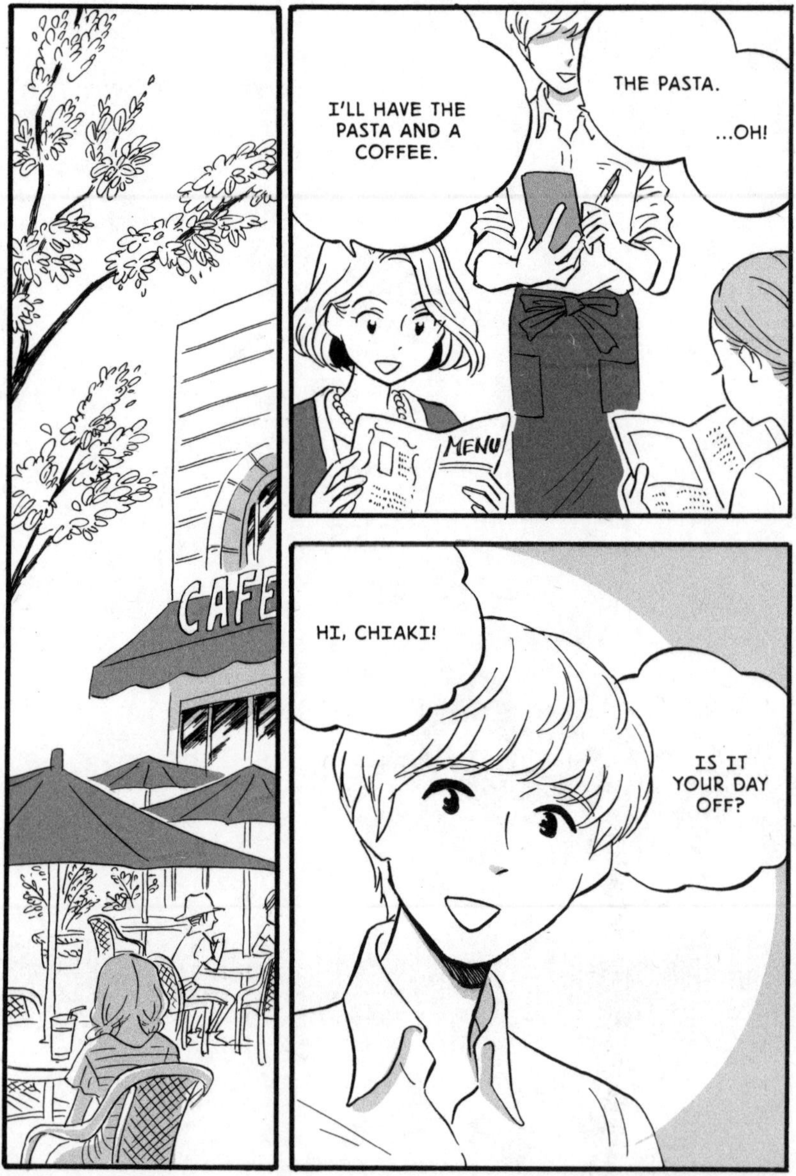
CAFE
I'LL HAVE THE PASTA AND A COFFEE.
THE PASTA.
...OH!
MENU
HI, CHIAKI!
IS IT YOUR DAY OFF?

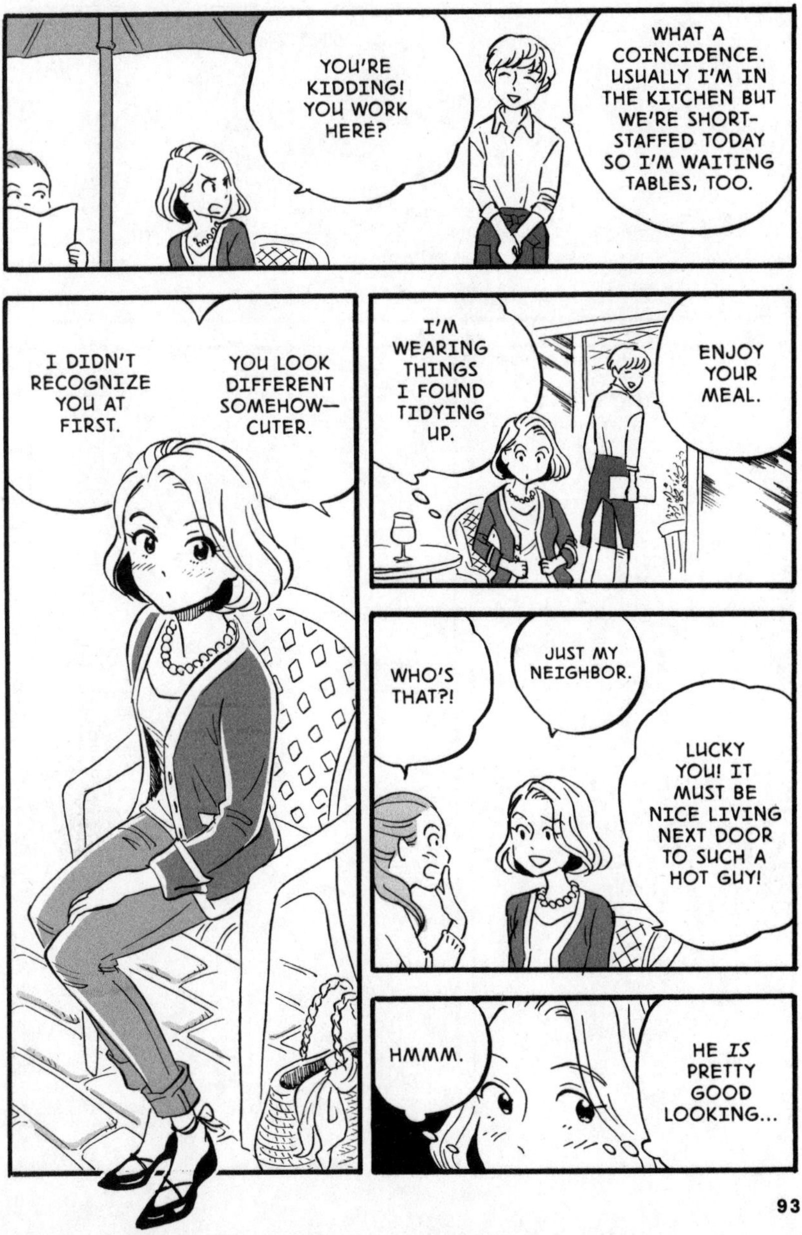
YOU'RE KIDDING! YOU WORK HERE?
WHAT A COINCIDENCE. USUALLY I'M IN THE KITCHEN BUT WE'RE SHORT-STAFFED TODAY SO I'M WAITING TABLES, TOO.
I DIDN'T RECOGNIZE YOU AT FIRST.
YOU LOOK DIFFERENT SOMEHOW—CUTER.
I'M WEARING THINGS I FOUND TIDYING UP.
ENJOY YOUR MEAL.
WHO'S THAT?!
JUST MY NEIGHBOR.
LUCKY YOU! IT MUST BE NICE LIVING NEXT DOOR TO SUCH A HOT GUY!
HMMM.
HE *IS* PRETTY GOOD LOOKING...

CUTE.

GIGGLE

DID HE SAY CUTE...?

MAYBE 'CUZ I'M WEARING "JOY" FROM MY CLOSET.

bounce

CHIAKI

CUTE

I'M HOME!

CLICK

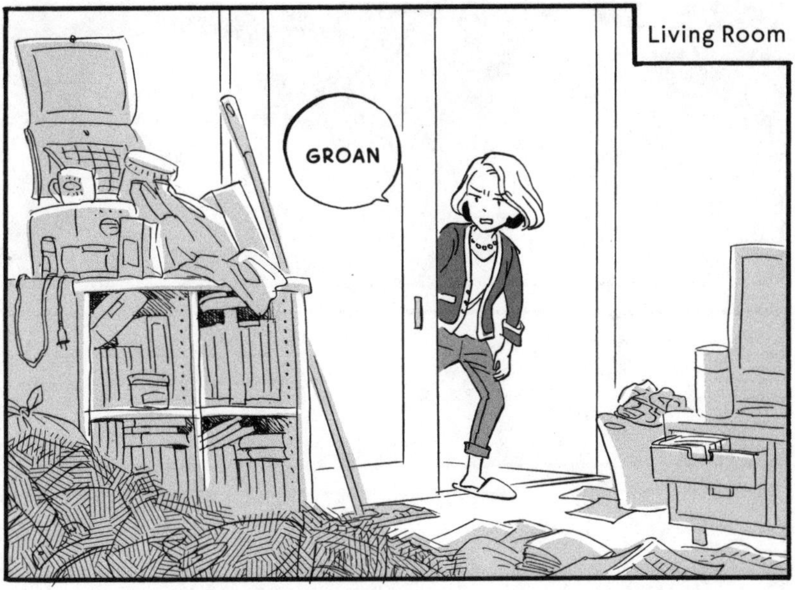
Living Room
GROAN

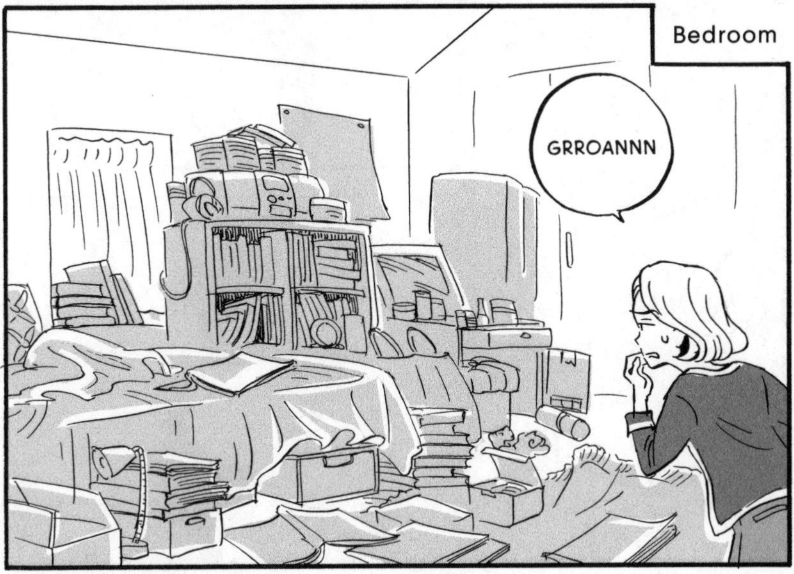
Bedroom
GRROANNN

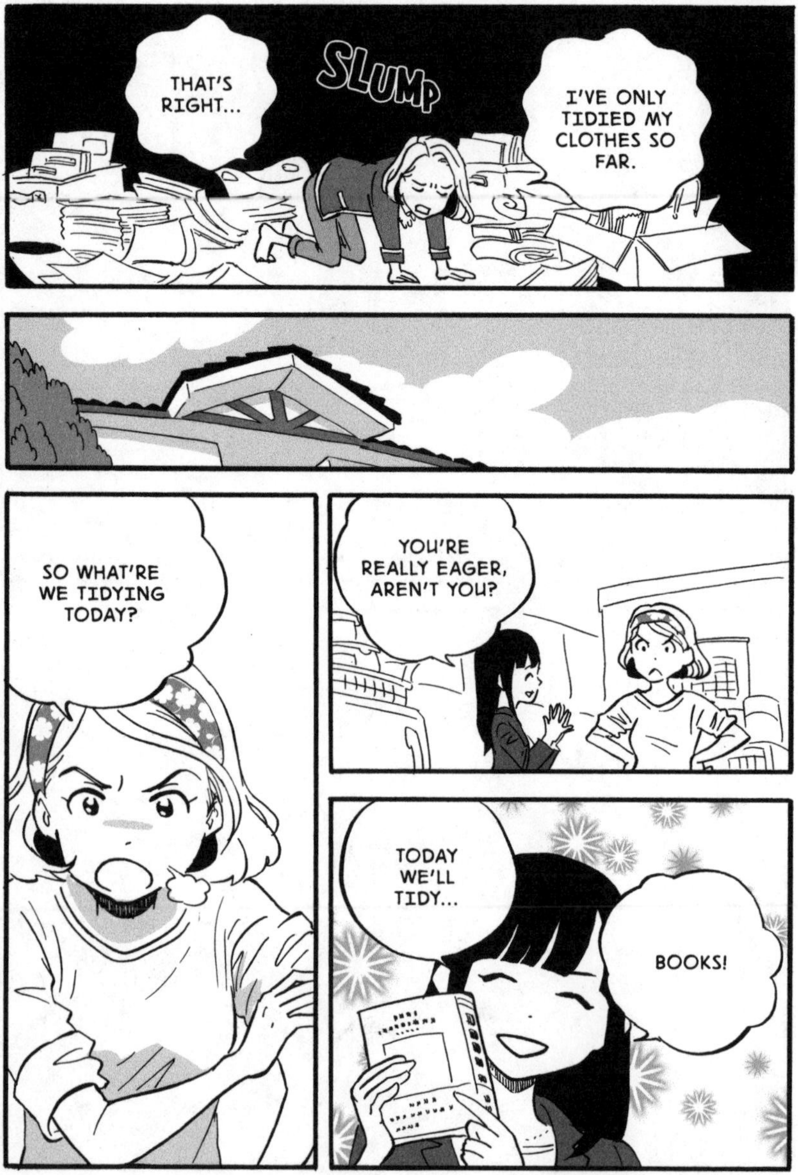
THAT'S RIGHT...
SLUMP
I'VE ONLY TIDIED MY CLOTHES SO FAR.
SO WHAT'RE WE TIDYING TODAY?
YOU'RE REALLY EAGER, AREN'T YOU?
TODAY WE'LL TIDY...
BOOKS!

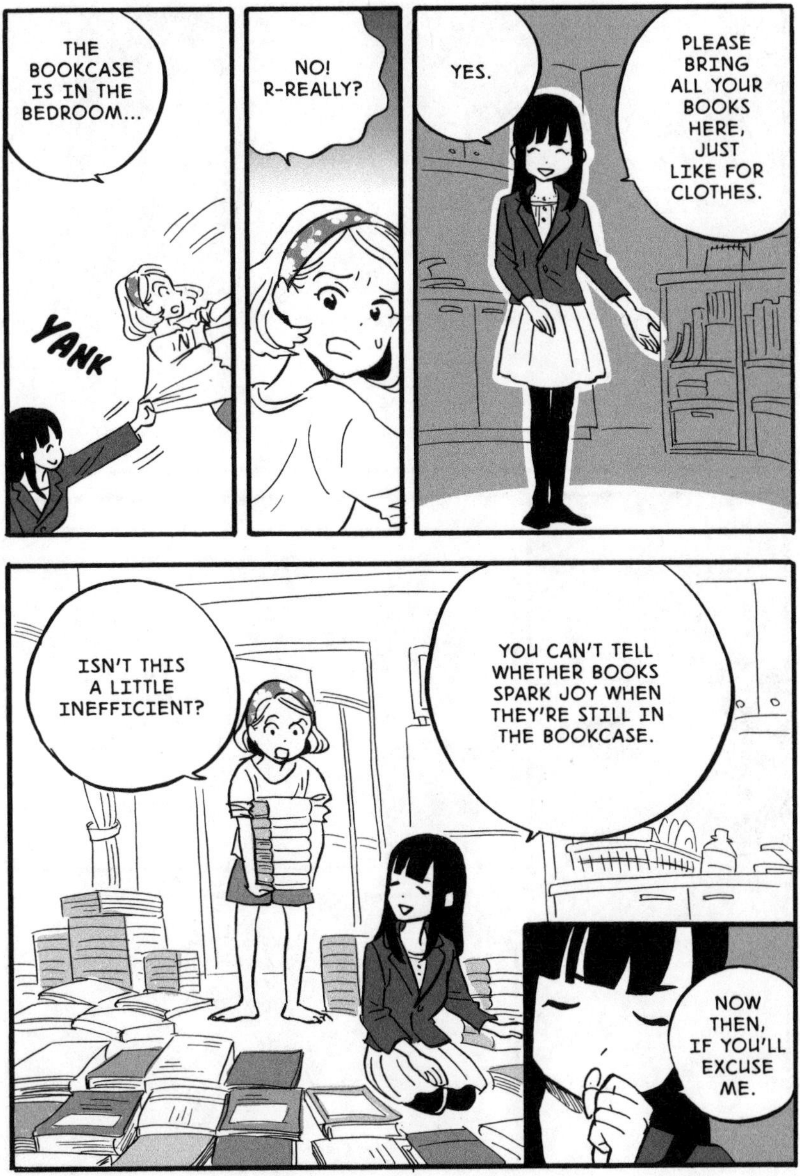
THE BOOKCASE IS IN THE BEDROOM...
YANK
NO! R-REALLY?
YES.
PLEASE BRING ALL YOUR BOOKS HERE, JUST LIKE FOR CLOTHES.
ISN'T THIS A LITTLE INEFFICIENT?
YOU CAN'T TELL WHETHER BOOKS SPARK JOY WHEN THEY'RE STILL IN THE BOOKCASE.
NOW THEN, IF YOU'LL EXCUSE ME.

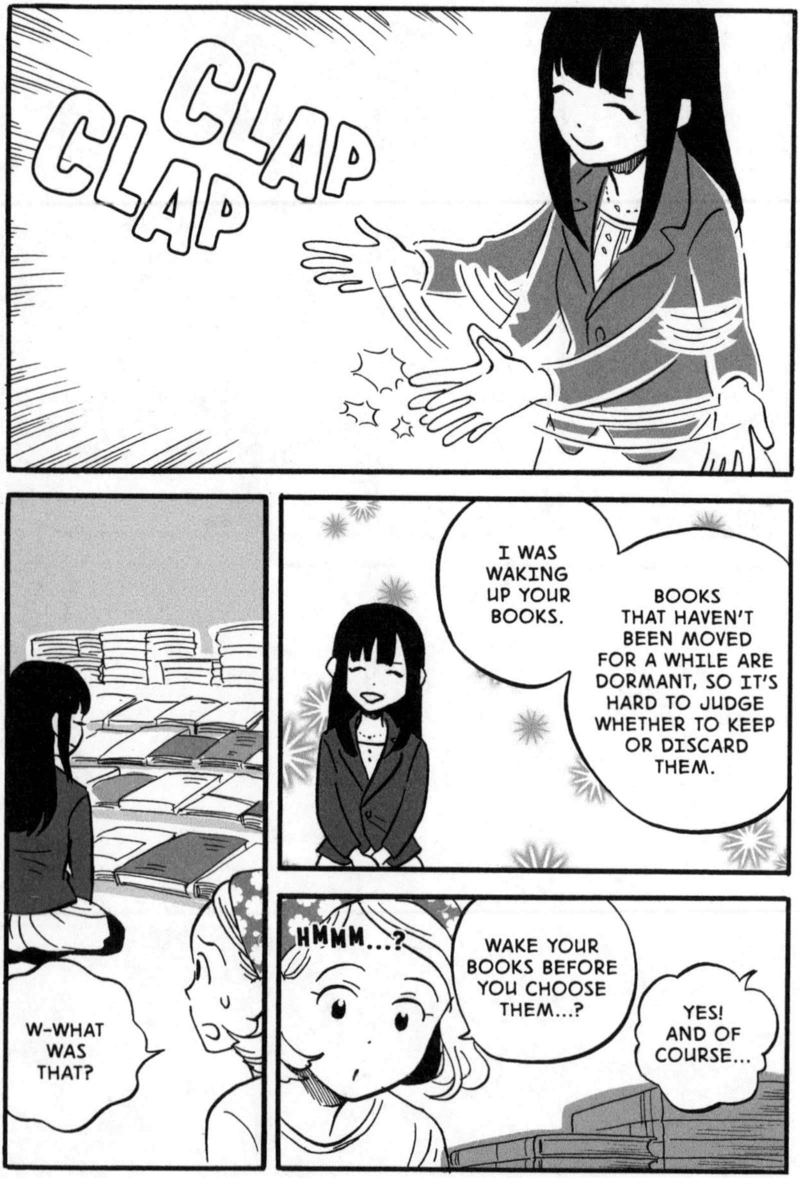
CLAP CLAP
W-WHAT WAS THAT?
I WAS WAKING UP YOUR BOOKS.
BOOKS THAT HAVEN'T BEEN MOVED FOR A WHILE ARE DORMANT, SO IT'S HARD TO JUDGE WHETHER TO KEEP OR DISCARD THEM.
HMMM...?
WAKE YOUR BOOKS BEFORE YOU CHOOSE THEM...?
YES! AND OF COURSE...

JUST LIKE CLOTHES

THE CRITERION FOR CHOOSING IS JOY.

IT'S GOING TO TAKE A LONG TIME TO DECIDE IF THEY SPARK JOY OR NOT...

OH! DON'T OPEN THEM!

FLIP FLIP

JUST SEE IF YOU FEEL ANY JOY WHEN YOU TOUCH THEM.

READING BLUNTS YOUR JOY DETECTOR. YOU'LL START THINKING ABOUT WHETHER YOU NEED A BOOK INSTEAD OF HOW IT MAKES YOU FEEL.

BUT, BUT...

THEY'RE BOOKS!

99

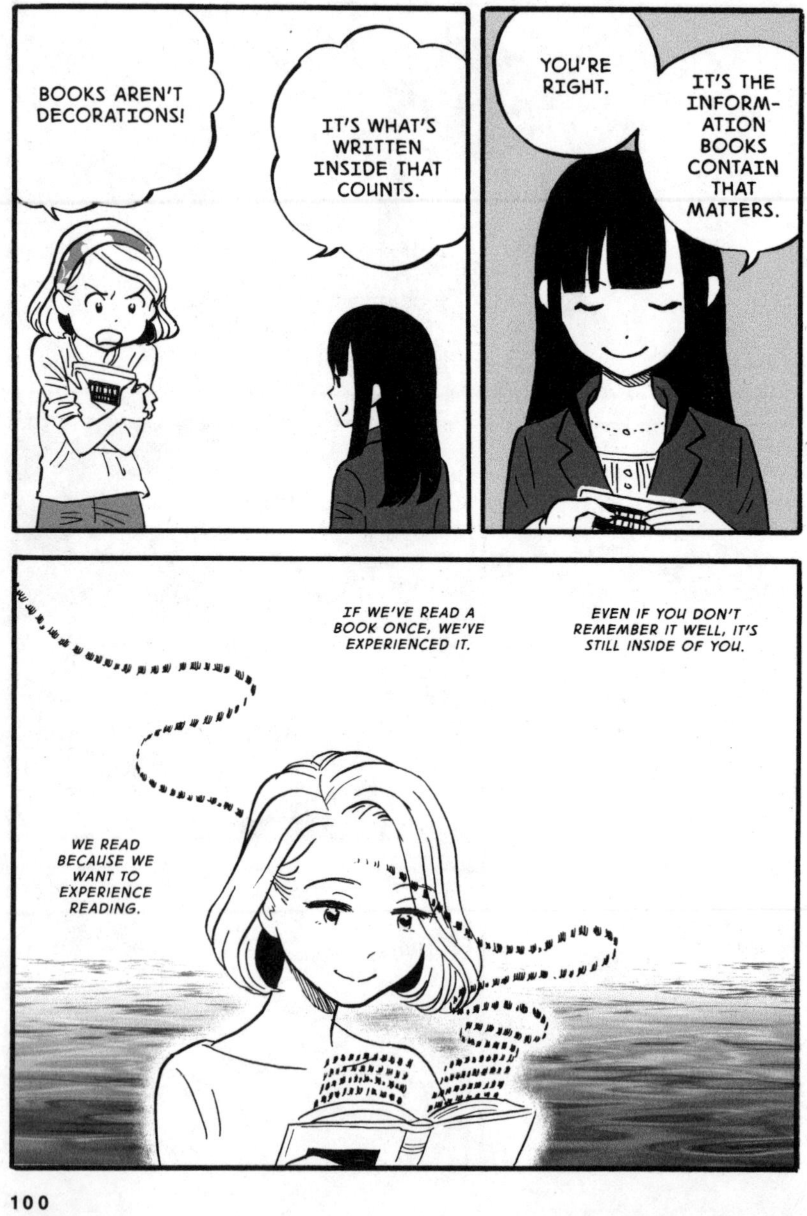
BOOKS AREN'T DECORATIONS!
IT'S WHAT'S WRITTEN INSIDE THAT COUNTS.
YOU'RE RIGHT.
IT'S THE INFORMATION BOOKS CONTAIN THAT MATTERS.
IF WE'VE READ A BOOK ONCE, WE'VE EXPERIENCED IT.
EVEN IF YOU DON'T REMEMBER IT WELL, IT'S STILL INSIDE OF YOU.
WE READ BECAUSE WE WANT TO EXPERIENCE READING.

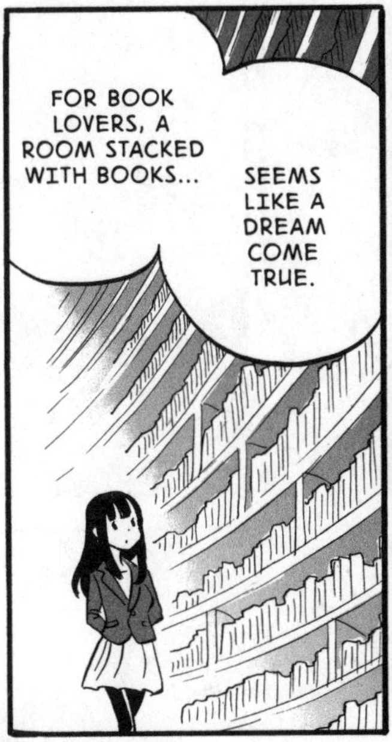
FOR BOOK LOVERS, A ROOM STACKED WITH BOOKS...
SEEMS LIKE A DREAM COME TRUE.

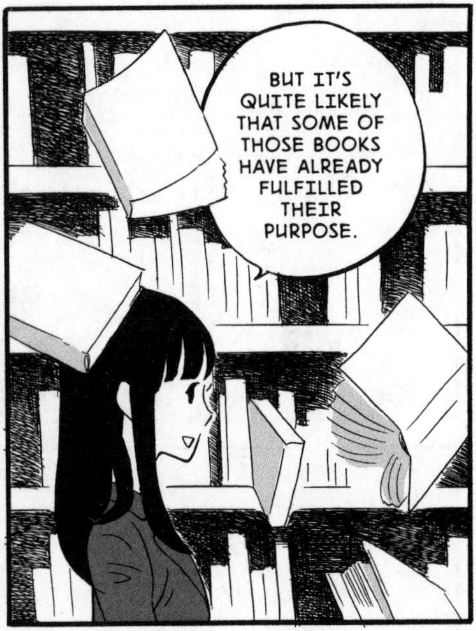
BUT IT'S QUITE LIKELY THAT SOME OF THOSE BOOKS HAVE ALREADY FULFILLED THEIR PURPOSE.

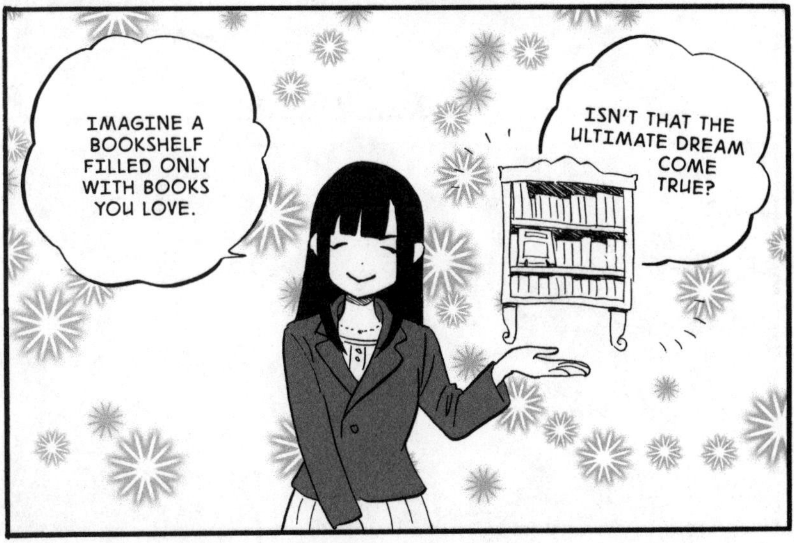
IMAGINE A BOOKSHELF FILLED ONLY WITH BOOKS YOU LOVE.
ISN'T THAT THE ULTIMATE DREAM COME TRUE?

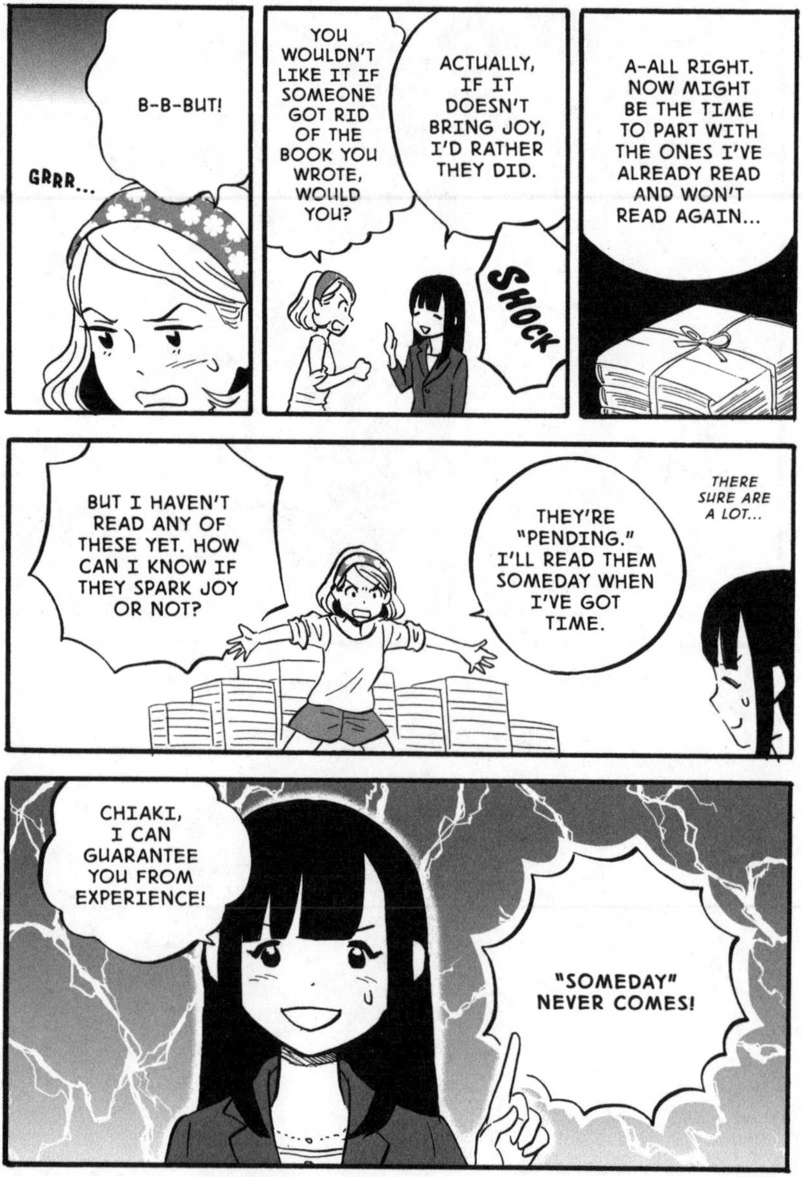

B-B-BUT!
GRRR...
YOU WOULDN'T LIKE IT IF SOMEONE GOT RID OF THE BOOK YOU WROTE, WOULD YOU?
ACTUALLY, IF IT DOESN'T BRING JOY, I'D RATHER THEY DID.
SHOCK
A-ALL RIGHT. NOW MIGHT BE THE TIME TO PART WITH THE ONES I'VE ALREADY READ AND WON'T READ AGAIN...
BUT I HAVEN'T READ ANY OF THESE YET. HOW CAN I KNOW IF THEY SPARK JOY OR NOT?
THEY'RE "PENDING." I'LL READ THEM SOMEDAY WHEN I'VE GOT TIME.
THERE SURE ARE A LOT...
CHIAKI, I CAN GUARANTEE YOU FROM EXPERIENCE!
"SOMEDAY" NEVER COMES!

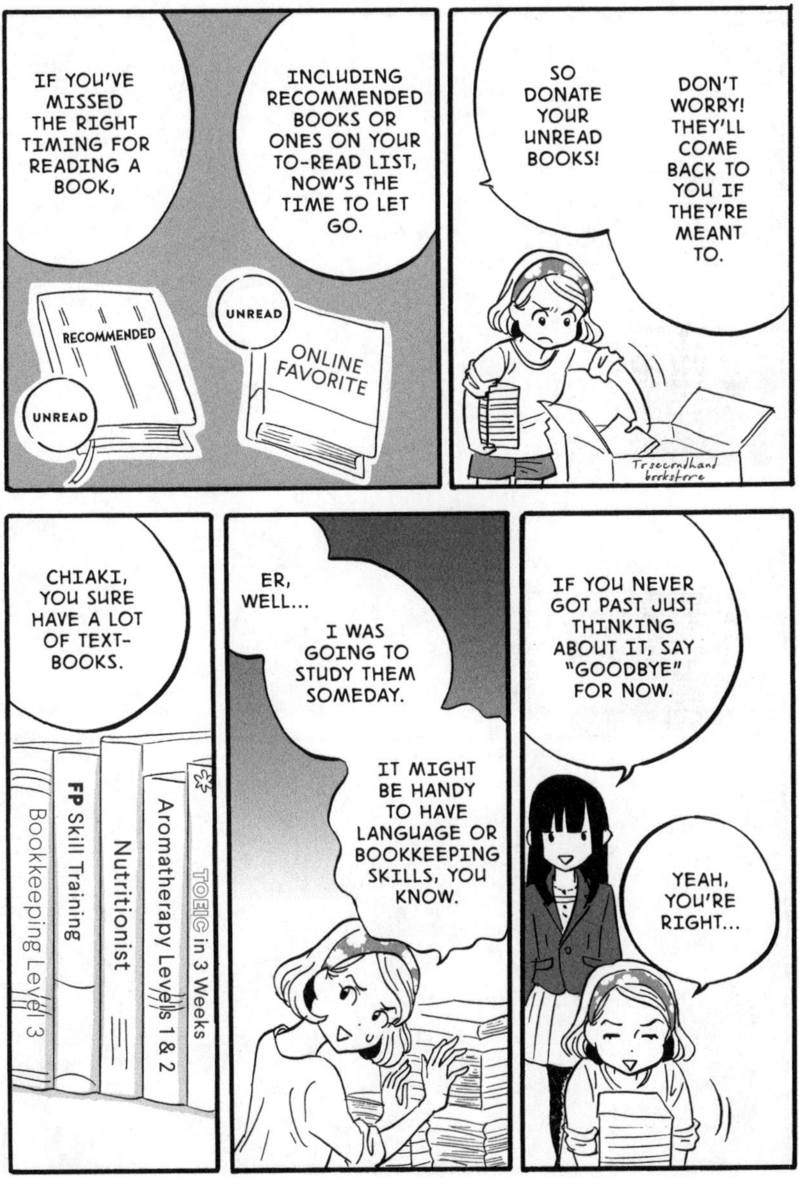
IF YOU'VE MISSED THE RIGHT TIMING FOR READING A BOOK,
INCLUDING RECOMMENDED BOOKS OR ONES ON YOUR TO-READ LIST, NOW'S THE TIME TO LET GO.
RECOMMENDED
UNREAD
UNREAD
ONLINE FAVORITE
SO DONATE YOUR UNREAD BOOKS!
DON'T WORRY! THEY'LL COME BACK TO YOU IF THEY'RE MEANT TO.
To secondhand bookstore
CHIAKI, YOU SURE HAVE A LOT OF TEXT-BOOKS.
Bookkeeping Level 3
FP Skill Training
Nutritionist
Aromatherapy Levels 1 & 2
TOEIC in 3 Weeks
ER, WELL...
I WAS GOING TO STUDY THEM SOMEDAY.
IT MIGHT BE HANDY TO HAVE LANGUAGE OR BOOKKEEPING SKILLS, YOU KNOW.
IF YOU NEVER GOT PAST JUST THINKING ABOUT IT, SAY "GOODBYE" FOR NOW.
YEAH, YOU'RE RIGHT...

WAIT! WHY DON'T I FILE THEM?

I COULD TEAR OUT PICTURES

AND COPY THE IMPORTANT POINTS INTO A NOTEBOOK...

I HATE TO BREAK THIS TO YOU...

BUT I'VE ALREADY TRIED THAT...

EVEN IF YOU MAKE A FILE, YOU'LL NEVER LOOK AT IT.

WHEN IT COMES TO BOOKS, TIMING IS EVERYTHING! THE TIME TO READ EACH BOOK IS THE MOMENT YOU GET IT.

...

DID I JUST SEE YOU HIDE SOMETHING?
WHOOSH!
I...
I JUST CAN'T
FLUTTER
PART WITH THIS ONE!

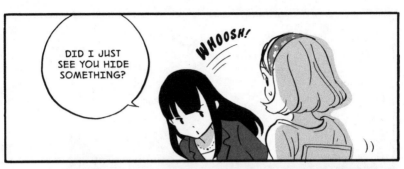

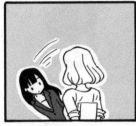

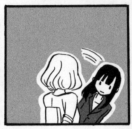

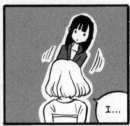

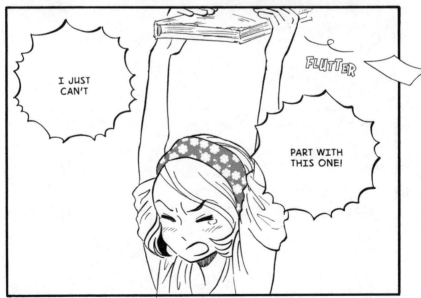

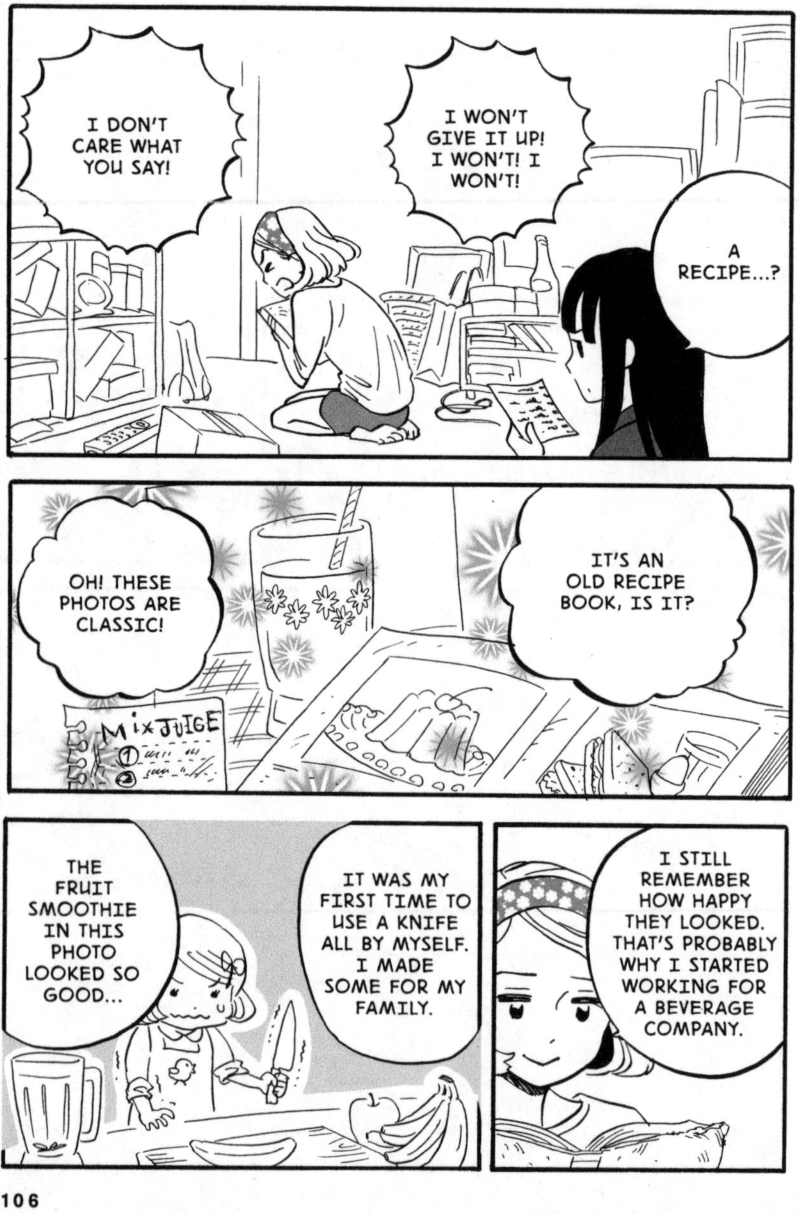
I DON'T CARE WHAT YOU SAY!
I WON'T GIVE IT UP! I WON'T! I WON'T!
A RECIPE...?
OH! THESE PHOTOS ARE CLASSIC!
IT'S AN OLD RECIPE BOOK, IS IT?
THE FRUIT SMOOTHIE IN THIS PHOTO LOOKED SO GOOD...
IT WAS MY FIRST TIME TO USE A KNIFE ALL BY MYSELF. I MADE SOME FOR MY FAMILY.
I STILL REMEMBER HOW HAPPY THEY LOOKED. THAT'S PROBABLY WHY I STARTED WORKING FOR A BEVERAGE COMPANY.

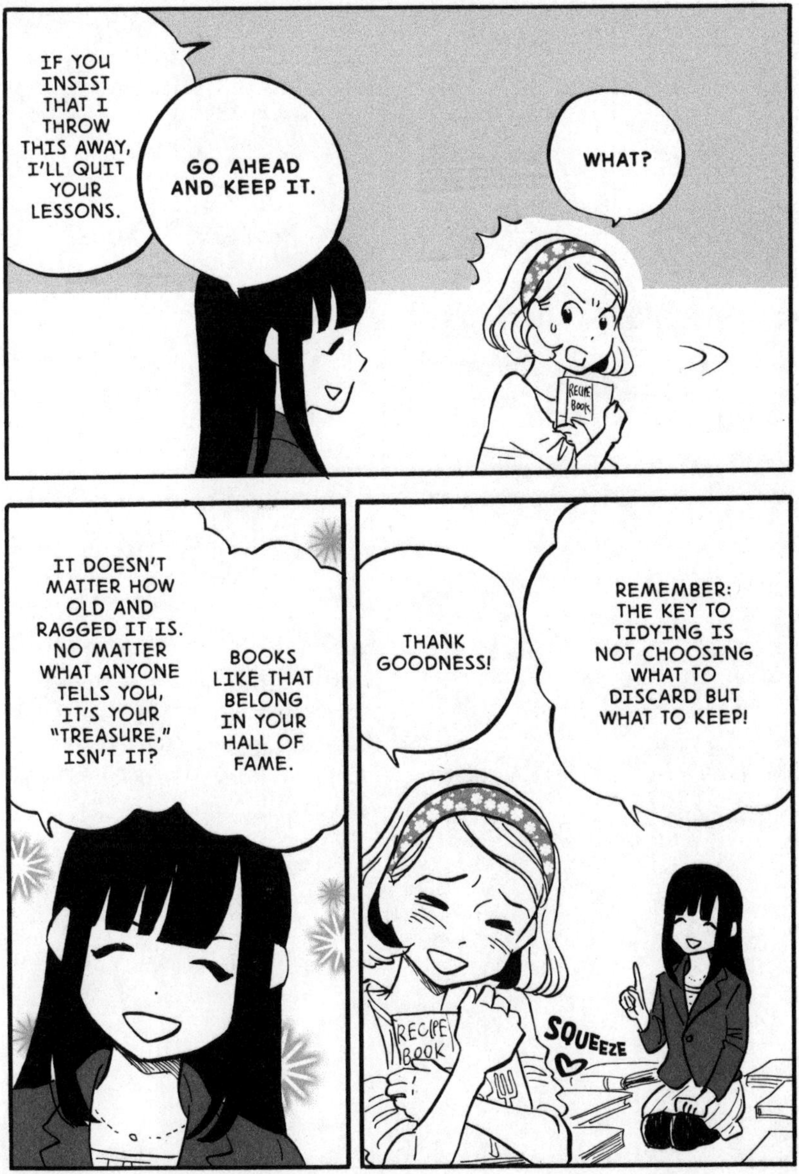
IF YOU INSIST THAT I THROW THIS AWAY, I'LL QUIT YOUR LESSONS.
GO AHEAD AND KEEP IT.
WHAT?
RECIPE BOOK
IT DOESN'T MATTER HOW OLD AND RAGGED IT IS. NO MATTER WHAT ANYONE TELLS YOU, IT'S YOUR "TREASURE," ISN'T IT?
BOOKS LIKE THAT BELONG IN YOUR HALL OF FAME.
THANK GOODNESS!
REMEMBER: THE KEY TO TIDYING IS NOT CHOOSING WHAT TO DISCARD BUT WHAT TO KEEP!
RECIPE BOOK
SQUEEZE

Do you have unread books that you intend to read "someday"? Believe me. "Someday" never comes.

———

Take all your books off the shelf and put them on the floor. Pick them up one by one and choose which ones you want to keep. Of course, the criterion is whether or not they spark joy. Keep those that belong in your personal Hall of Fame and treasure them.

Take this opportunity to get rid of all your unread, neglected books. When you're left with only those that spark joy, you'll find that the quality of information that comes your way changes dramatically.

By discarding books, you create space for an equivalent amount of information, and you'll soon see that the information you need comes right when you need it.

7

papers and *komono*

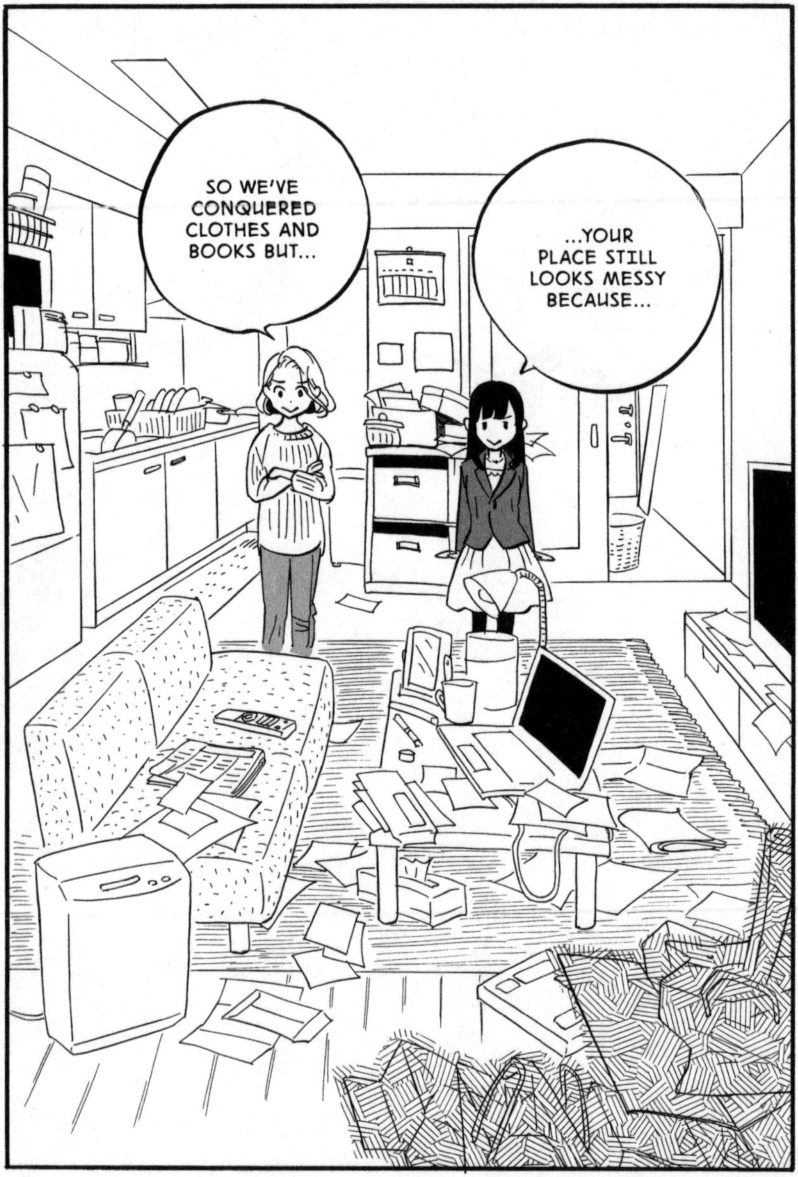
SO WE'VE CONQUERED CLOTHES AND BOOKS BUT...
...YOUR PLACE STILL LOOKS MESSY BECAUSE...

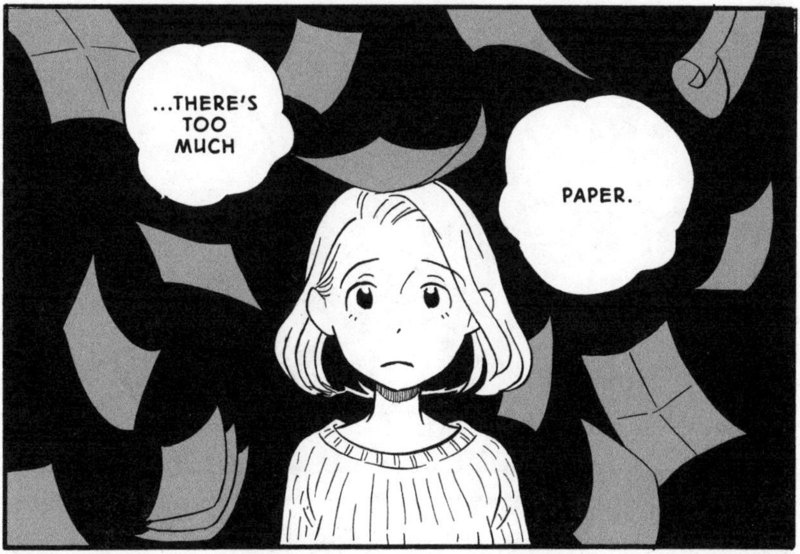
...THERE'S TOO MUCH
PAPER.

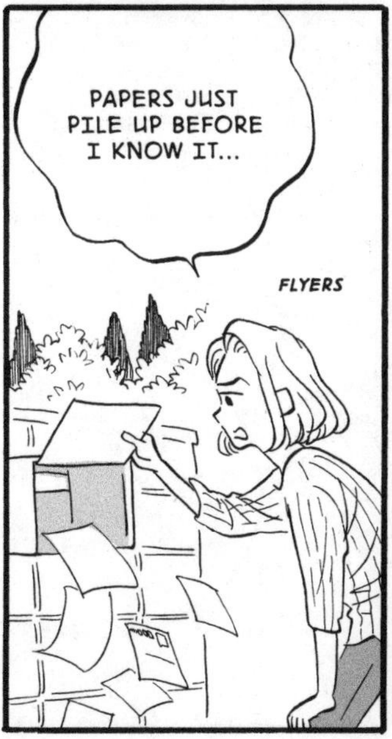
PAPERS JUST PILE UP BEFORE I KNOW IT...
FLYERS

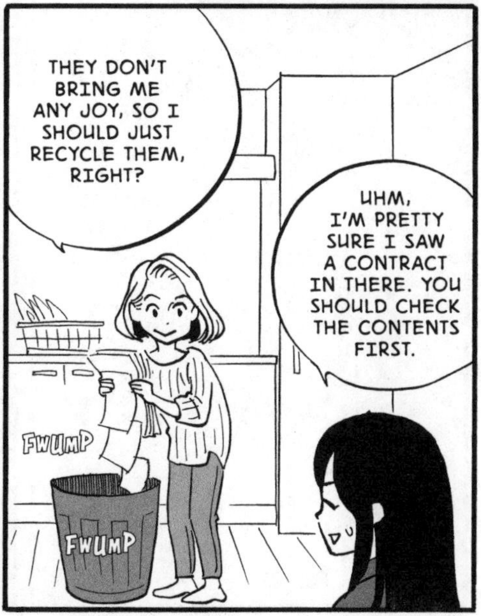
THEY DON'T BRING ME ANY JOY, SO I SHOULD JUST RECYCLE THEM, RIGHT?
UHM, I'M PRETTY SURE I SAW A CONTRACT IN THERE. YOU SHOULD CHECK THE CONTENTS FIRST.
FWUMP
FWUMP

BUT, YES, IN THE END...

THE RULE OF THUMB IS TO DISCARD THEM ALL.

SEE?

I KNEW IT!

ON THE TV, THE TABLE...I SEEM TO LEAVE PAPERS EVERYWHERE.

PAPERS ACTUALLY TEND TO PILE UP IN CERTAIN PLACES, LIKE SNOWDRIFTS.

PEOPLE OFTEN THINK A HOME HAS LESS PAPER THAN AN OFFICE,

BUT WHEN YOU GATHER THEM ALL TOGETHER, THERE'S QUITE A LOT.

SHREDDER GOING FULL BLAST

ONE OF MY CLIENTS HAD FIFTEEN BAGS OF PAPER RECYCLING.

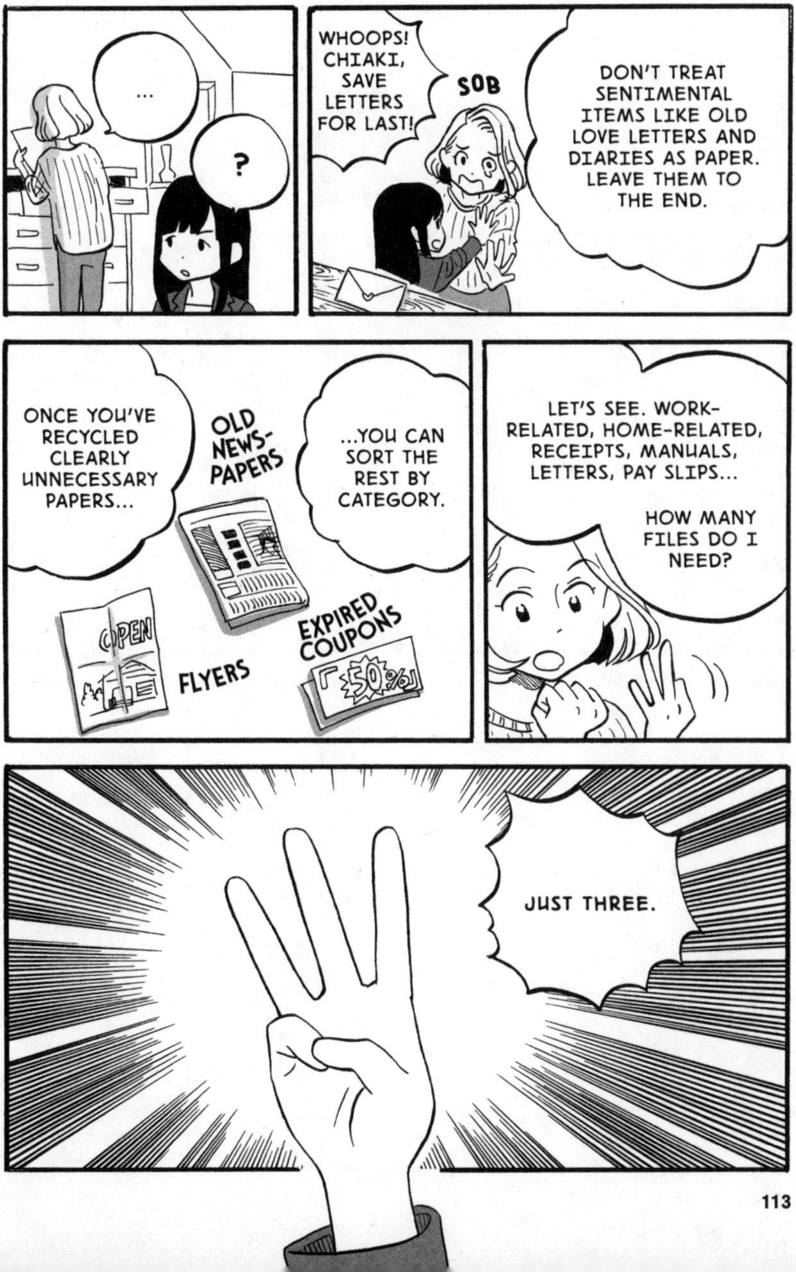
...
?
WHOOPS! CHIAKI, SAVE LETTERS FOR LAST!
SOB
DON'T TREAT SENTIMENTAL ITEMS LIKE OLD LOVE LETTERS AND DIARIES AS PAPER. LEAVE THEM TO THE END.
ONCE YOU'VE RECYCLED CLEARLY UNNECESSARY PAPERS...
OLD NEWS-PAPERS
...YOU CAN SORT THE REST BY CATEGORY.
OPEN
FLYERS
EXPIRED COUPONS
50%
LET'S SEE. WORK-RELATED, HOME-RELATED, RECEIPTS, MANUALS, LETTERS, PAY SLIPS...
HOW MANY FILES DO I NEED?
JUST THREE.

THREE?

YES. YOU CAN USE UP TO THREE FOLDERS OR CONTAINERS.

Needs Attention

Save (contractual)

Save (other)

JUST THESE THREE.

I GET THE FIRST ONE— PENDING.

LETTERS I NEED TO ANSWER, RECEIPTS FOR MY BUDGET...

PLOP PLOP

THE IDEAL IS TO KEEP THIS BOX EMPTY.

I DON'T ALWAYS MAN- AGE IT MYSELF.

I'M NOT SURE ABOUT CATEGORIES TWO AND THREE, "CONTRACTUAL" AND "OTHER."

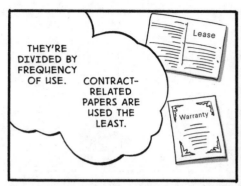

THEY'RE DIVIDED BY FREQUENCY OF USE.
CONTRACT-RELATED PAPERS ARE USED THE LEAST.
Lease
Warranty
YOU HARDLY EVER LOOK AT THESE, RIGHT?
Lease contract
Insurance Policy
PUT THEM ALL IN ONE CLEAR PLASTIC FILE.
IT'S THAT SIMPLE?
JUST BECAUSE THEY'RE IMPORTANT DOESN'T MEAN YOU NEED TO KEEP THEM IN IMPRESSIVE FILES. IT'S BEST TO SIMPLIFY WHEN YOU CAN.
I THOUGHT I HAD TO STORE THIS FOR LIFE IN A REALLY STURDY FILE...
THIS IS SO THIN!
CATEGORY THREE, "OTHER"...
...IS EVERYTHING ELSE BESIDES ONE AND TWO.
THIS MEANS PAPERS YOU USE FAIRLY FREQUENTLY
BUT THAT YOU DON'T NEED TO SAVE AS LONG AS CONTRACTS.

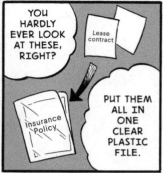

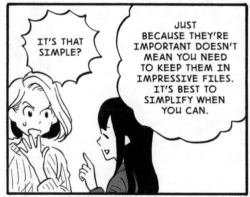

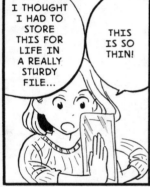

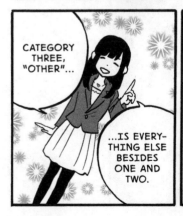

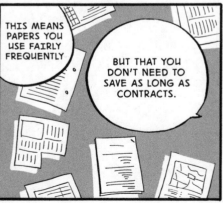

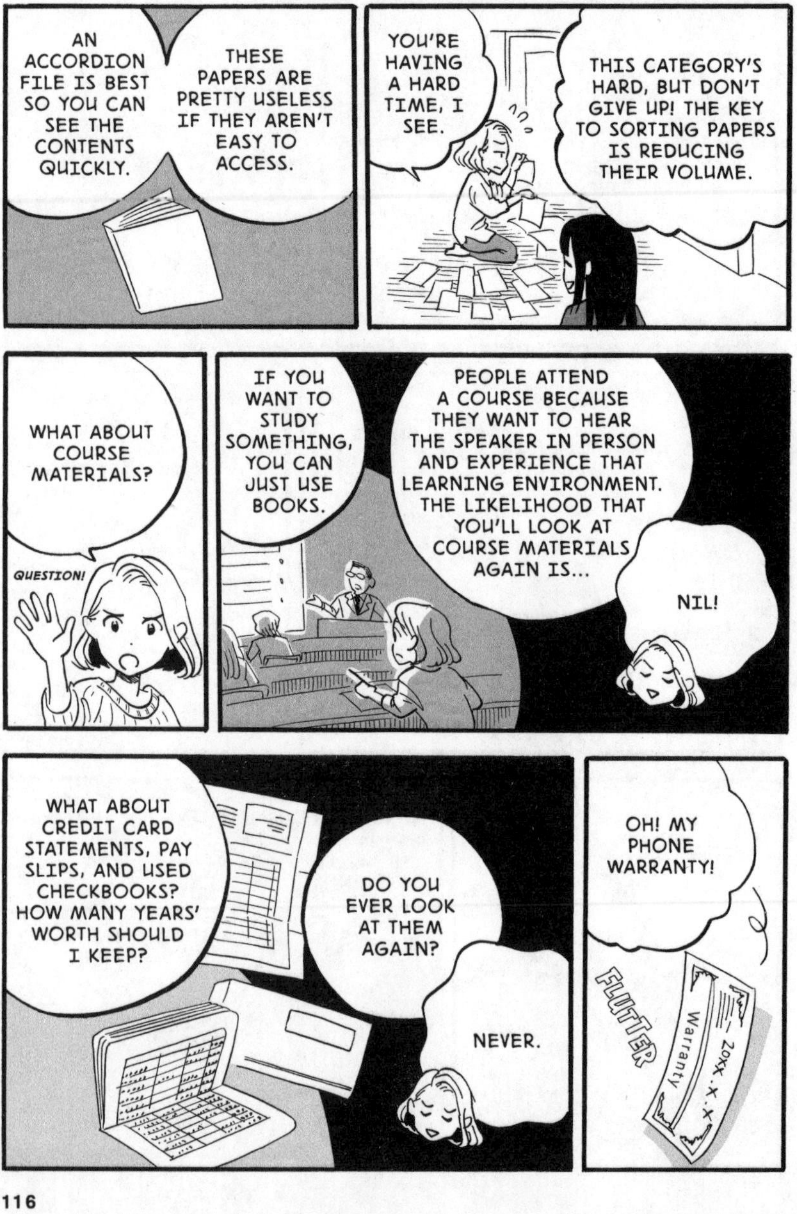
AN ACCORDION FILE IS BEST SO YOU CAN SEE THE CONTENTS QUICKLY.
THESE PAPERS ARE PRETTY USELESS IF THEY AREN'T EASY TO ACCESS.
YOU'RE HAVING A HARD TIME, I SEE.
THIS CATEGORY'S HARD, BUT DON'T GIVE UP! THE KEY TO SORTING PAPERS IS REDUCING THEIR VOLUME.
WHAT ABOUT COURSE MATERIALS?
QUESTION!
IF YOU WANT TO STUDY SOMETHING, YOU CAN JUST USE BOOKS.
PEOPLE ATTEND A COURSE BECAUSE THEY WANT TO HEAR THE SPEAKER IN PERSON AND EXPERIENCE THAT LEARNING ENVIRONMENT. THE LIKELIHOOD THAT YOU'LL LOOK AT COURSE MATERIALS AGAIN IS...
NIL!
WHAT ABOUT CREDIT CARD STATEMENTS, PAY SLIPS, AND USED CHECKBOOKS? HOW MANY YEARS' WORTH SHOULD I KEEP?
DO YOU EVER LOOK AT THEM AGAIN?
NEVER.
OH! MY PHONE WARRANTY!
FLUTTER
Warranty
20XX.X.X

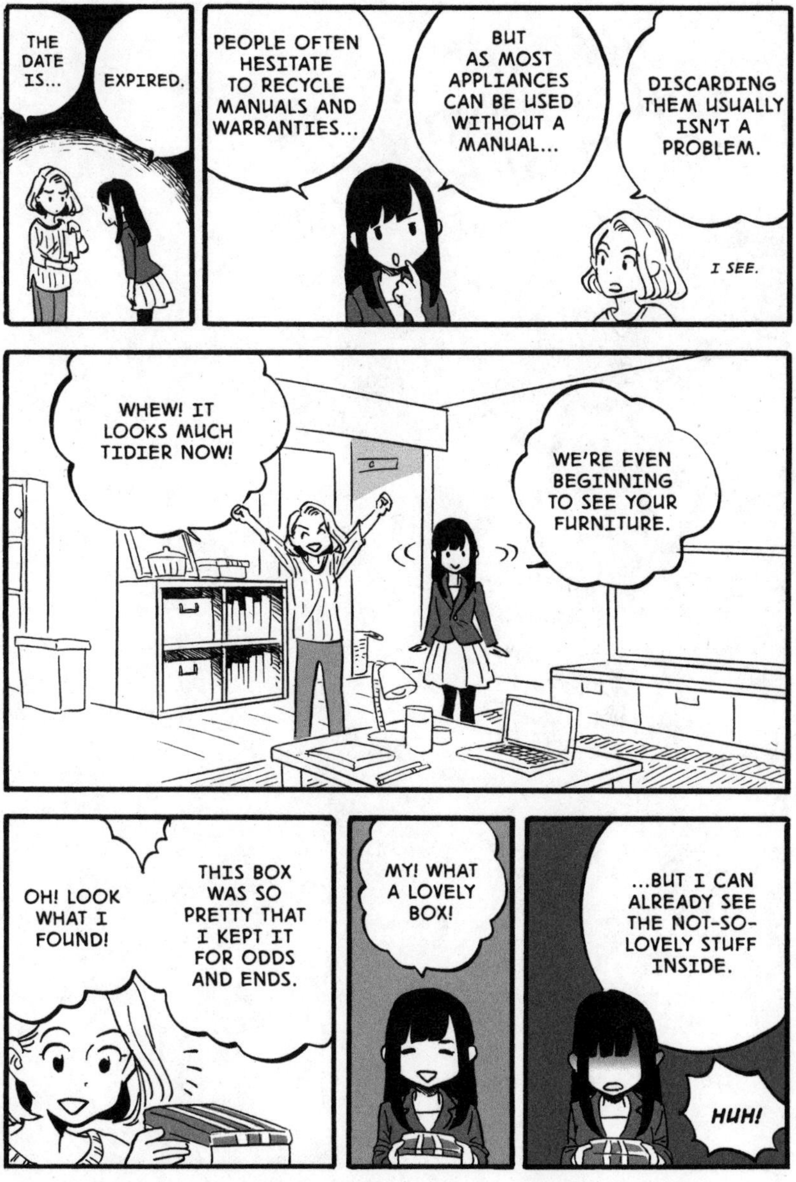
THE DATE IS...
EXPIRED.
PEOPLE OFTEN HESITATE TO RECYCLE MANUALS AND WARRANTIES...
BUT AS MOST APPLIANCES CAN BE USED WITHOUT A MANUAL...
DISCARDING THEM USUALLY ISN'T A PROBLEM.
I SEE.
WHEW! IT LOOKS MUCH TIDIER NOW!
WE'RE EVEN BEGINNING TO SEE YOUR FURNITURE.
OH! LOOK WHAT I FOUND!
THIS BOX WAS SO PRETTY THAT I KEPT IT FOR ODDS AND ENDS.
MY! WHAT A LOVELY BOX!
...BUT I CAN ALREADY SEE THE NOT-SO-LOVELY STUFF INSIDE.
HUH!

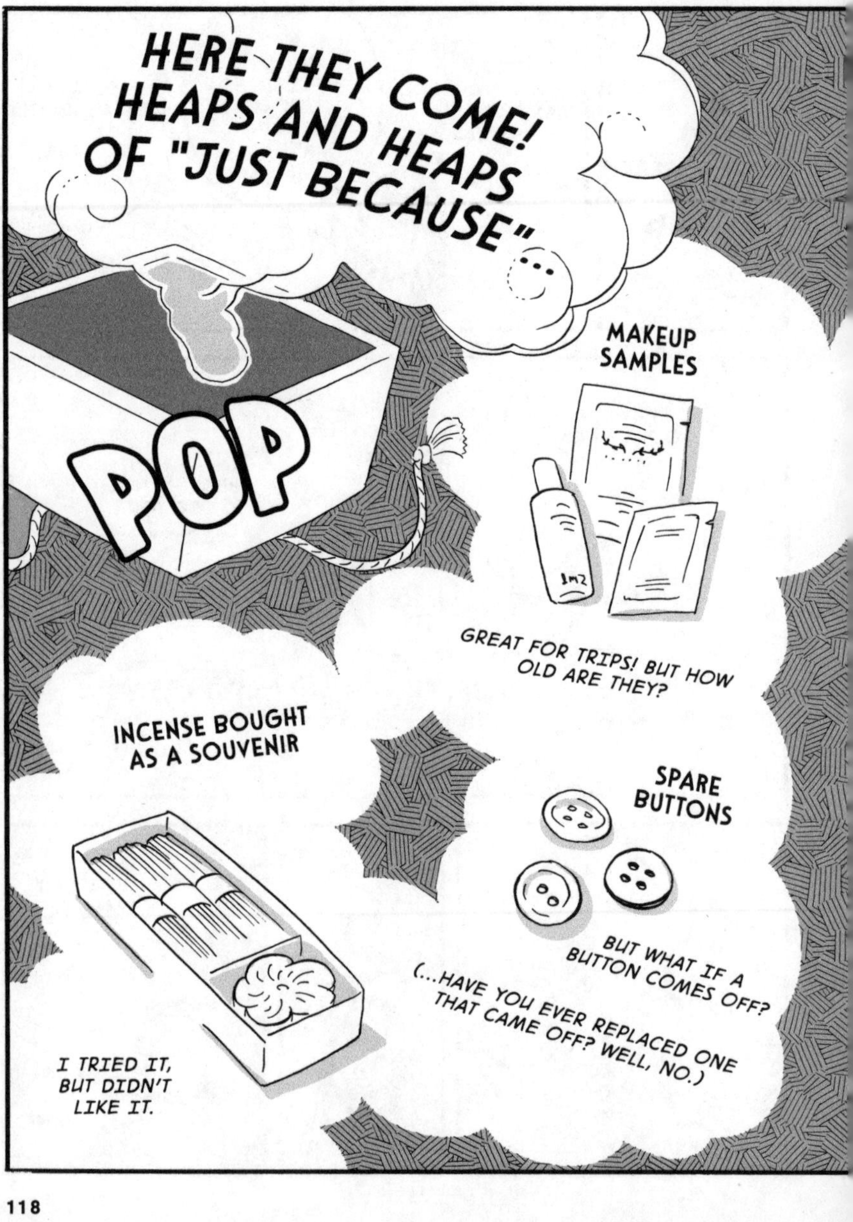
HERE THEY COME! HEAPS AND HEAPS OF "JUST BECAUSE"...
POP
MAKEUP SAMPLES
GREAT FOR TRIPS! BUT HOW OLD ARE THEY?
INCENSE BOUGHT AS A SOUVENIR
I TRIED IT, BUT DIDN'T LIKE IT.
SPARE BUTTONS
BUT WHAT IF A BUTTON COMES OFF?
(...HAVE YOU EVER REPLACED ONE THAT CAME OFF? WELL, NO.)

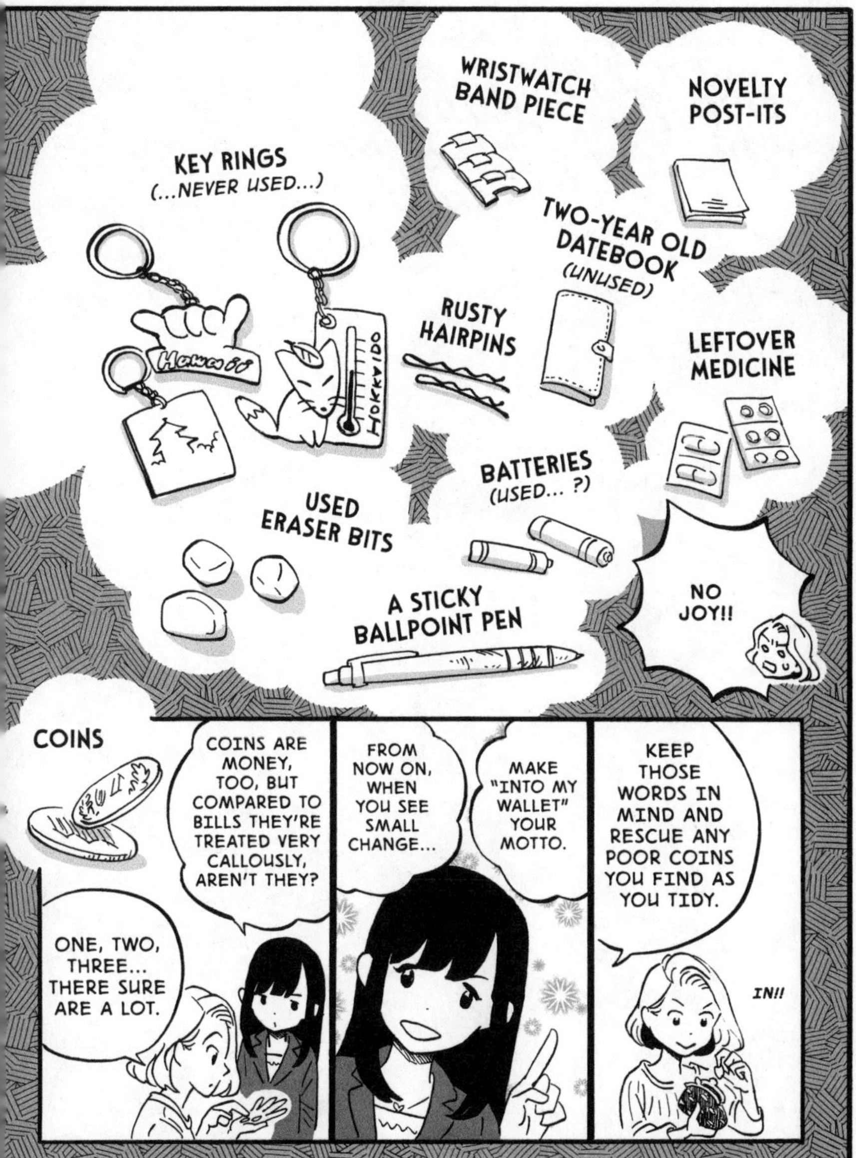
KEY RINGS
(...NEVER USED...)
WRISTWATCH BAND PIECE
NOVELTY POST-ITS
TWO-YEAR OLD DATEBOOK
(UNUSED)
RUSTY HAIRPINS
LEFTOVER MEDICINE
BATTERIES
(USED... ?)
USED ERASER BITS
A STICKY BALLPOINT PEN
NO JOY!!
COINS
COINS ARE MONEY, TOO, BUT COMPARED TO BILLS THEY'RE TREATED VERY CALLOUSLY, AREN'T THEY?
ONE, TWO, THREE... THERE SURE ARE A LOT.
FROM NOW ON, WHEN YOU SEE SMALL CHANGE...
MAKE "INTO MY WALLET" YOUR MOTTO.
KEEP THOSE WORDS IN MIND AND RESCUE ANY POOR COINS YOU FIND AS YOU TIDY.
IN!!

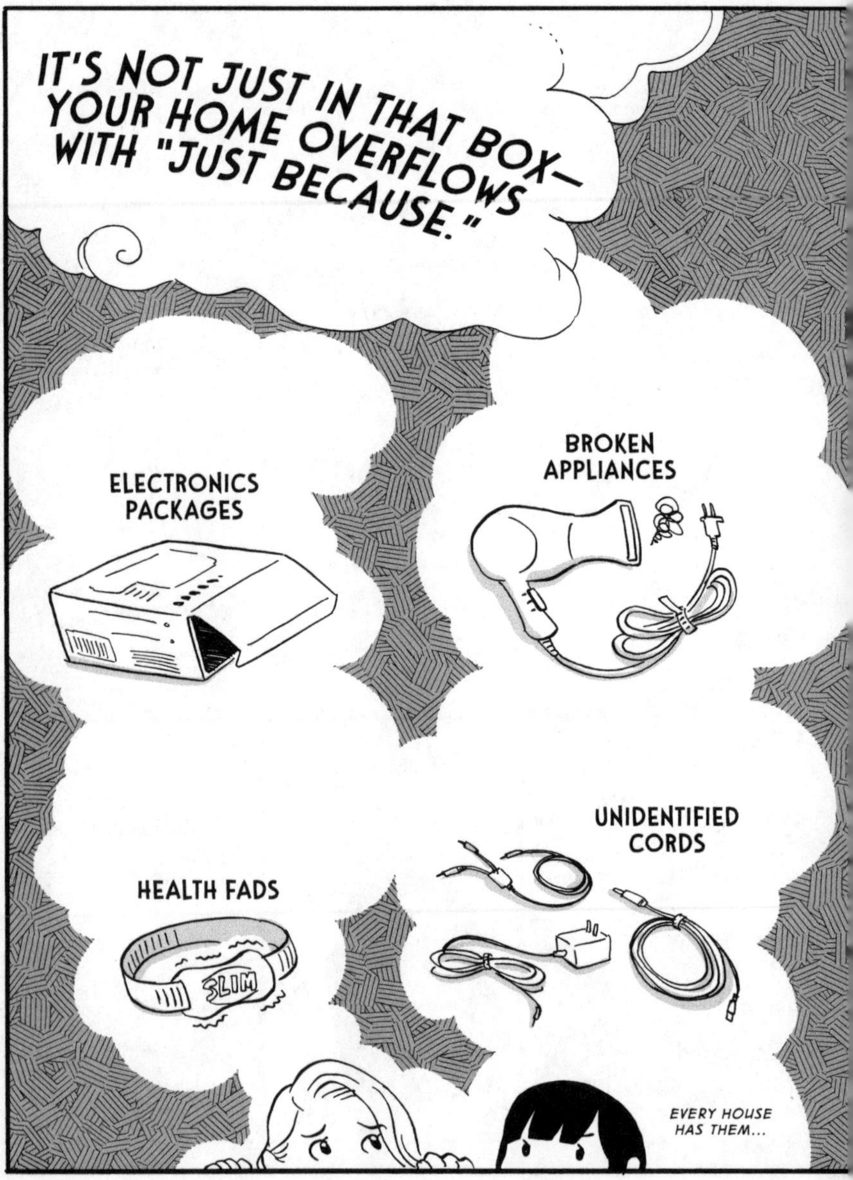
IT'S NOT JUST IN THAT BOX—YOUR HOME OVERFLOWS WITH "JUST BECAUSE."
ELECTRONICS PACKAGES
BROKEN APPLIANCES
HEALTH FADS
SLIM
UNIDENTIFIED CORDS
EVERY HOUSE HAS THEM...

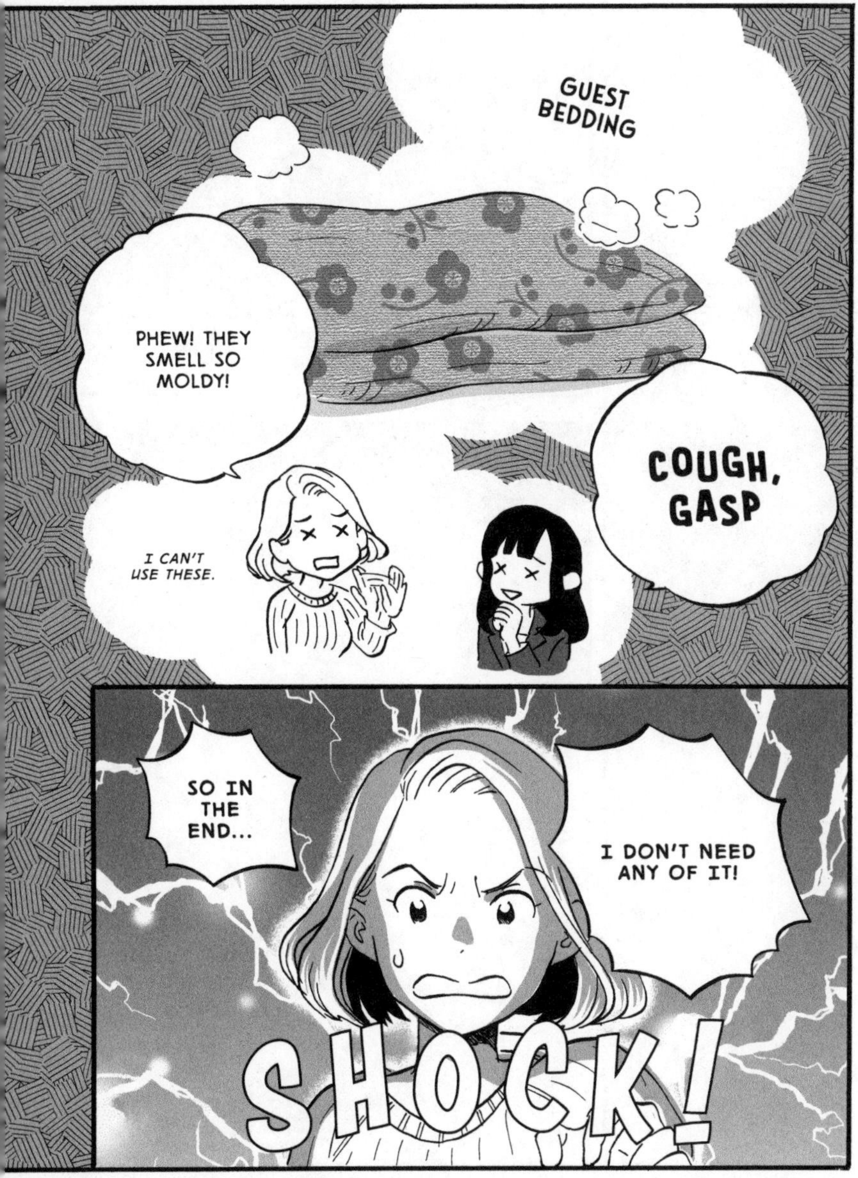
GUEST BEDDING
PHEW! THEY SMELL SO MOLDY!
I CAN'T USE THESE.
COUGH, GASP
SO IN THE END...
I DON'T NEED ANY OF IT!
SHOCK!

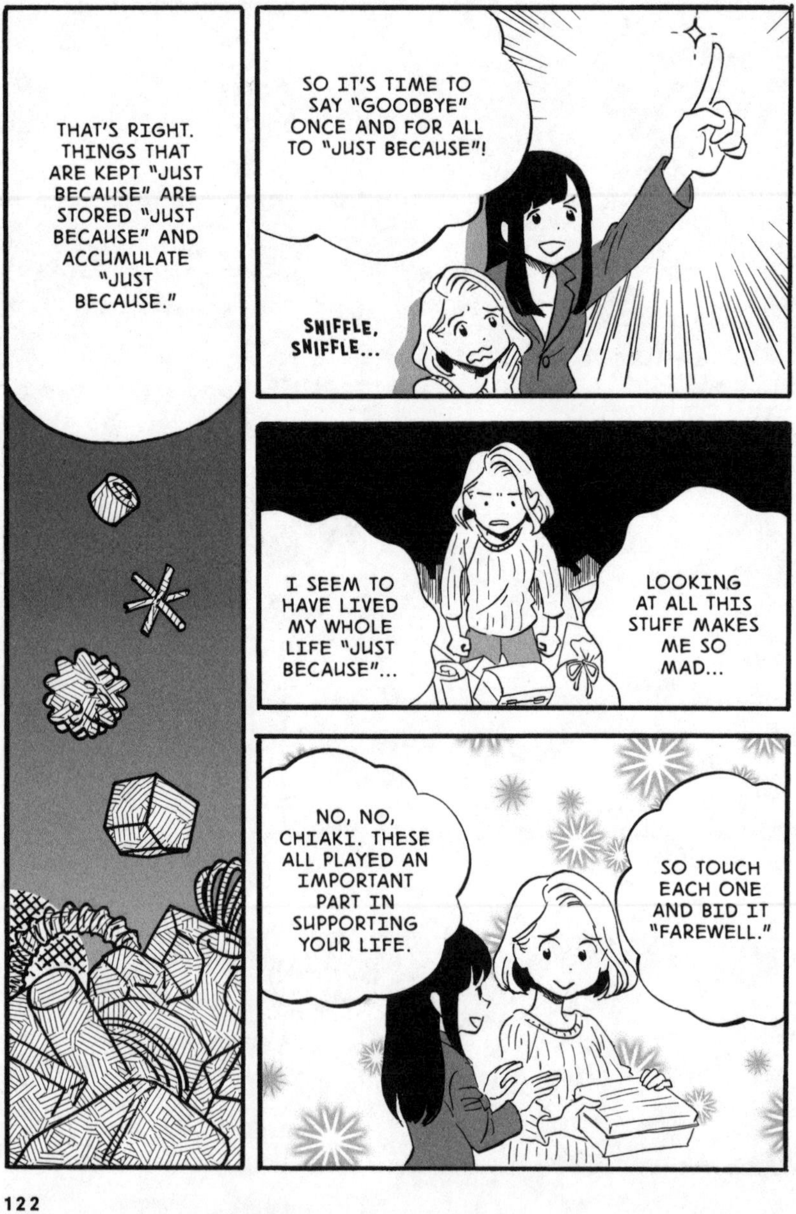

THAT'S RIGHT. THINGS THAT ARE KEPT "JUST BECAUSE" ARE STORED "JUST BECAUSE" AND ACCUMULATE "JUST BECAUSE."
SO IT'S TIME TO SAY "GOODBYE" ONCE AND FOR ALL TO "JUST BECAUSE"!
SNIFFLE, SNIFFLE...
I SEEM TO HAVE LIVED MY WHOLE LIFE "JUST BECAUSE"...
LOOKING AT ALL THIS STUFF MAKES ME SO MAD...
NO, NO, CHIAKI. THESE ALL PLAYED AN IMPORTANT PART IN SUPPORTING YOUR LIFE.
SO TOUCH EACH ONE AND BID IT "FAREWELL."

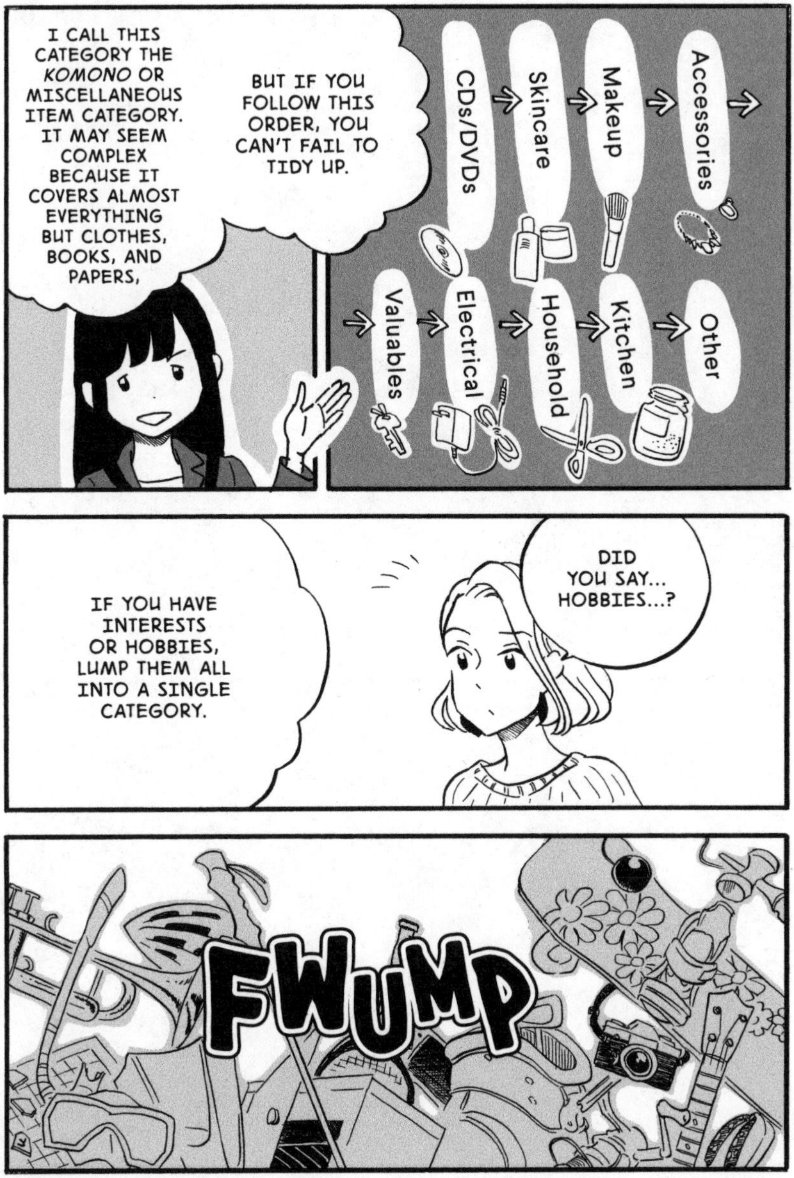
I CALL THIS CATEGORY THE *KOMONO* OR MISCELLANEOUS ITEM CATEGORY. IT MAY SEEM COMPLEX BECAUSE IT COVERS ALMOST EVERYTHING BUT CLOTHES, BOOKS, AND PAPERS,
BUT IF YOU FOLLOW THIS ORDER, YOU CAN'T FAIL TO TIDY UP.
CDs/DVDs
Skincare
Makeup
Accessories
Valuables
Electrical
Household
Kitchen
Other
IF YOU HAVE INTERESTS OR HOBBIES, LUMP THEM ALL INTO A SINGLE CATEGORY.
DID YOU SAY... HOBBIES...?
FWUMP

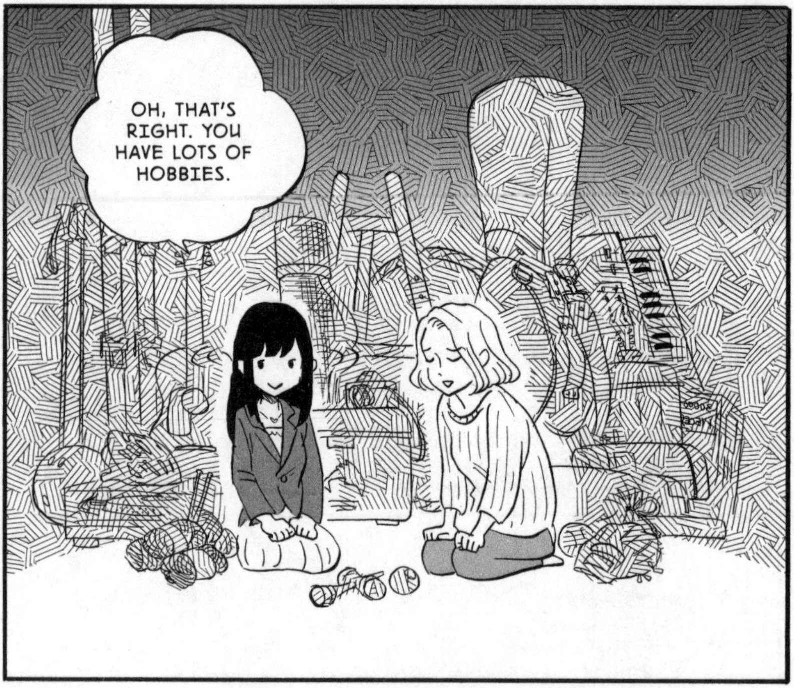
OH, THAT'S RIGHT. YOU HAVE LOTS OF HOBBIES.

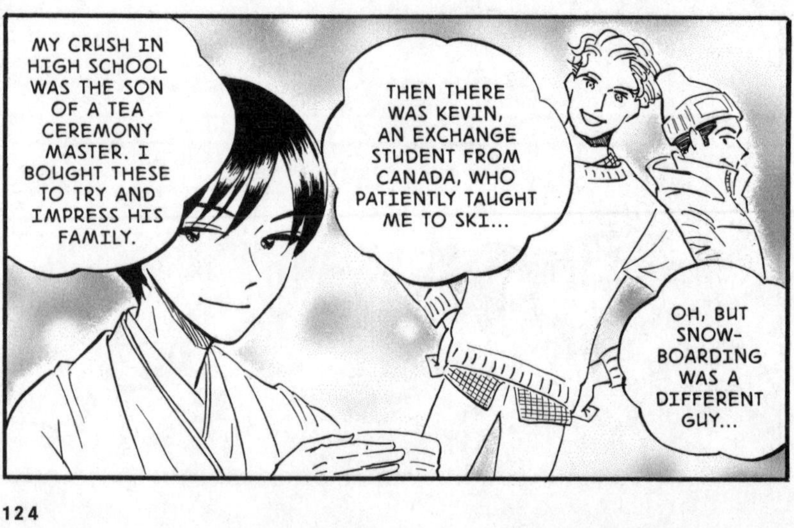
MY CRUSH IN HIGH SCHOOL WAS THE SON OF A TEA CEREMONY MASTER. I BOUGHT THESE TO TRY AND IMPRESS HIS FAMILY.
THEN THERE WAS KEVIN, AN EXCHANGE STUDENT FROM CANADA, WHO PATIENTLY TAUGHT ME TO SKI...
OH, BUT SNOW-BOARDING WAS A DIFFERENT GUY...

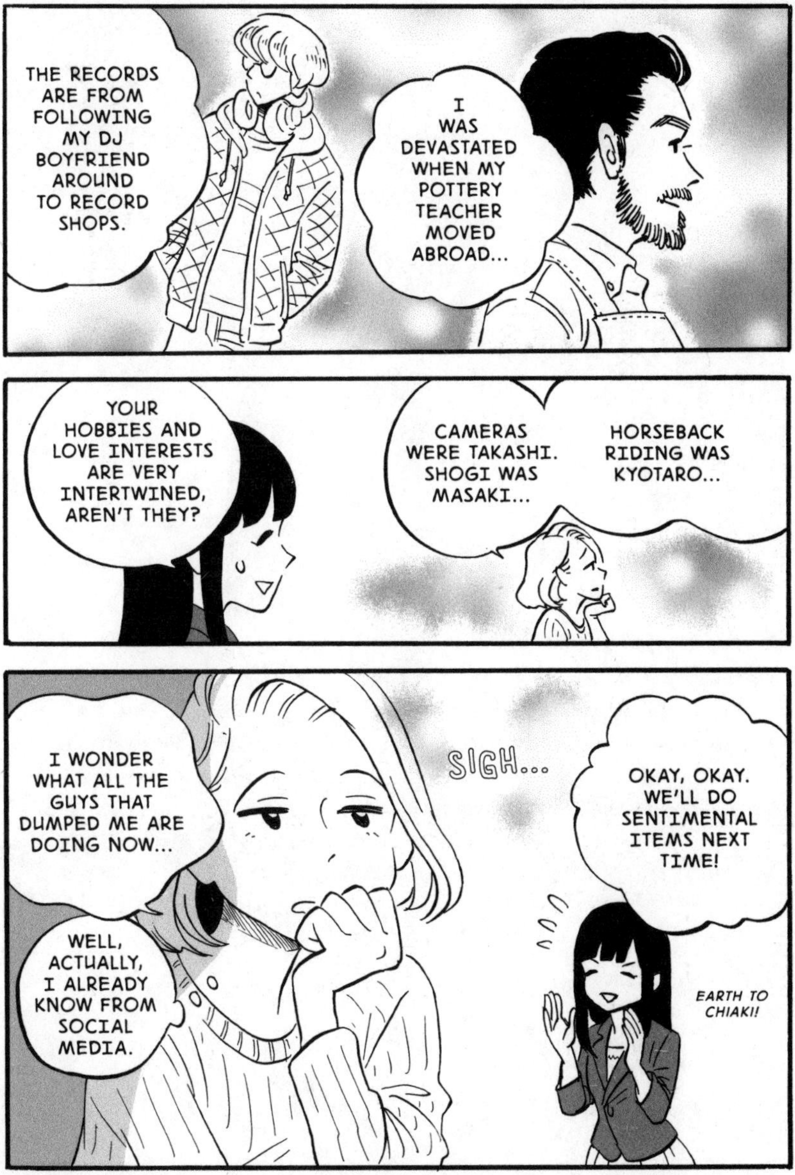
THE RECORDS ARE FROM FOLLOWING MY DJ BOYFRIEND AROUND TO RECORD SHOPS.
I WAS DEVASTATED WHEN MY POTTERY TEACHER MOVED ABROAD...
YOUR HOBBIES AND LOVE INTERESTS ARE VERY INTERTWINED, AREN'T THEY?
CAMERAS WERE TAKASHI. SHOGI WAS MASAKI...
HORSEBACK RIDING WAS KYOTARO...
I WONDER WHAT ALL THE GUYS THAT DUMPED ME ARE DOING NOW...
SIGH...
OKAY, OKAY. WE'LL DO SENTIMENTAL ITEMS NEXT TIME!
WELL, ACTUALLY, I ALREADY KNOW FROM SOCIAL MEDIA.
EARTH TO CHIAKI!

The rule of thumb for papers is to discard them all. Keep only those that you're certain you will use in the future.

———

Discard any papers that don't fall into one of the following three categories: those you are currently using, those you will need for a limited period of time, and those that you need to keep indefinitely.

Put all those papers that require action, such as letters you need to respond to or bills you need to pay, in a "Pending" box, set a date for dealing with them, and tackle them all in one go. Unfinished business like this weighs on the mind far more than we realize. You'll feel much better if you get this job out of the way quickly.

8

leave
sentimental
items
for last

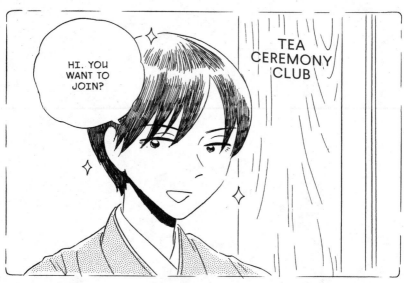

HI. YOU WANT TO JOIN?
TEA CEREMONY CLUB
...YES!
CRUMPLE
Application for the School Movie Club
CHIAKI AGE SIXTEEN
YOU'RE ALWAYS SO ENTHUSI-ASTIC, CHIAKI.
THANKS! I'M GOING SHOPPING AGAIN THIS WEEKEND FOR TEA CEREMONY THINGS. WOULD YOU COME AND HELP ME?
OH, SORRY. I HAVE A DATE WITH MY GIRLFRIEND.
SHOCK
G-G-GIRLFRIEND

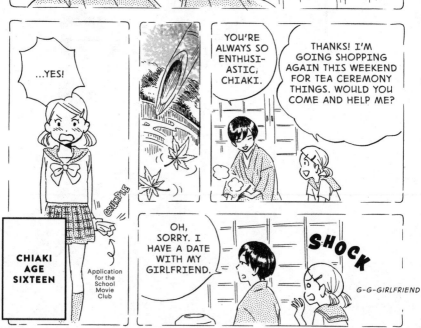

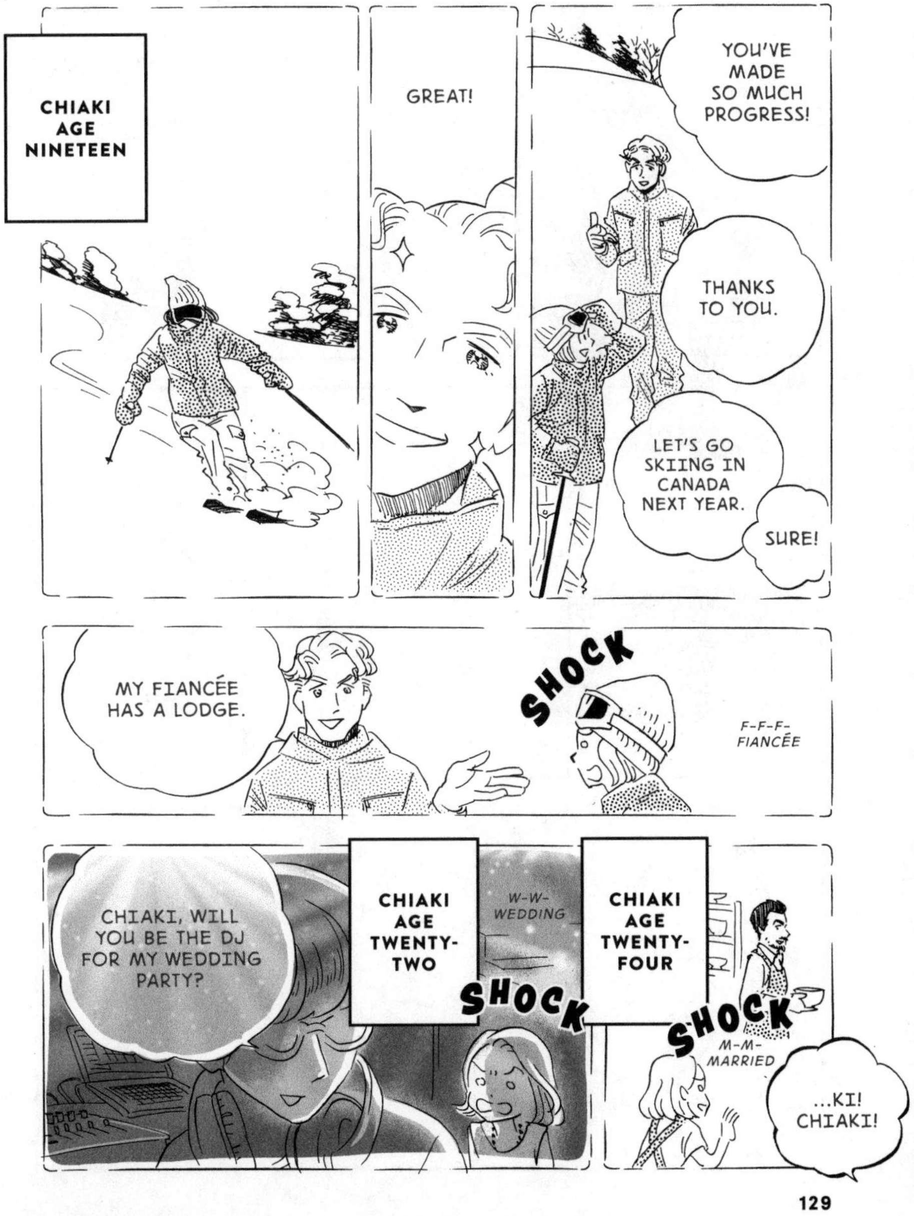
CHIAKI AGE NINETEEN
GREAT!
YOU'VE MADE SO MUCH PROGRESS!
THANKS TO YOU.
LET'S GO SKIING IN CANADA NEXT YEAR.
SURE!
MY FIANCÉE HAS A LODGE.
SHOCK
F-F-F-FIANCÉE
CHIAKI AGE TWENTY-TWO
CHIAKI, WILL YOU BE THE DJ FOR MY WEDDING PARTY?
W-W-WEDDING
SHOCK
CHIAKI AGE TWENTY-FOUR
SHOCK
M-M-MARRIED
...KI! CHIAKI!

CHIAKI!

ZONED OUT

HUH?

WAKE UP, CHIAKI! IT'S TIME TO TIDY YOUR HOBBY-RELATED ITEMS.

CLAP-CLAP

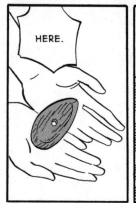

HERE.

DOES THIS SPARK JOY?

WHAT'S THIS?

UHM, SO KONMARI, GUESS WHAT THIS IS FOR.

?

IT'S NO USE ASKING ME...

OH! NOW I REMEMBER! IT'S FOR POTTERY.

Finishing tool

I'LL GET RID OF MY ENTIRE POTTERY KIT.

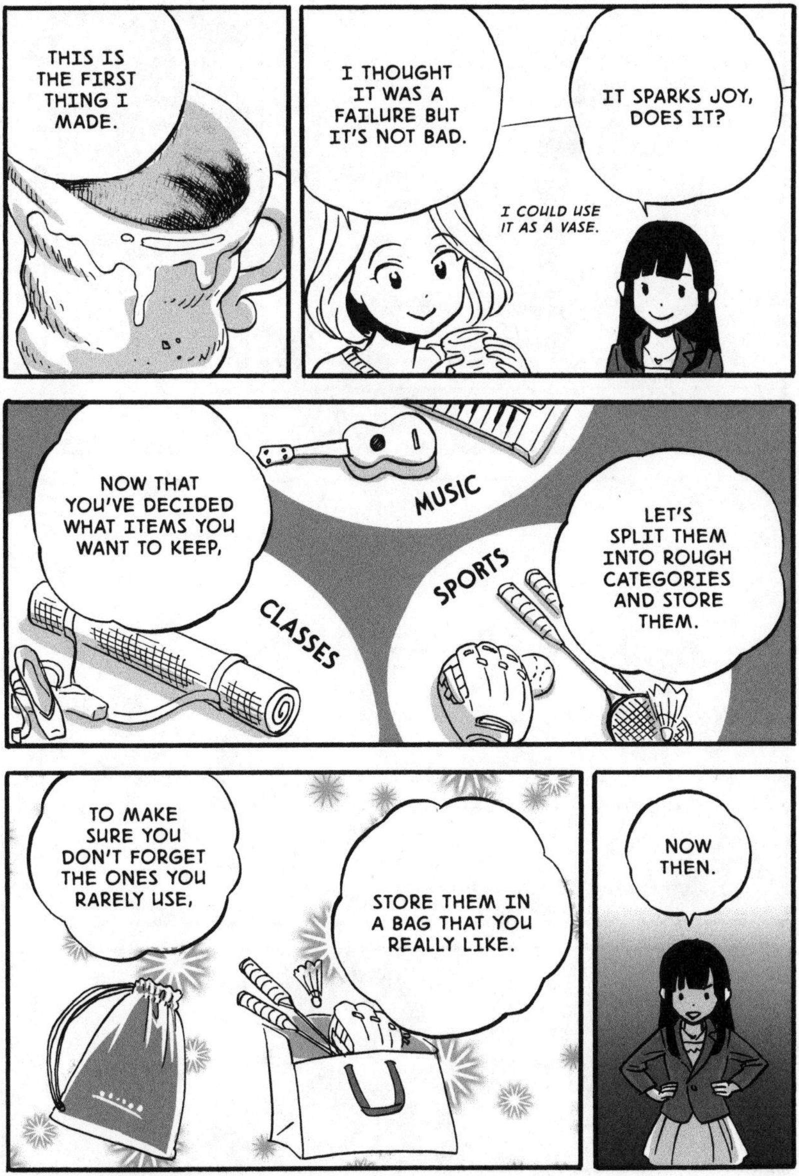
THIS IS THE FIRST THING I MADE.
I THOUGHT IT WAS A FAILURE BUT IT'S NOT BAD.
IT SPARKS JOY, DOES IT?
I COULD USE IT AS A VASE.
NOW THAT YOU'VE DECIDED WHAT ITEMS YOU WANT TO KEEP,
MUSIC
LET'S SPLIT THEM INTO ROUGH CATEGORIES AND STORE THEM.
SPORTS
CLASSES
TO MAKE SURE YOU DON'T FORGET THE ONES YOU RARELY USE,
STORE THEM IN A BAG THAT YOU REALLY LIKE.
NOW THEN.

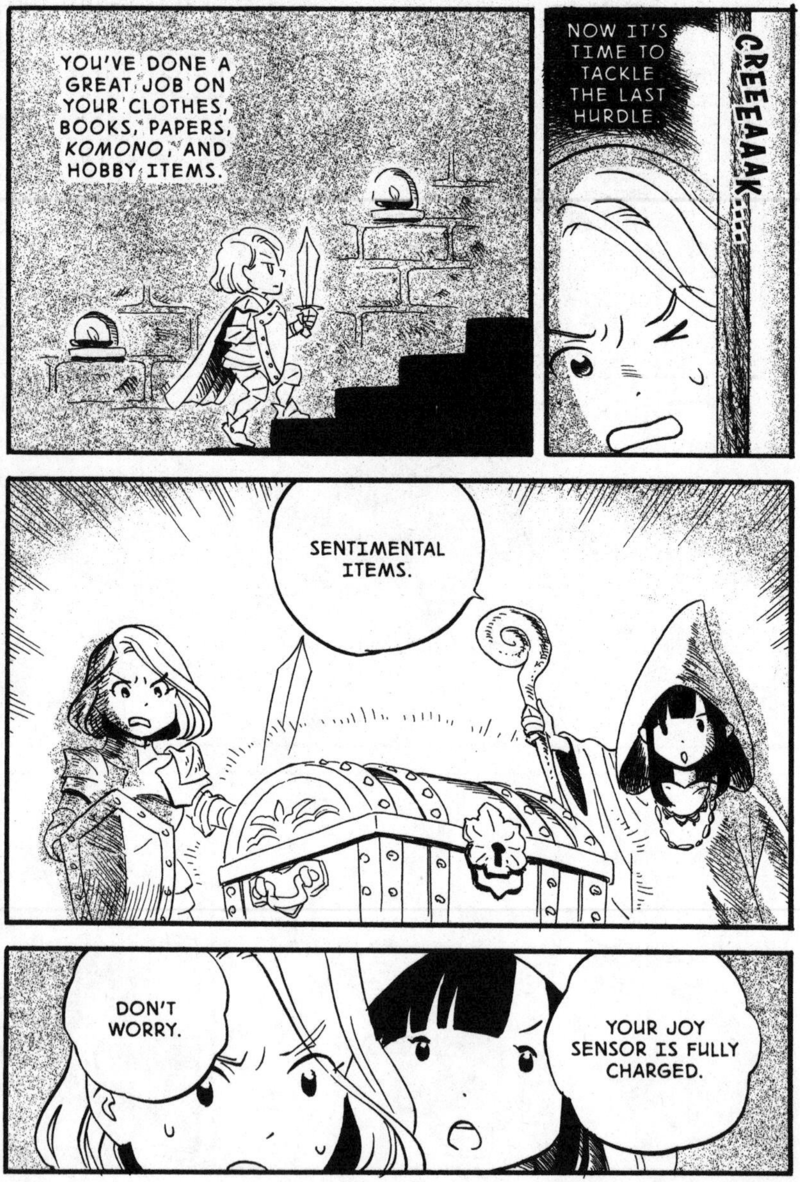
YOU'VE DONE A GREAT JOB ON YOUR CLOTHES, BOOKS, PAPERS, *KOMONO*, AND HOBBY ITEMS.
NOW IT'S TIME TO TACKLE THE LAST HURDLE.
CREEEAAAK....
SENTIMENTAL ITEMS.
DON'T WORRY.
YOUR JOY SENSOR IS FULLY CHARGED.

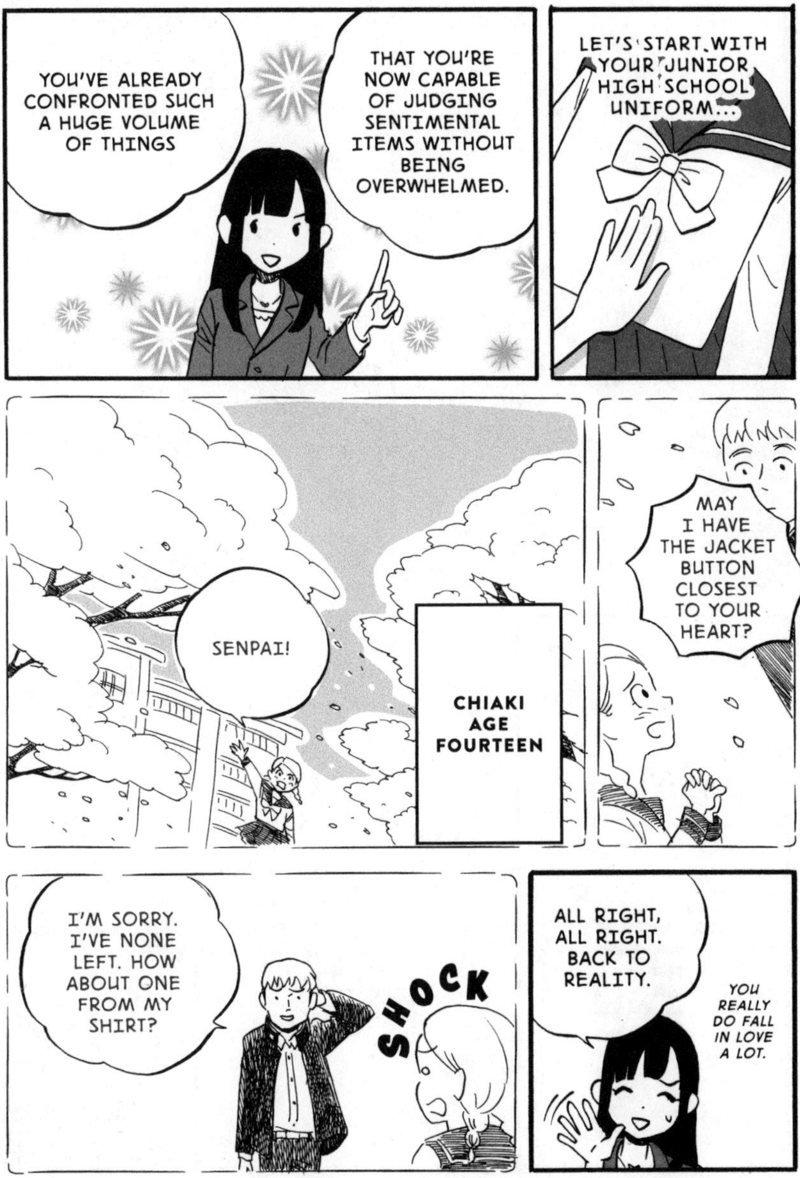
YOU'VE ALREADY CONFRONTED SUCH A HUGE VOLUME OF THINGS
THAT YOU'RE NOW CAPABLE OF JUDGING SENTIMENTAL ITEMS WITHOUT BEING OVERWHELMED.
LET'S START WITH YOUR JUNIOR HIGH SCHOOL UNIFORM...
SENPAI!
CHIAKI AGE FOURTEEN
MAY I HAVE THE JACKET BUTTON CLOSEST TO YOUR HEART?
I'M SORRY. I'VE NONE LEFT. HOW ABOUT ONE FROM MY SHIRT?
SHOCK
ALL RIGHT, ALL RIGHT. BACK TO REALITY.
YOU REALLY DO FALL IN LOVE A LOT.

A SCHOOL MEMORY, I SEE.

YES! THE BUTTON OF A BOY I LIKED WAS IN THE POCKET.

SIGH!

WHY DON'T YOU PUT IT ON AND LET YOURSELF BASK IN MEMORIES?

IT'S... TOO... TIGHT...

I RECOMMEND PUTTING ALL YOUR DIPLOMAS IN THE SAME TUBE.

Diary with a lock

DIARY

MY FIRST TIME LIVING ALONE

HELLO NEW ME.

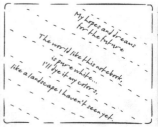

My hopes and dreams for the future

The world like this notebook, is pure white...

I'll dye it my colors,

like a landscape I haven't seen yet.

...BUT WHY DID I WRITE IT IN VERSE?

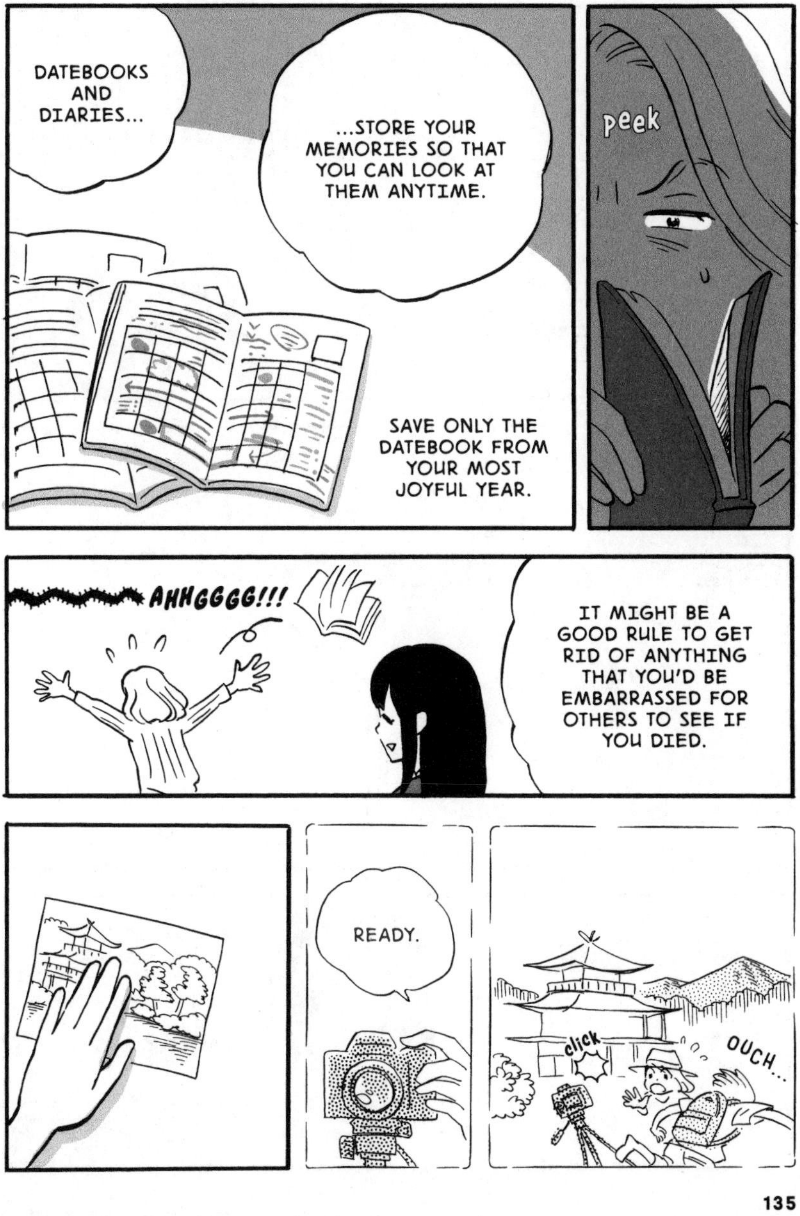
DATEBOOKS AND DIARIES...
...STORE YOUR MEMORIES SO THAT YOU CAN LOOK AT THEM ANYTIME.
SAVE ONLY THE DATEBOOK FROM YOUR MOST JOYFUL YEAR.
peek
AHHGGGG!!!
IT MIGHT BE A GOOD RULE TO GET RID OF ANYTHING THAT YOU'D BE EMBARRASSED FOR OTHERS TO SEE IF YOU DIED.
READY.
click
OUCH...

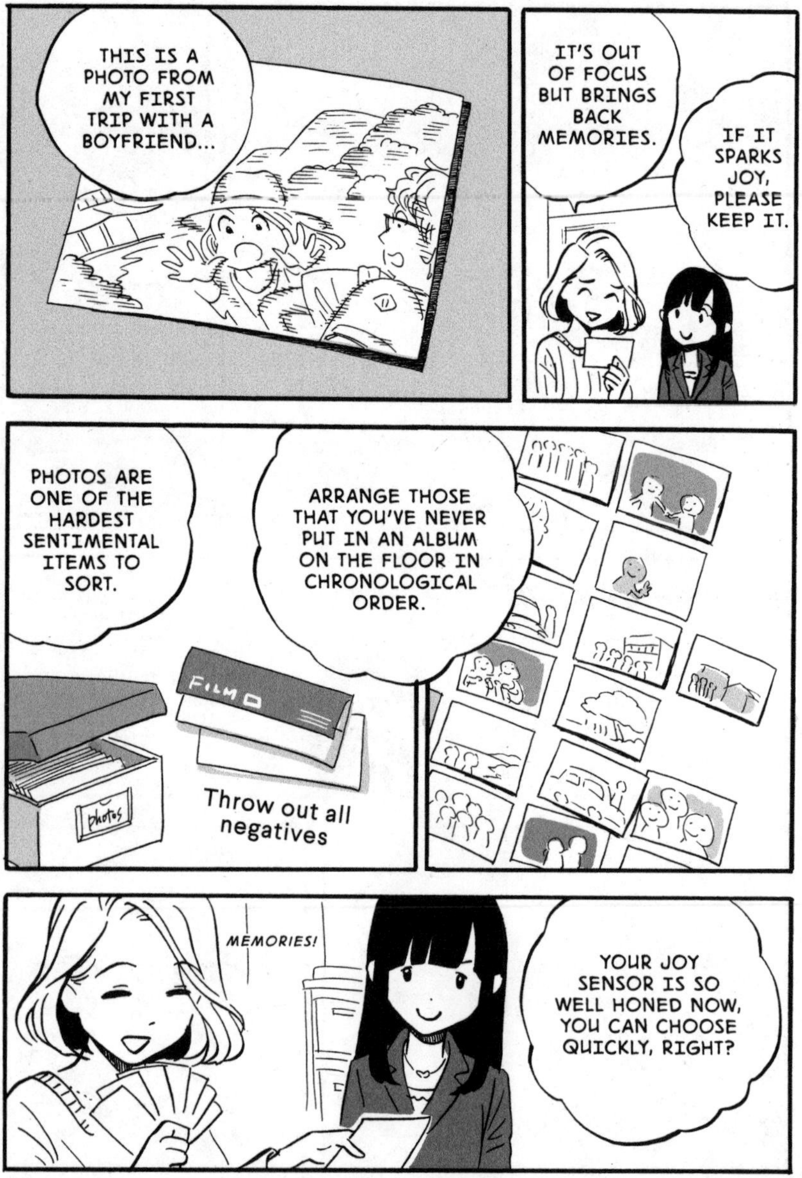
THIS IS A PHOTO FROM MY FIRST TRIP WITH A BOYFRIEND...
IT'S OUT OF FOCUS BUT BRINGS BACK MEMORIES.
IF IT SPARKS JOY, PLEASE KEEP IT.
PHOTOS ARE ONE OF THE HARDEST SENTIMENTAL ITEMS TO SORT.
ARRANGE THOSE THAT YOU'VE NEVER PUT IN AN ALBUM ON THE FLOOR IN CHRONOLOGICAL ORDER.
FILM
photos
Throw out all negatives
MEMORIES!
YOUR JOY SENSOR IS SO WELL HONED NOW, YOU CAN CHOOSE QUICKLY, RIGHT?

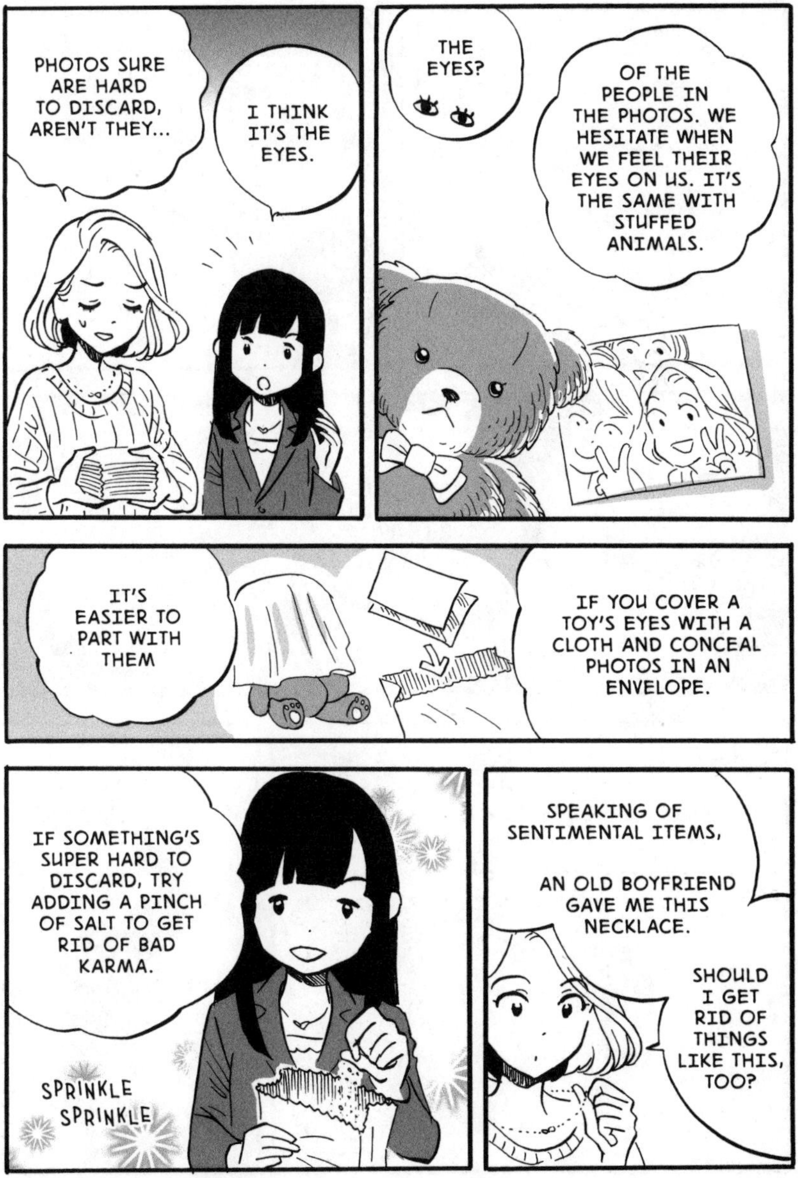
PHOTOS SURE ARE HARD TO DISCARD, AREN'T THEY...
I THINK IT'S THE EYES.
THE EYES?
OF THE PEOPLE IN THE PHOTOS. WE HESITATE WHEN WE FEEL THEIR EYES ON US. IT'S THE SAME WITH STUFFED ANIMALS.
IT'S EASIER TO PART WITH THEM
IF YOU COVER A TOY'S EYES WITH A CLOTH AND CONCEAL PHOTOS IN AN ENVELOPE.
IF SOMETHING'S SUPER HARD TO DISCARD, TRY ADDING A PINCH OF SALT TO GET RID OF BAD KARMA.
SPRINKLE SPRINKLE
SPEAKING OF SENTIMENTAL ITEMS,
AN OLD BOYFRIEND GAVE ME THIS NECKLACE.
SHOULD I GET RID OF THINGS LIKE THIS, TOO?

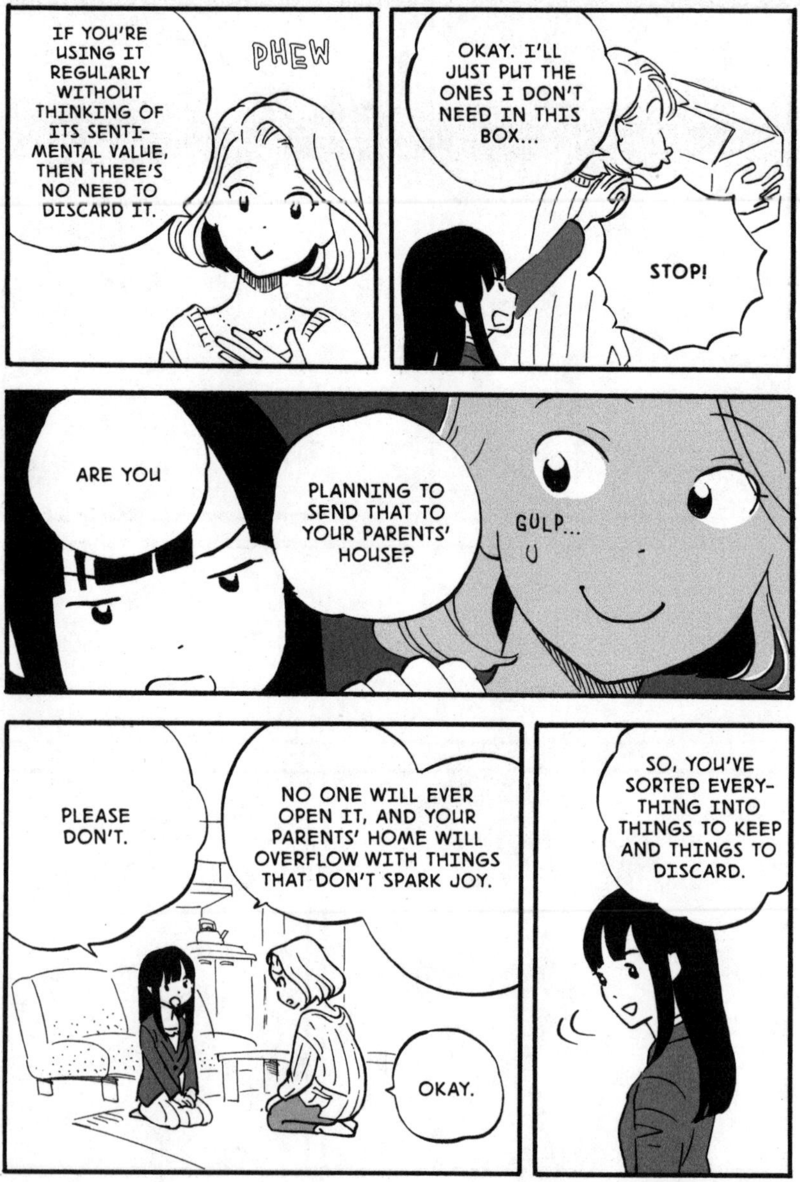
IF YOU'RE USING IT REGULARLY WITHOUT THINKING OF ITS SENTI-MENTAL VALUE, THEN THERE'S NO NEED TO DISCARD IT.
PHEW
OKAY. I'LL JUST PUT THE ONES I DON'T NEED IN THIS BOX...
STOP!
ARE YOU
PLANNING TO SEND THAT TO YOUR PARENTS' HOUSE?
GULP...
PLEASE DON'T.
NO ONE WILL EVER OPEN IT, AND YOUR PARENTS' HOME WILL OVERFLOW WITH THINGS THAT DON'T SPARK JOY.
OKAY.
SO, YOU'VE SORTED EVERY-THING INTO THINGS TO KEEP AND THINGS TO DISCARD.

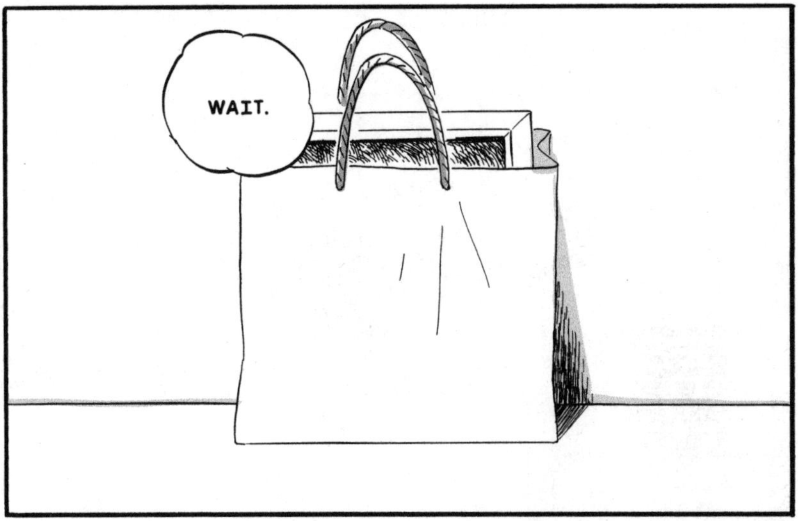
WAIT.

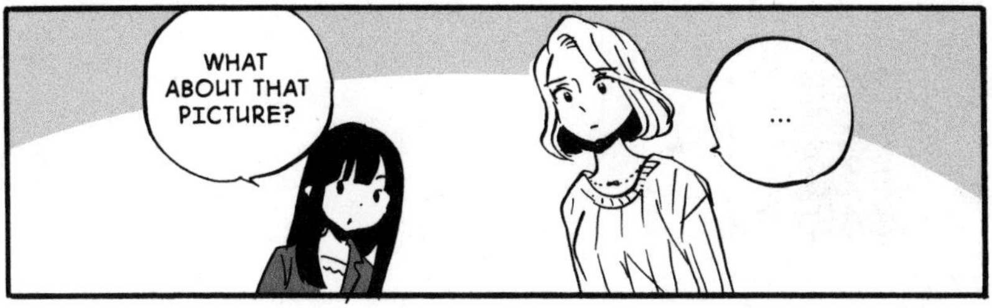
WHAT ABOUT THAT PICTURE?
...

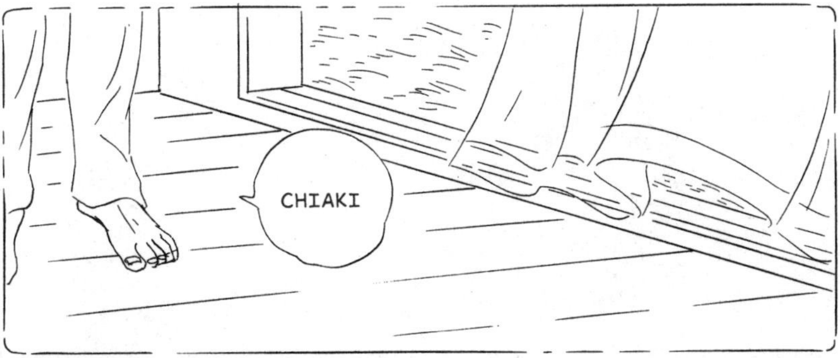
CHIAKI

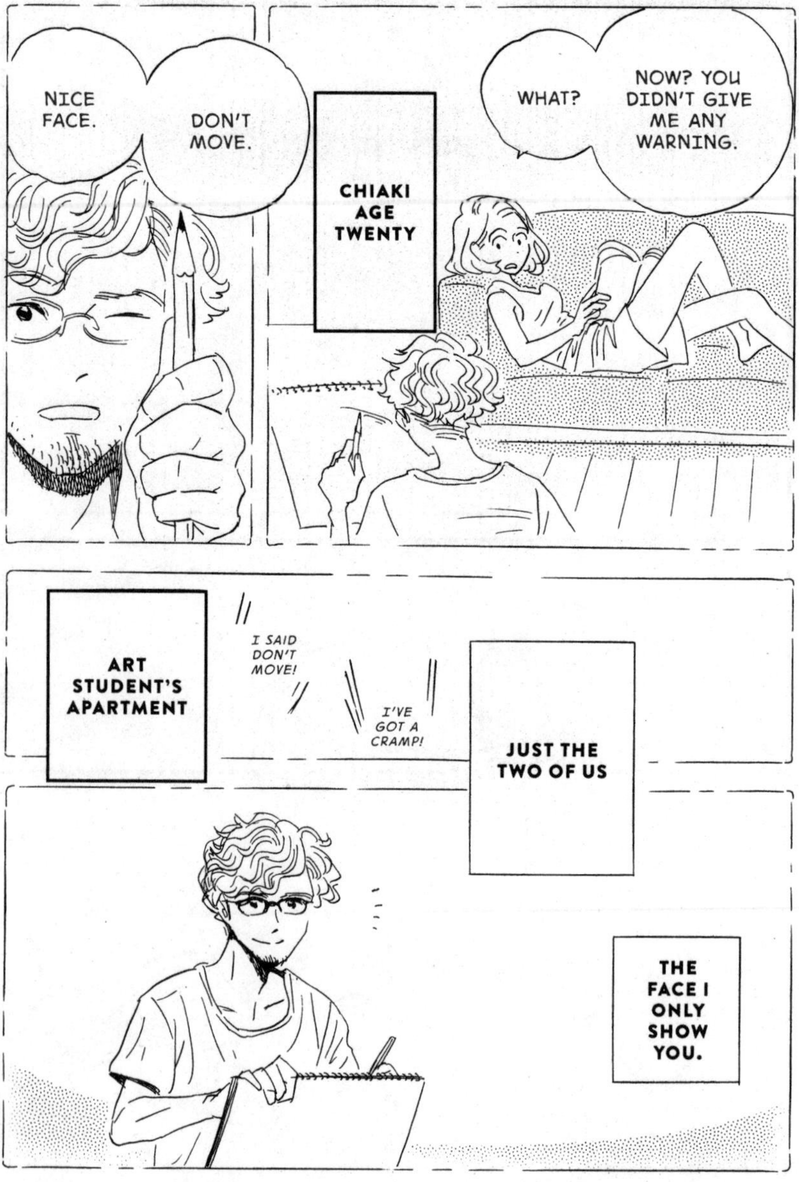
NICE FACE.
DON'T MOVE.
CHIAKI AGE TWENTY
WHAT?
NOW? YOU DIDN'T GIVE ME ANY WARNING.
ART STUDENT'S APARTMENT
I SAID DON'T MOVE!
I'VE GOT A CRAMP!
JUST THE TWO OF US
THE FACE I ONLY SHOW YOU.

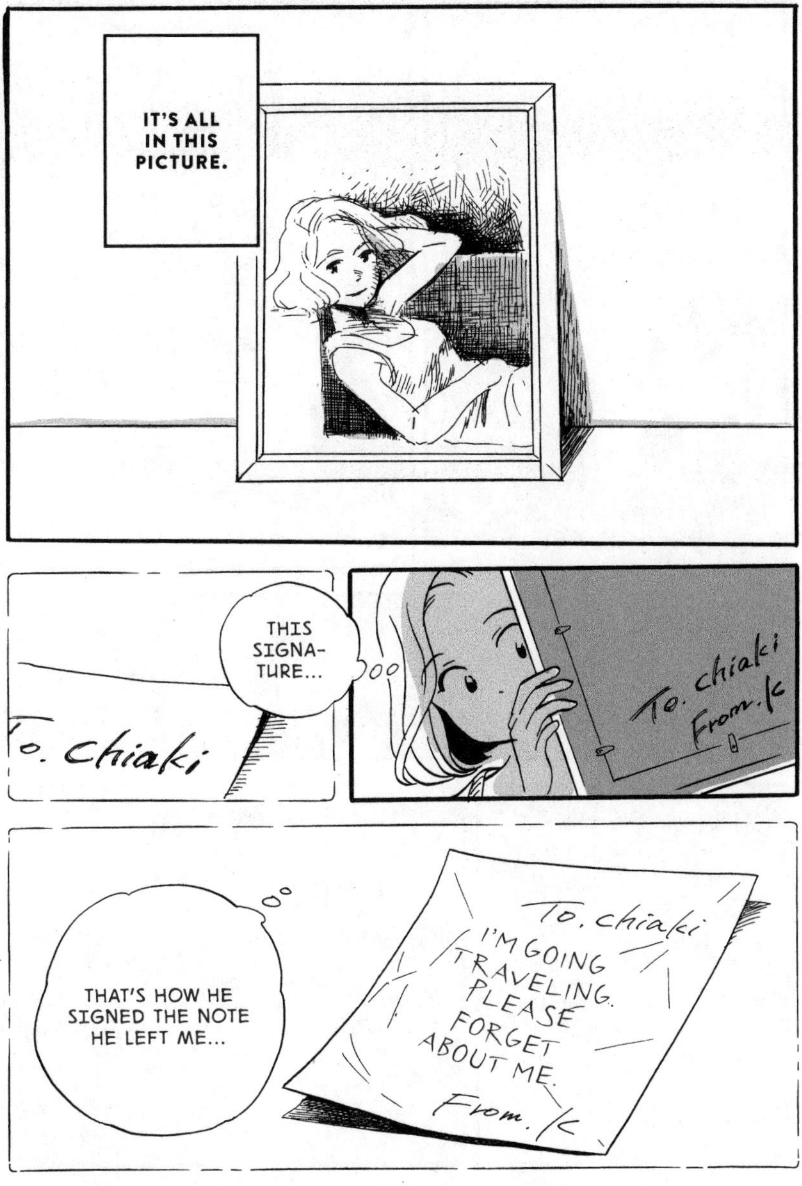
IT'S ALL IN THIS PICTURE.
THIS SIGNATURE...
To. chiaki
To. chiaki From. K
THAT'S HOW HE SIGNED THE NOTE HE LEFT ME...
To. chiaki I'M GOING TRAVELING. PLEASE FORGET ABOUT ME. From. K

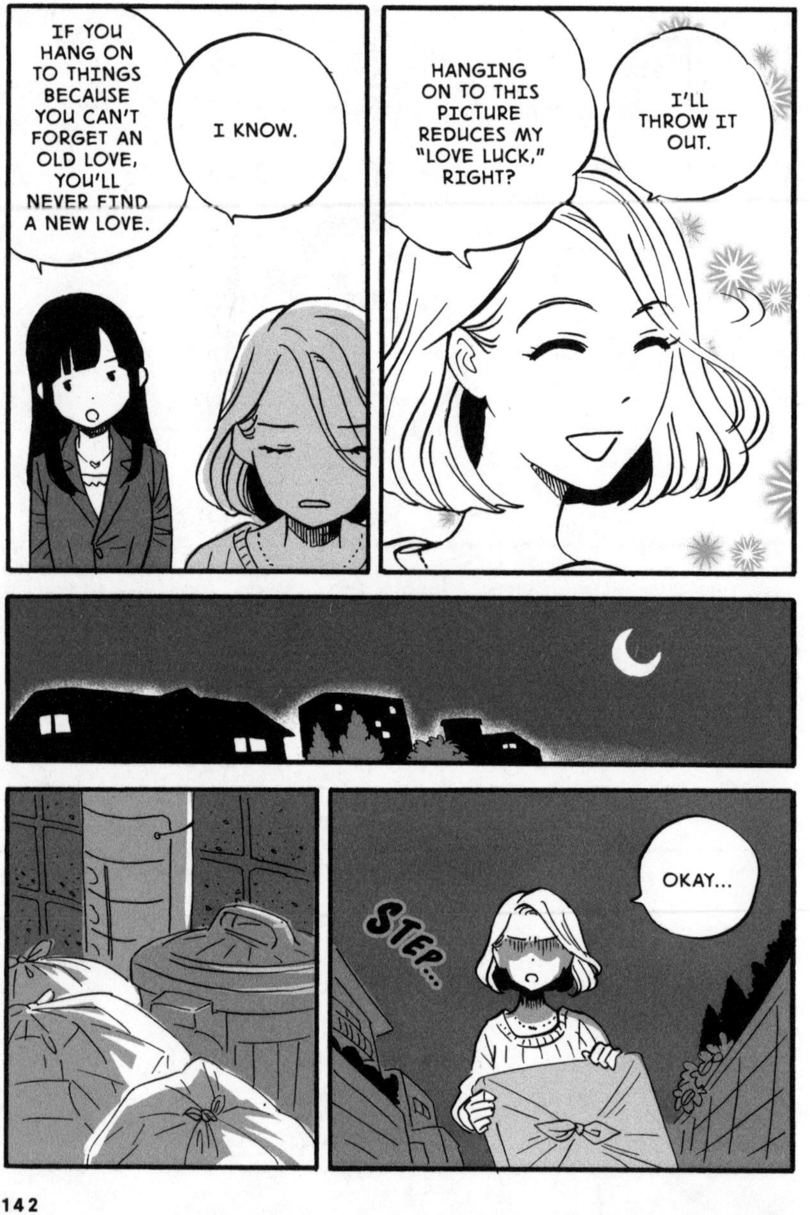
IF YOU HANG ON TO THINGS BECAUSE YOU CAN'T FORGET AN OLD LOVE, YOU'LL NEVER FIND A NEW LOVE.
I KNOW.
HANGING ON TO THIS PICTURE REDUCES MY "LOVE LUCK," RIGHT?
I'LL THROW IT OUT.
STEP...
OKAY...

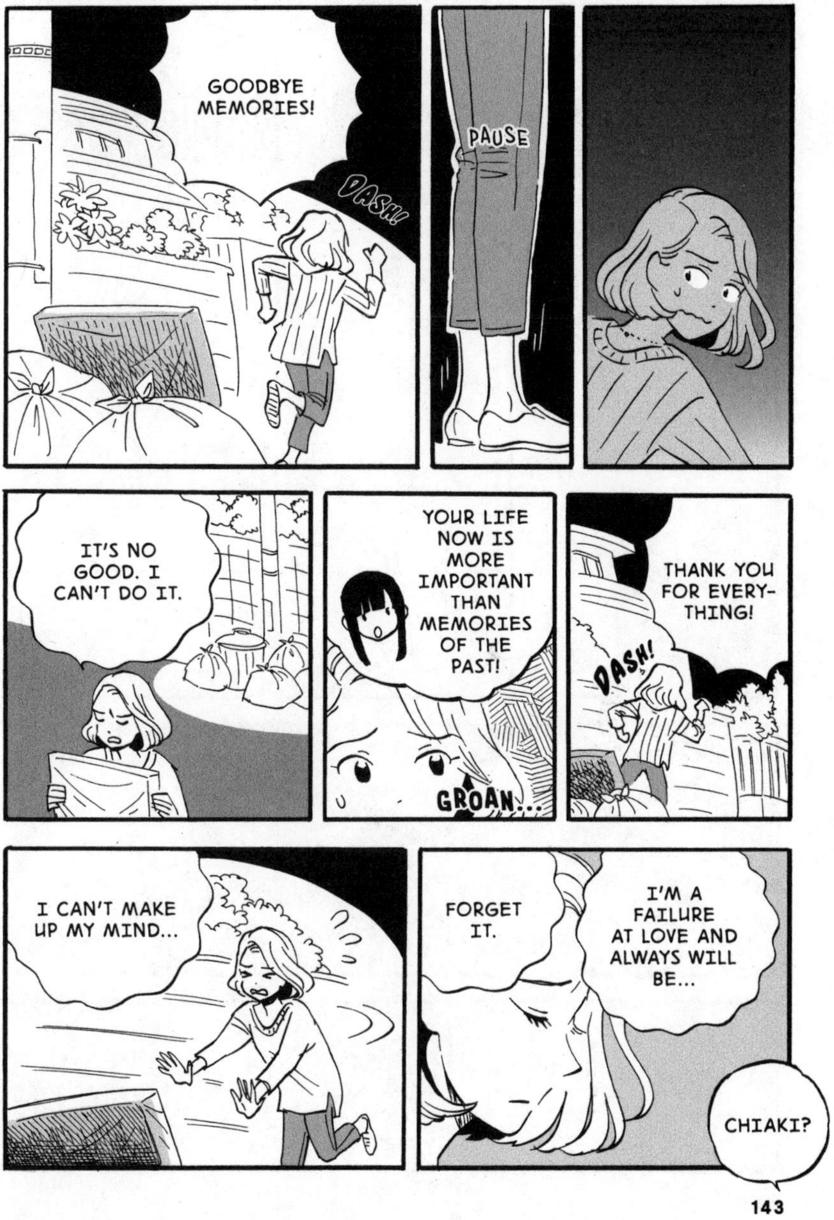
GOODBYE MEMORIES!
DASH!
PAUSE
IT'S NO GOOD. I CAN'T DO IT.
YOUR LIFE NOW IS MORE IMPORTANT THAN MEMORIES OF THE PAST!
GROAN...
THANK YOU FOR EVERY-THING!
DASH!
I CAN'T MAKE UP MY MIND...
FORGET IT.
I'M A FAILURE AT LOVE AND ALWAYS WILL BE...
CHIAKI?

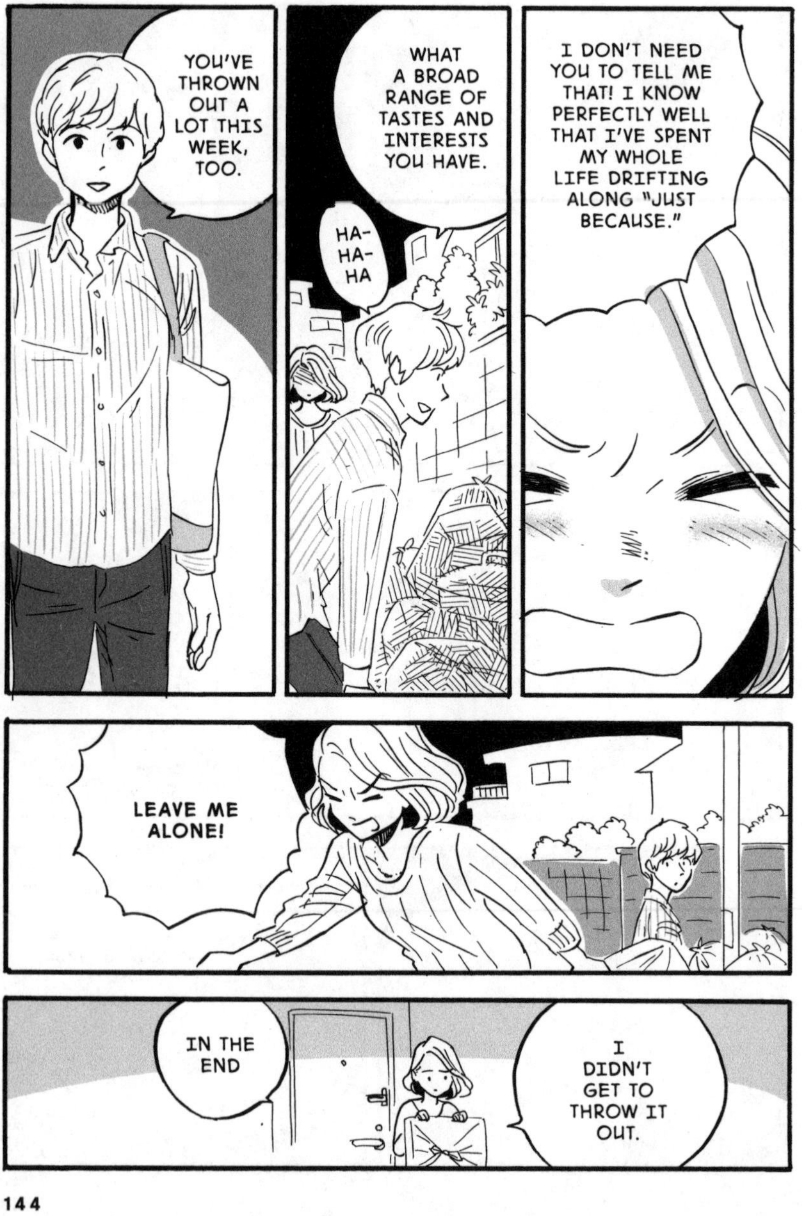
YOU'VE THROWN OUT A LOT THIS WEEK, TOO.
WHAT A BROAD RANGE OF TASTES AND INTERESTS YOU HAVE.
HA-HA-HA
I DON'T NEED YOU TO TELL ME THAT! I KNOW PERFECTLY WELL THAT I'VE SPENT MY WHOLE LIFE DRIFTING ALONG "JUST BECAUSE."
LEAVE ME ALONE!
IN THE END
I DIDN'T GET TO THROW IT OUT.

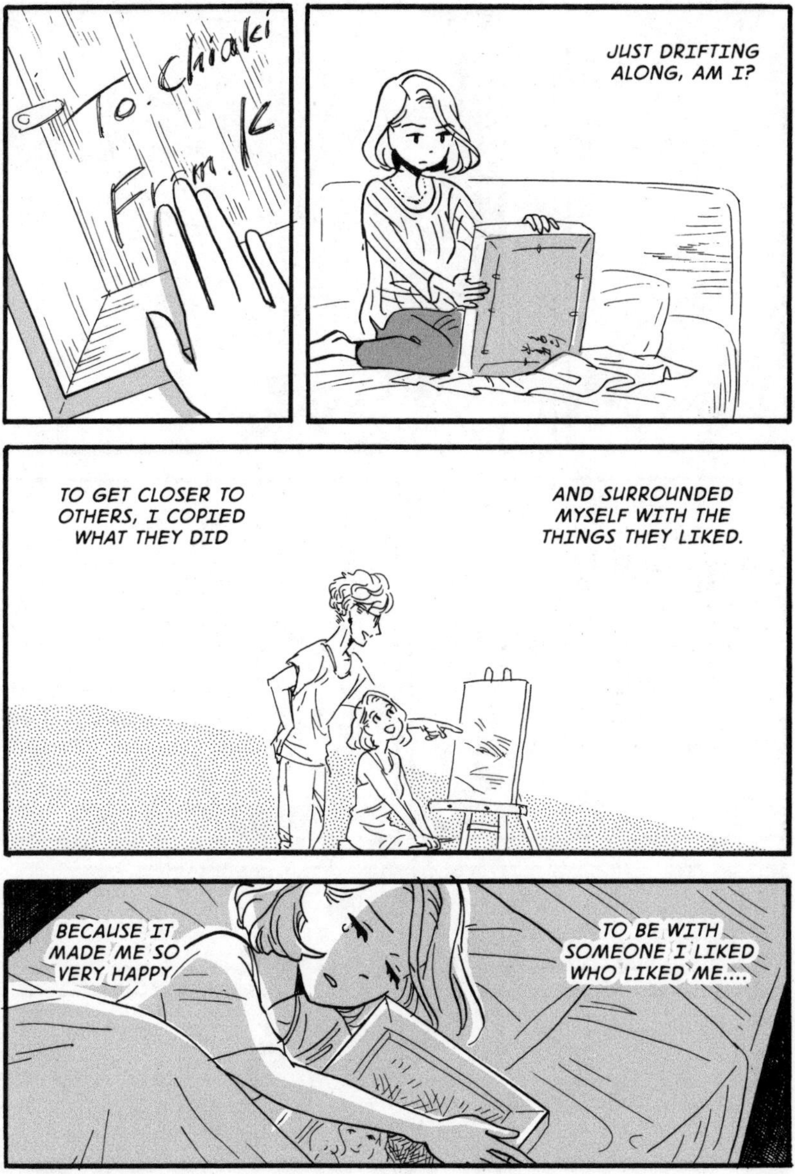
To Chiaki
From K
JUST DRIFTING ALONG, AM I?
TO GET CLOSER TO OTHERS, I COPIED WHAT THEY DID
AND SURROUNDED MYSELF WITH THE THINGS THEY LIKED.
BECAUSE IT MADE ME SO VERY HAPPY
TO BE WITH SOMEONE I LIKED WHO LIKED ME....

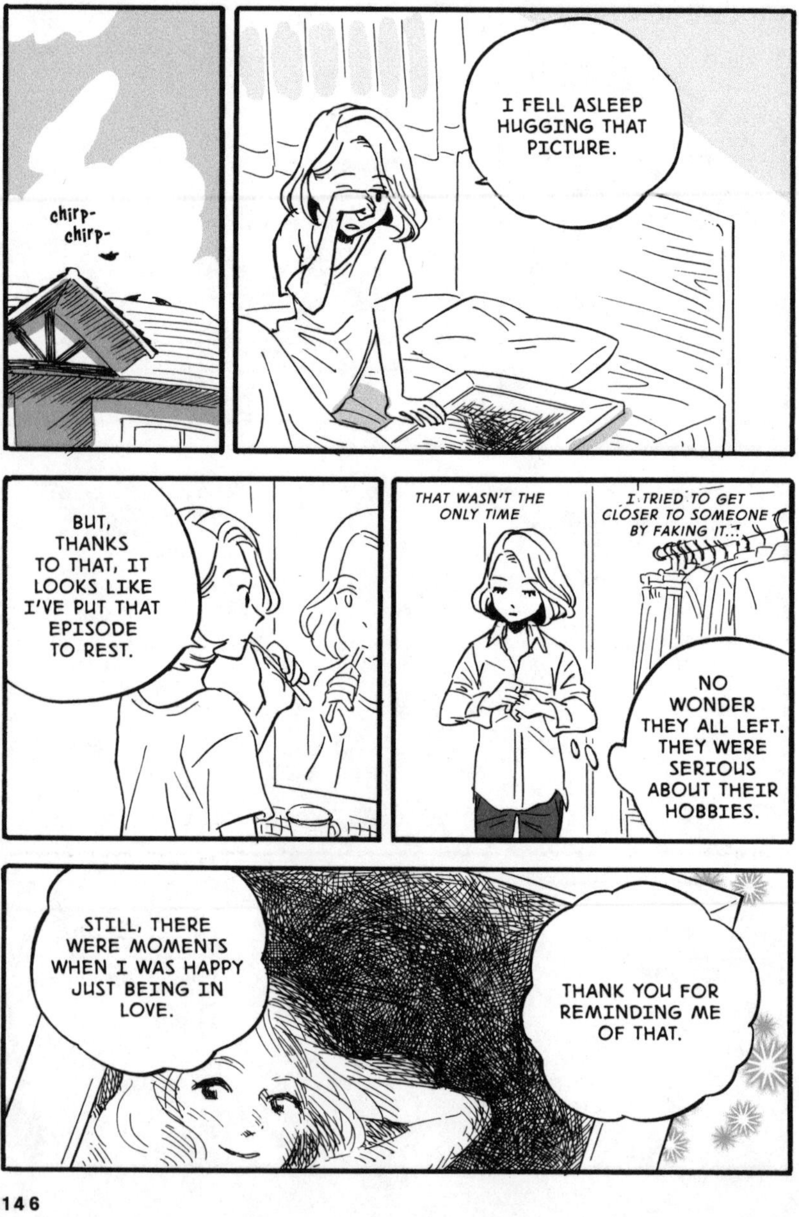
chirp-
chirp-
I FELL ASLEEP HUGGING THAT PICTURE.
BUT, THANKS TO THAT, IT LOOKS LIKE I'VE PUT THAT EPISODE TO REST.
THAT WASN'T THE ONLY TIME
I TRIED TO GET CLOSER TO SOMEONE BY FAKING IT...
NO WONDER THEY ALL LEFT. THEY WERE SERIOUS ABOUT THEIR HOBBIES.
STILL, THERE WERE MOMENTS WHEN I WAS HAPPY JUST BEING IN LOVE.
THANK YOU FOR REMINDING ME OF THAT.

OH NO! THE GARBAGE TRUCK!
WAIT! WAIT! MORE TRASH!
TH-THANK YOU! I'M SO GLAD YOU STOPPED HIM.
I THOUGHT IT WAS MY FAULT THAT YOU DIDN'T GET TO THROW IT OUT LAST NIGHT.
SORRY FOR BEING SO INSEN-SITIVE.
NO, I'M SORRY FOR BEHAVING LIKE THAT.
BUT THANKS TO YOU, I FEEL LIKE I CAN MOVE FORWARD NOW.
thump-thump
WHAT DID YOU THROW AWAY?
IT'S A SECRET.

We live in this moment. Who you
are now is more important than
memories of your past. Be good
to yourself.

———

It is so hard to let go of things that once brought us joy and are filled with precious memories. It feels like we are losing the memories along with them. But that is not the case. Memories that are truly precious will never be forgotten, even if we discard an item associated with them.

What really matters is not the past but the person we have now become, thanks to those past experiences. We should use our space not for the person we once were, but for our future selves.

9 store things where they belong

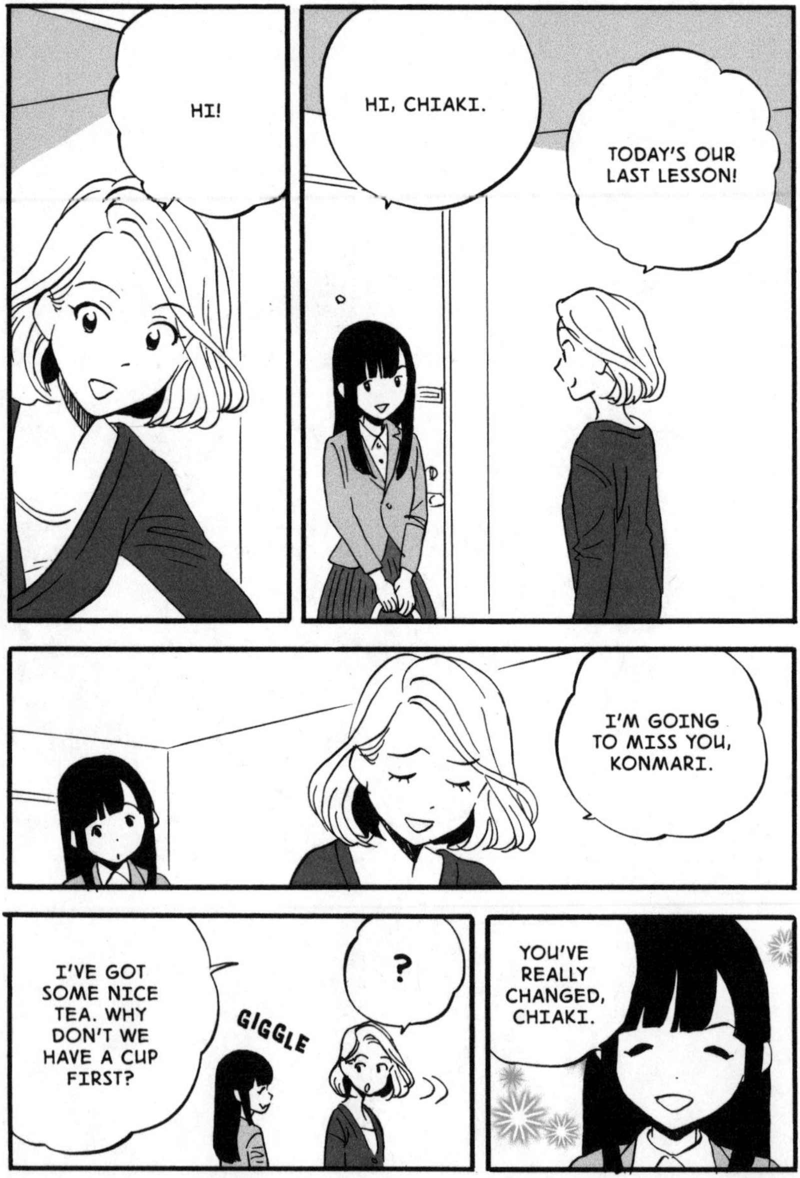
HI!
HI, CHIAKI.
TODAY'S OUR LAST LESSON!
I'M GOING TO MISS YOU, KONMARI.
I'VE GOT SOME NICE TEA. WHY DON'T WE HAVE A CUP FIRST?
GIGGLE
?
YOU'VE REALLY CHANGED, CHIAKI.

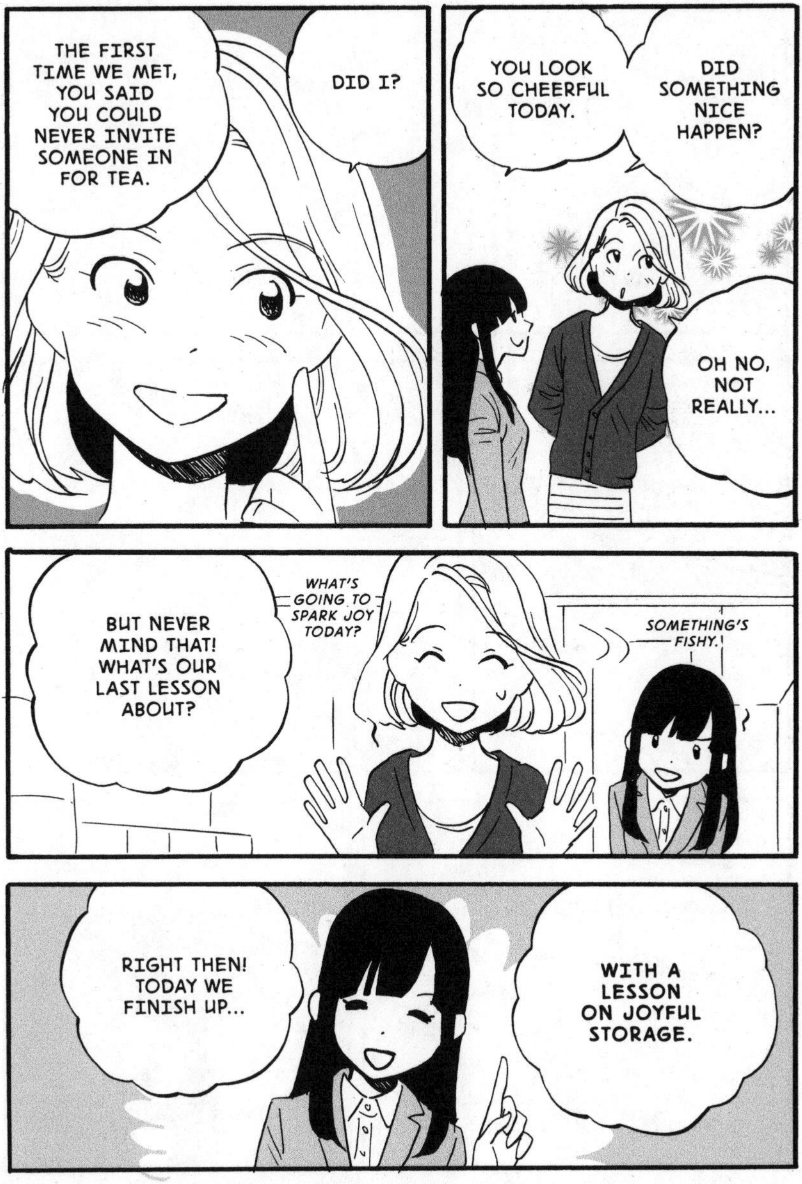
THE FIRST TIME WE MET, YOU SAID YOU COULD NEVER INVITE SOMEONE IN FOR TEA.
DID I?
YOU LOOK SO CHEERFUL TODAY.
DID SOMETHING NICE HAPPEN?
OH NO, NOT REALLY...
BUT NEVER MIND THAT! WHAT'S OUR LAST LESSON ABOUT?
WHAT'S GOING TO SPARK JOY TODAY?
SOMETHING'S FISHY.
RIGHT THEN! TODAY WE FINISH UP...
WITH A LESSON ON JOYFUL STORAGE.

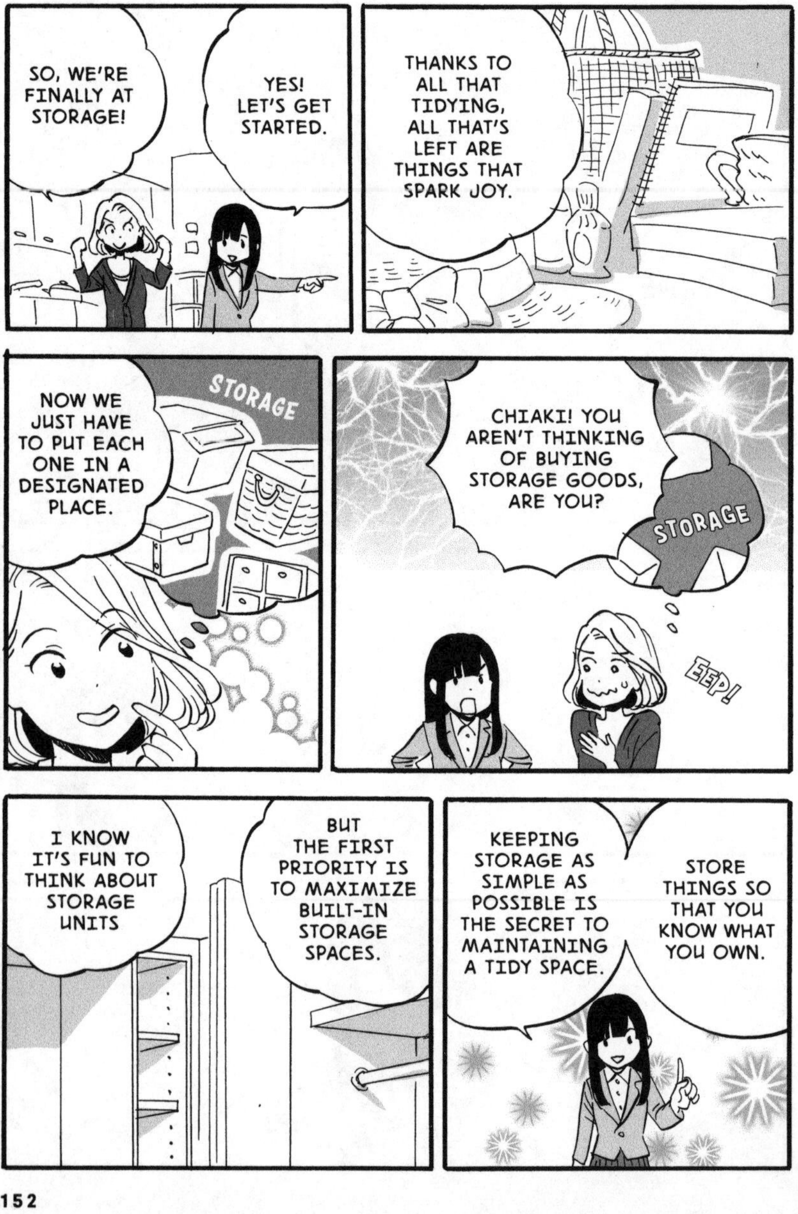
SO, WE'RE FINALLY AT STORAGE!
YES! LET'S GET STARTED.
THANKS TO ALL THAT TIDYING, ALL THAT'S LEFT ARE THINGS THAT SPARK JOY.
NOW WE JUST HAVE TO PUT EACH ONE IN A DESIGNATED PLACE.
STORAGE
CHIAKI! YOU AREN'T THINKING OF BUYING STORAGE GOODS, ARE YOU?
STORAGE
EEP!
I KNOW IT'S FUN TO THINK ABOUT STORAGE UNITS
BUT THE FIRST PRIORITY IS TO MAXIMIZE BUILT-IN STORAGE SPACES.
KEEPING STORAGE AS SIMPLE AS POSSIBLE IS THE SECRET TO MAINTAINING A TIDY SPACE.
STORE THINGS SO THAT YOU KNOW WHAT YOU OWN.

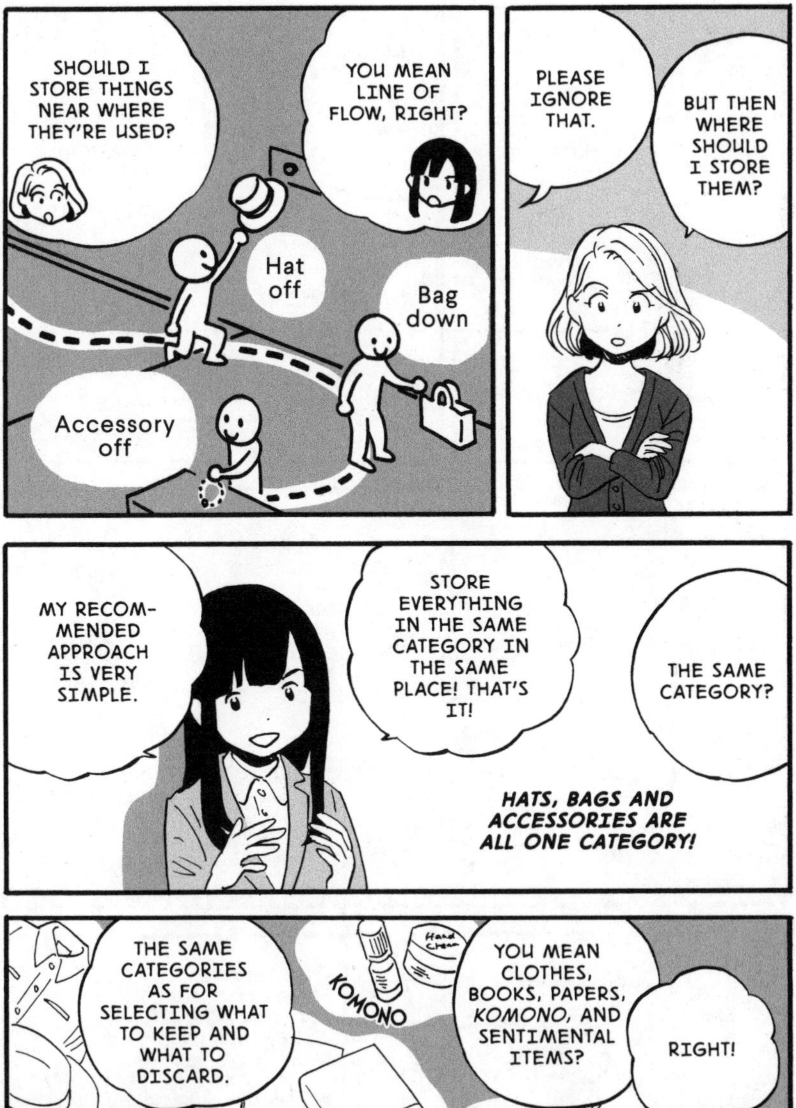
SHOULD I STORE THINGS NEAR WHERE THEY'RE USED?
YOU MEAN LINE OF FLOW, RIGHT?
Hat off
Bag down
Accessory off
PLEASE IGNORE THAT.
BUT THEN WHERE SHOULD I STORE THEM?
MY RECOM-MENDED APPROACH IS VERY SIMPLE.
STORE EVERYTHING IN THE SAME CATEGORY IN THE SAME PLACE! THAT'S IT!
THE SAME CATEGORY?
HATS, BAGS AND ACCESSORIES ARE ALL ONE CATEGORY!
THE SAME CATEGORIES AS FOR SELECTING WHAT TO KEEP AND WHAT TO DISCARD.
KOMONO
Hand Cream
YOU MEAN CLOTHES, BOOKS, PAPERS, KOMONO, AND SENTIMENTAL ITEMS?
RIGHT!
CLOTHES
BOOKS
PAPERS

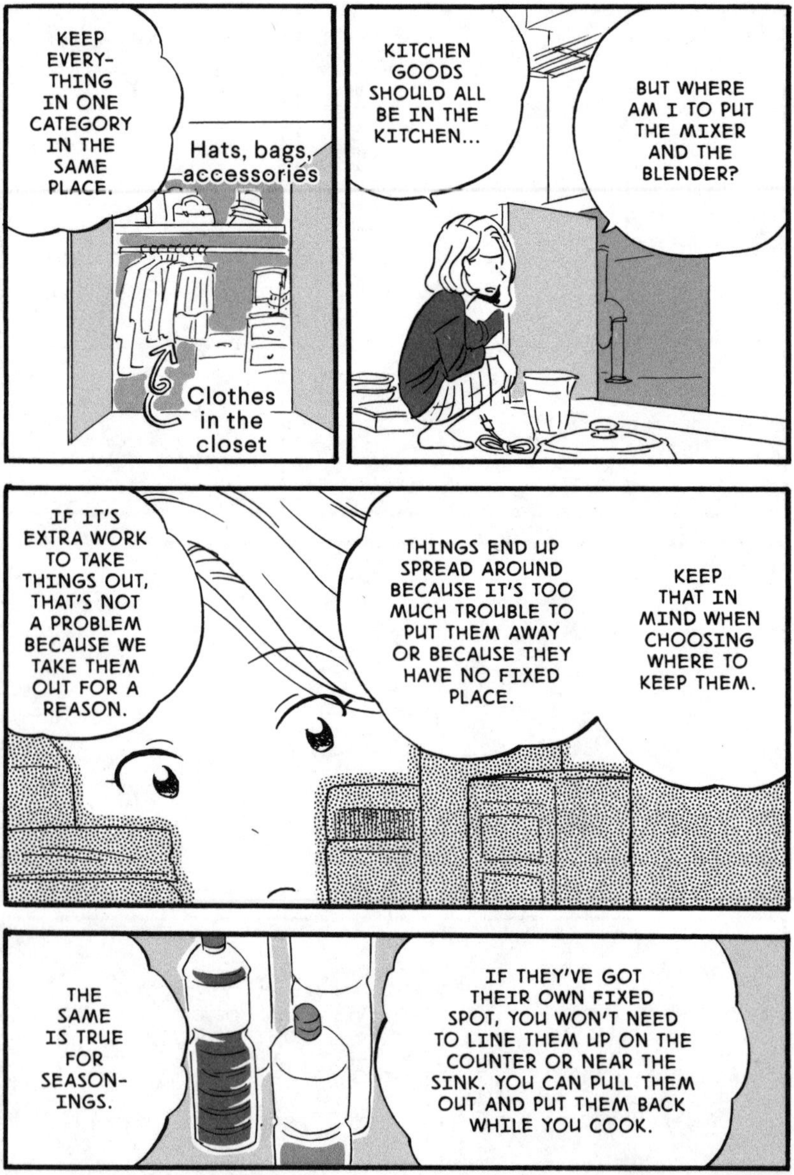
KEEP EVERYTHING IN ONE CATEGORY IN THE SAME PLACE.
Hats, bags, accessories
Clothes in the closet
KITCHEN GOODS SHOULD ALL BE IN THE KITCHEN...
BUT WHERE AM I TO PUT THE MIXER AND THE BLENDER?
IF IT'S EXTRA WORK TO TAKE THINGS OUT, THAT'S NOT A PROBLEM BECAUSE WE TAKE THEM OUT FOR A REASON.
THINGS END UP SPREAD AROUND BECAUSE IT'S TOO MUCH TROUBLE TO PUT THEM AWAY OR BECAUSE THEY HAVE NO FIXED PLACE.
KEEP THAT IN MIND WHEN CHOOSING WHERE TO KEEP THEM.
THE SAME IS TRUE FOR SEASONINGS.
IF THEY'VE GOT THEIR OWN FIXED SPOT, YOU WON'T NEED TO LINE THEM UP ON THE COUNTER OR NEAR THE SINK. YOU CAN PULL THEM OUT AND PUT THEM BACK WHILE YOU COOK.

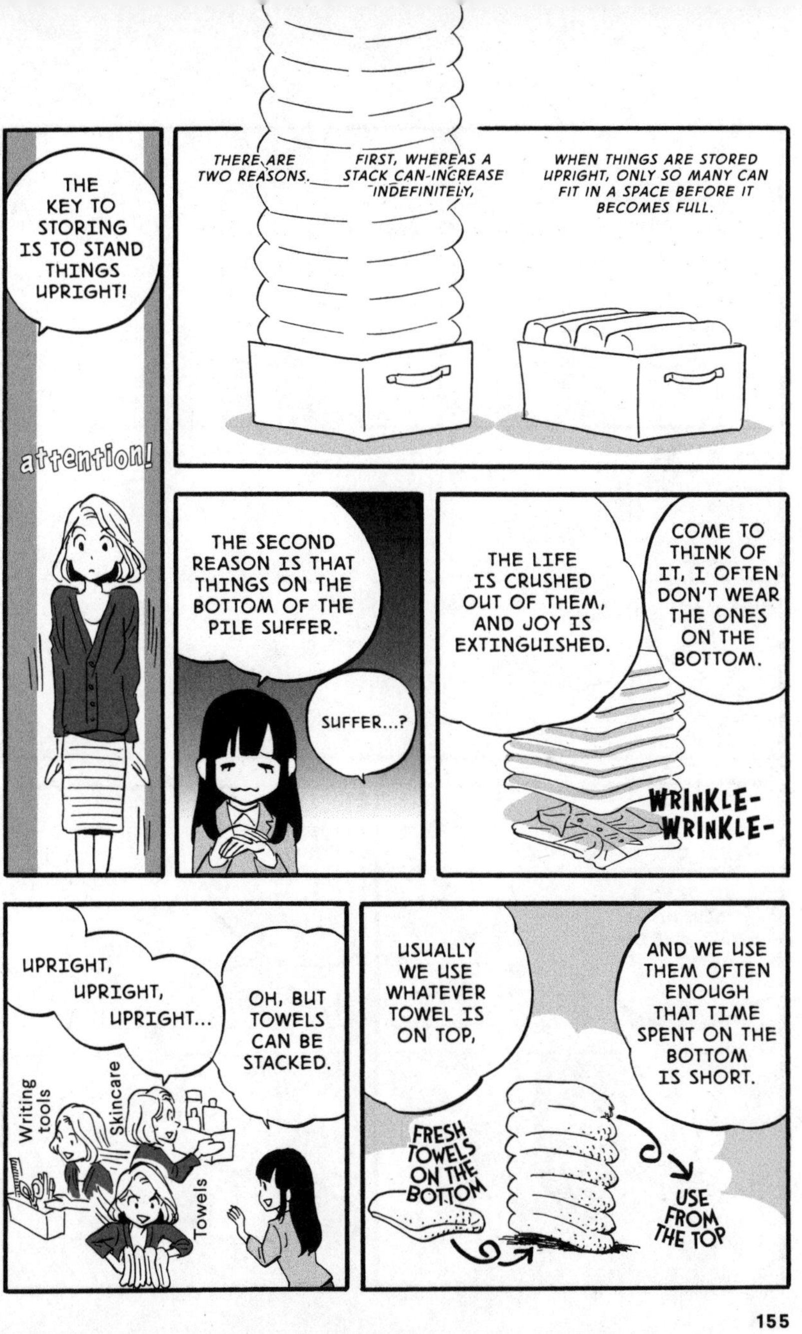
THE KEY TO STORING IS TO STAND THINGS UPRIGHT!
attention!
THERE ARE TWO REASONS.
FIRST, WHEREAS A STACK CAN INCREASE INDEFINITELY,
WHEN THINGS ARE STORED UPRIGHT, ONLY SO MANY CAN FIT IN A SPACE BEFORE IT BECOMES FULL.
THE SECOND REASON IS THAT THINGS ON THE BOTTOM OF THE PILE SUFFER.
SUFFER...?
THE LIFE IS CRUSHED OUT OF THEM, AND JOY IS EXTINGUISHED.
COME TO THINK OF IT, I OFTEN DON'T WEAR THE ONES ON THE BOTTOM.
WRINKLE-WRINKLE-
UPRIGHT, UPRIGHT, UPRIGHT...
Writing tools
Skincare
Towels
OH, BUT TOWELS CAN BE STACKED.
USUALLY WE USE WHATEVER TOWEL IS ON TOP,
AND WE USE THEM OFTEN ENOUGH THAT TIME SPENT ON THE BOTTOM IS SHORT.
FRESH TOWELS ON THE BOTTOM
USE FROM THE TOP

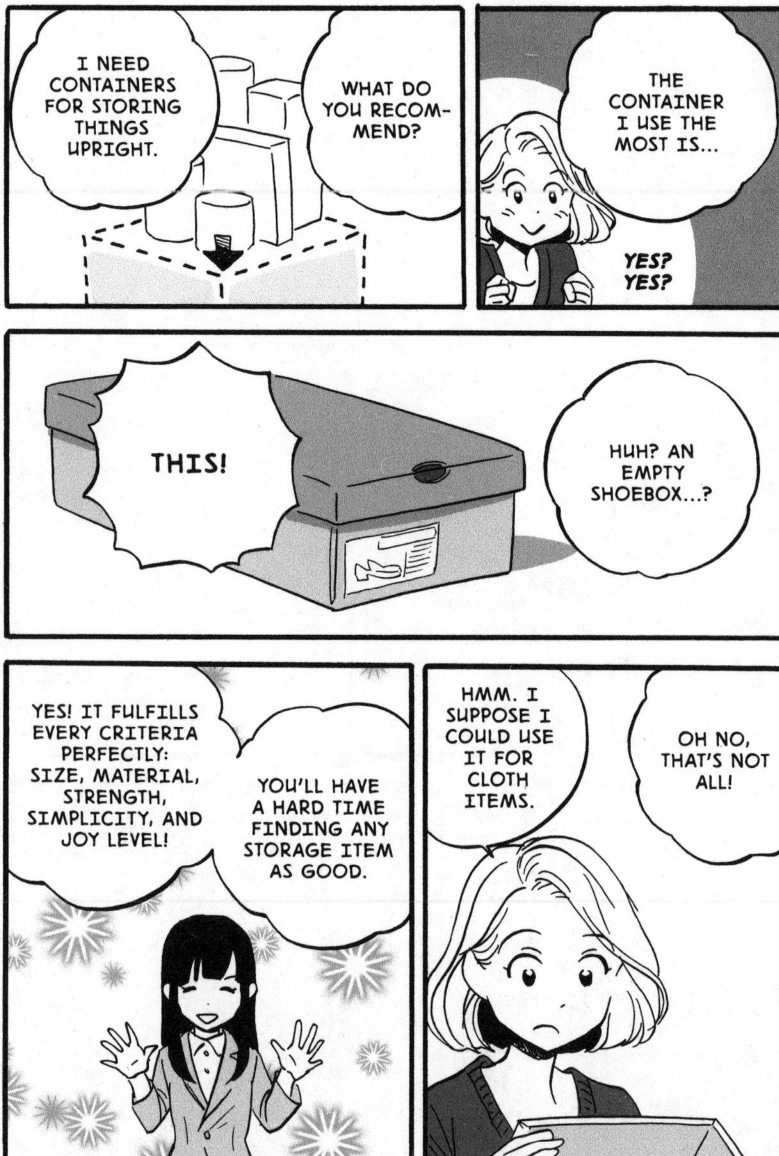
I NEED CONTAINERS FOR STORING THINGS UPRIGHT.
WHAT DO YOU RECOMMEND?
THE CONTAINER I USE THE MOST IS...
YES? YES?
THIS!
HUH? AN EMPTY SHOEBOX...?
YES! IT FULFILLS EVERY CRITERIA PERFECTLY: SIZE, MATERIAL, STRENGTH, SIMPLICITY, AND JOY LEVEL!
YOU'LL HAVE A HARD TIME FINDING ANY STORAGE ITEM AS GOOD.
HMM. I SUPPOSE I COULD USE IT FOR CLOTH ITEMS.
OH NO, THAT'S NOT ALL!

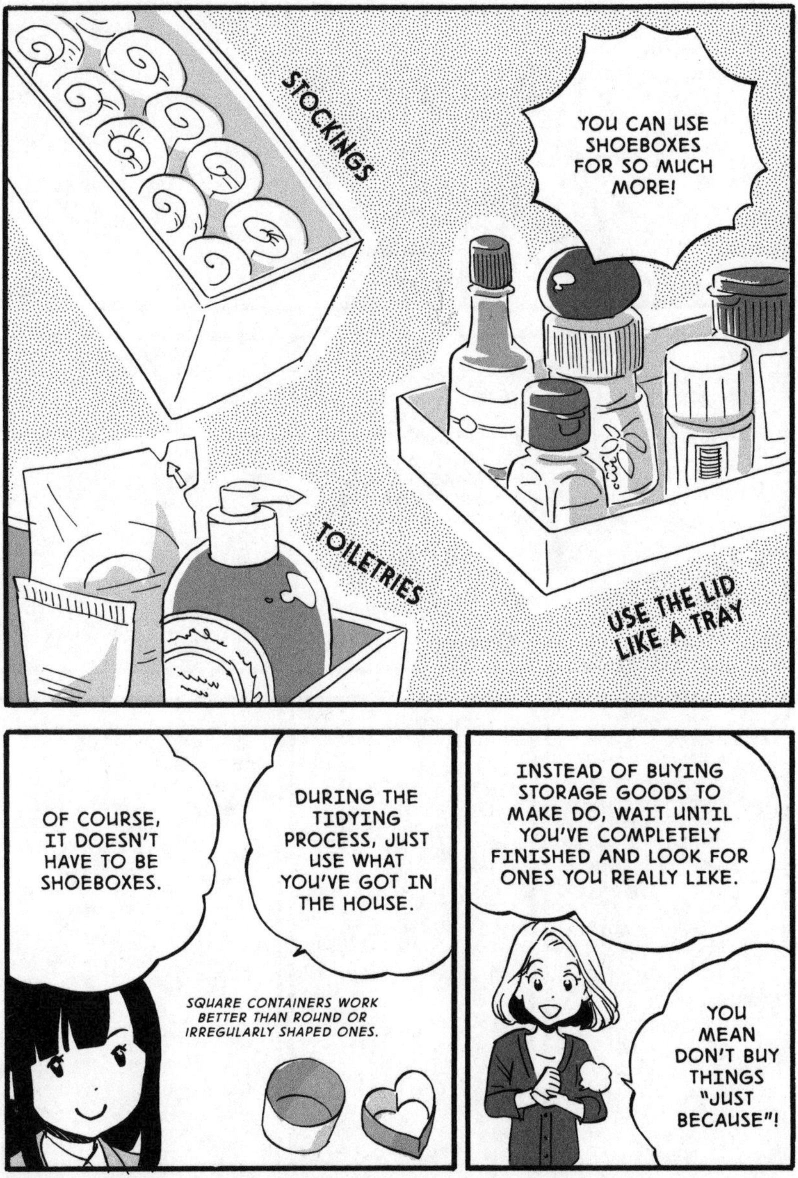
STOCKINGS
YOU CAN USE SHOEBOXES FOR SO MUCH MORE!
TOILETRIES
USE THE LID LIKE A TRAY
OF COURSE, IT DOESN'T HAVE TO BE SHOEBOXES.
DURING THE TIDYING PROCESS, JUST USE WHAT YOU'VE GOT IN THE HOUSE.
SQUARE CONTAINERS WORK BETTER THAN ROUND OR IRREGULARLY SHAPED ONES.
INSTEAD OF BUYING STORAGE GOODS TO MAKE DO, WAIT UNTIL YOU'VE COMPLETELY FINISHED AND LOOK FOR ONES YOU REALLY LIKE.
YOU MEAN DON'T BUY THINGS "JUST BECAUSE"!

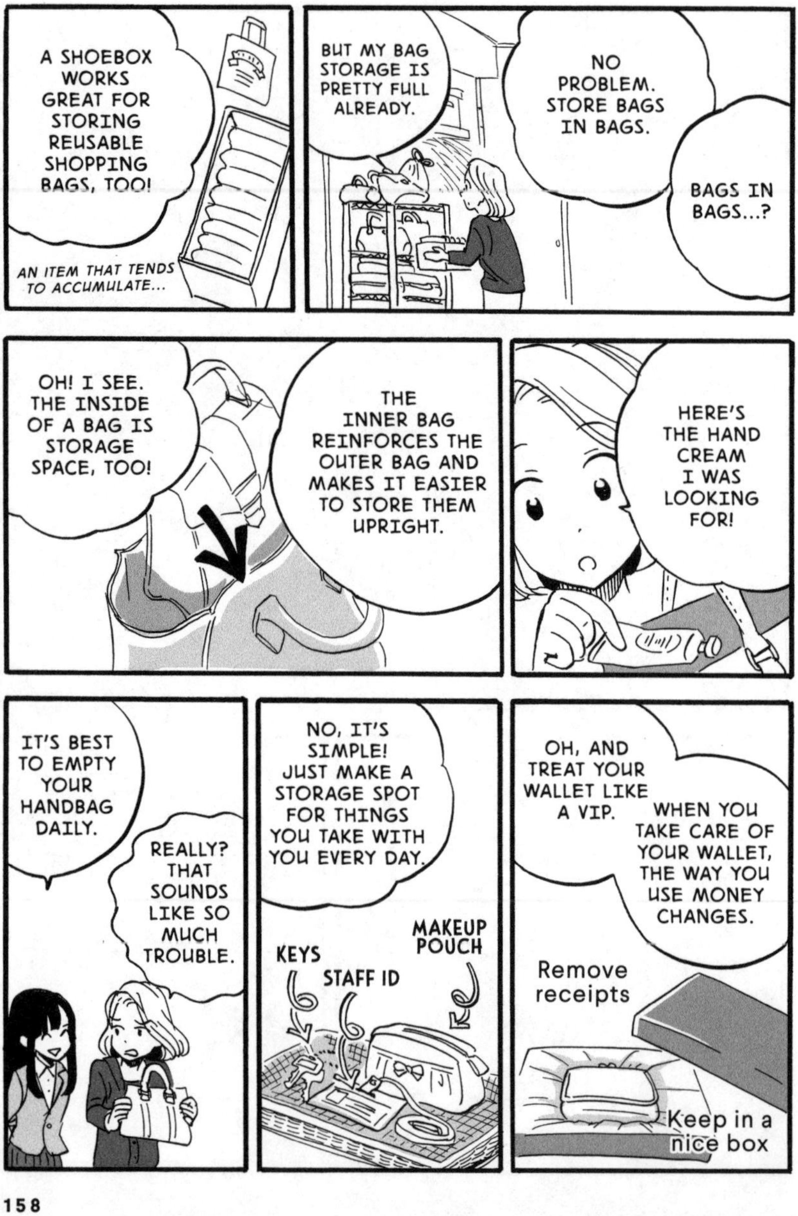
A SHOEBOX WORKS GREAT FOR STORING REUSABLE SHOPPING BAGS, TOO!
AN ITEM THAT TENDS TO ACCUMULATE...
BUT MY BAG STORAGE IS PRETTY FULL ALREADY.
NO PROBLEM. STORE BAGS IN BAGS.
BAGS IN BAGS...?
OH! I SEE. THE INSIDE OF A BAG IS STORAGE SPACE, TOO!
THE INNER BAG REINFORCES THE OUTER BAG AND MAKES IT EASIER TO STORE THEM UPRIGHT.
HERE'S THE HAND CREAM I WAS LOOKING FOR!
IT'S BEST TO EMPTY YOUR HANDBAG DAILY.
REALLY? THAT SOUNDS LIKE SO MUCH TROUBLE.
NO, IT'S SIMPLE! JUST MAKE A STORAGE SPOT FOR THINGS YOU TAKE WITH YOU EVERY DAY.
KEYS
STAFF ID
MAKEUP POUCH
OH, AND TREAT YOUR WALLET LIKE A VIP.
WHEN YOU TAKE CARE OF YOUR WALLET, THE WAY YOU USE MONEY CHANGES.
Remove receipts
Keep in a nice box

STORE THAT UPRIGHT. TIGHTEN THAT UP...

KONMARI...

I THOUGHT YOU WERE AN EXPERT AT MAKING PEOPLE DISCARD.

BUT YOU'RE ALSO A STORAGE PRO.

I'M MORE LIKE A STORAGE GEEK.

EHEHEH.

IT GOES BACK A LONG WAY.

I'M THE MIDDLE CHILD OF THREE.

MY MOTHER WAS BUSY TAKING CARE OF MY YOUNGER SISTER, AND MY OLDER BROTHER SPENT ALL HIS TIME PLAYING VIDEO GAMES.

I HAD A LOT OF TIME ON MY OWN AND MY FAVORITE PASTIME...

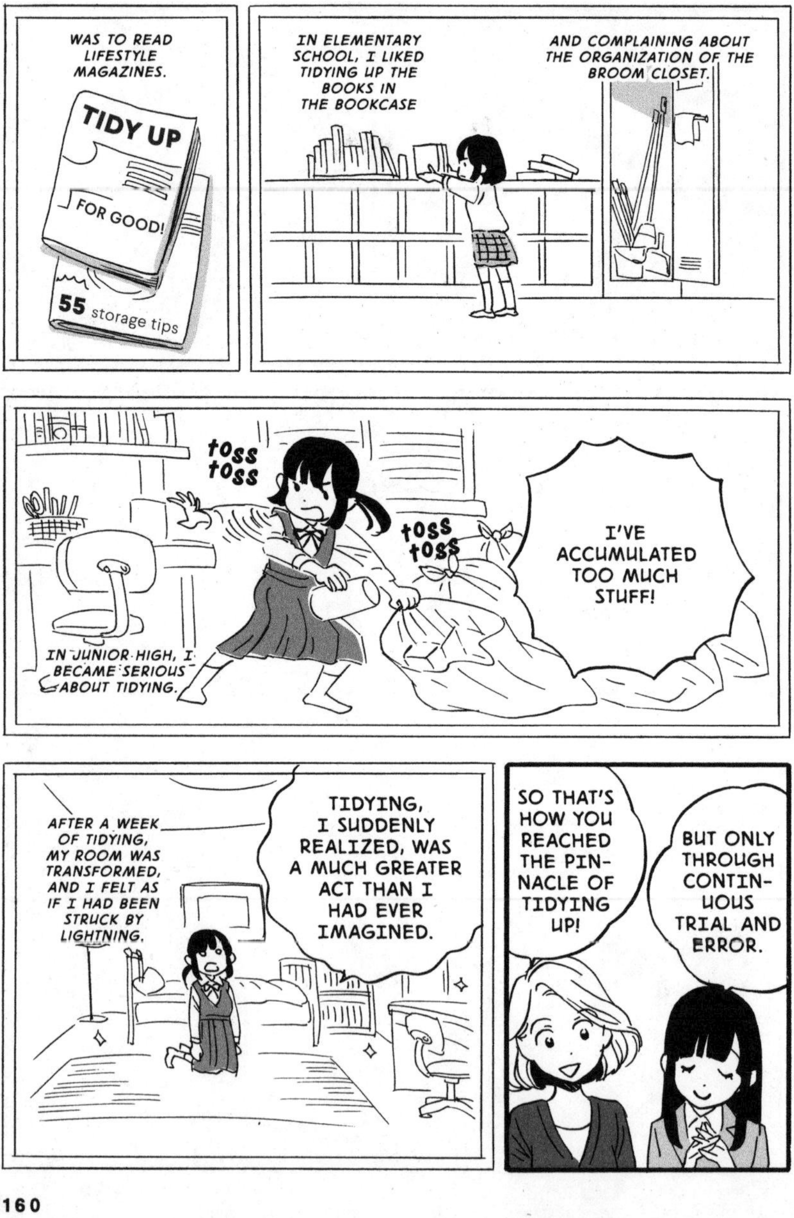
WAS TO READ LIFESTYLE MAGAZINES.
TIDY UP
FOR GOOD!
55 storage tips
IN ELEMENTARY SCHOOL, I LIKED TIDYING UP THE BOOKS IN THE BOOKCASE
AND COMPLAINING ABOUT THE ORGANIZATION OF THE BROOM CLOSET.
toss toss
toss toss
I'VE ACCUMULATED TOO MUCH STUFF!
IN JUNIOR HIGH, I BECAME SERIOUS ABOUT TIDYING.
AFTER A WEEK OF TIDYING, MY ROOM WAS TRANSFORMED, AND I FELT AS IF I HAD BEEN STRUCK BY LIGHTNING.
TIDYING, I SUDDENLY REALIZED, WAS A MUCH GREATER ACT THAN I HAD EVER IMAGINED.
SO THAT'S HOW YOU REACHED THE PIN-NACLE OF TIDYING UP!
BUT ONLY THROUGH CONTIN-UOUS TRIAL AND ERROR.

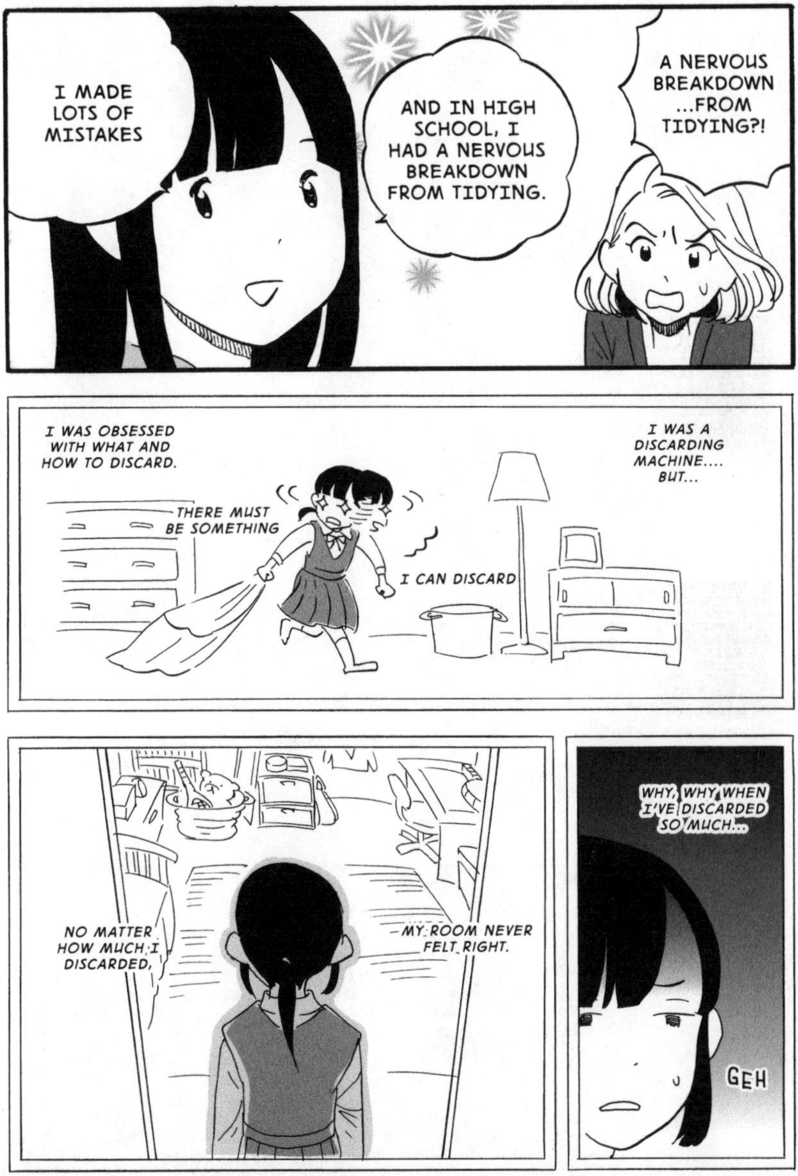

I MADE LOTS OF MISTAKES
AND IN HIGH SCHOOL, I HAD A NERVOUS BREAKDOWN FROM TIDYING.
A NERVOUS BREAKDOWN ...FROM TIDYING?!
I WAS OBSESSED WITH WHAT AND HOW TO DISCARD.
THERE MUST BE SOMETHING
I CAN DISCARD
I WAS A DISCARDING MACHINE.... BUT...
NO MATTER HOW MUCH I DISCARDED,
MY ROOM NEVER FELT RIGHT.
WHY, WHY WHEN I'VE DISCARDED SO MUCH...
GEH

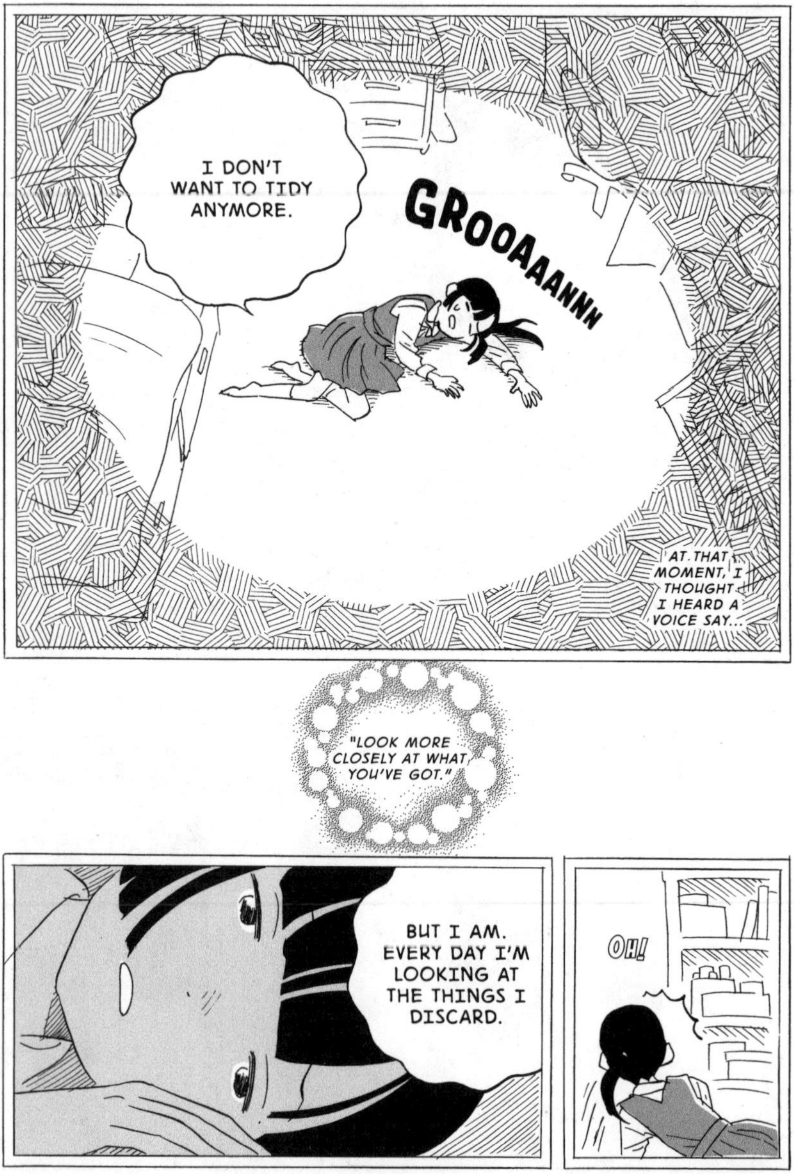
I DON'T WANT TO TIDY ANYMORE.
GROOAAANNN
AT THAT MOMENT, I THOUGHT I HEARD A VOICE SAY...
"LOOK MORE CLOSELY AT WHAT YOU'VE GOT."
BUT I AM. EVERY DAY I'M LOOKING AT THE THINGS I DISCARD.
OH!

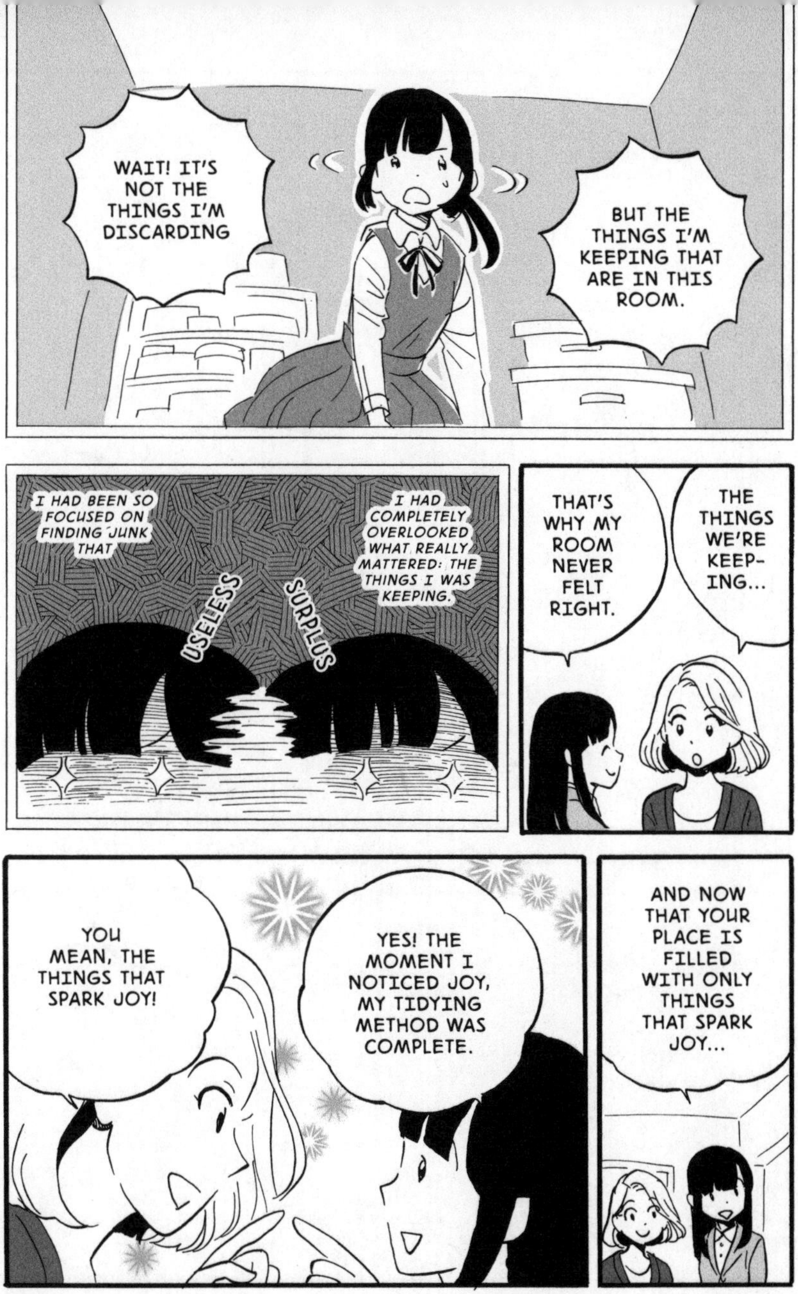
WAIT! IT'S NOT THE THINGS I'M DISCARDING
BUT THE THINGS I'M KEEPING THAT ARE IN THIS ROOM.
I HAD BEEN SO FOCUSED ON FINDING JUNK THAT
USELESS
SURPLUS
I HAD COMPLETELY OVERLOOKED WHAT REALLY MATTERED: THE THINGS I WAS KEEPING.
THAT'S WHY MY ROOM NEVER FELT RIGHT.
THE THINGS WE'RE KEEP- ING...
YOU MEAN, THE THINGS THAT SPARK JOY!
YES! THE MOMENT I NOTICED JOY, MY TIDYING METHOD WAS COMPLETE.
AND NOW THAT YOUR PLACE IS FILLED WITH ONLY THINGS THAT SPARK JOY...

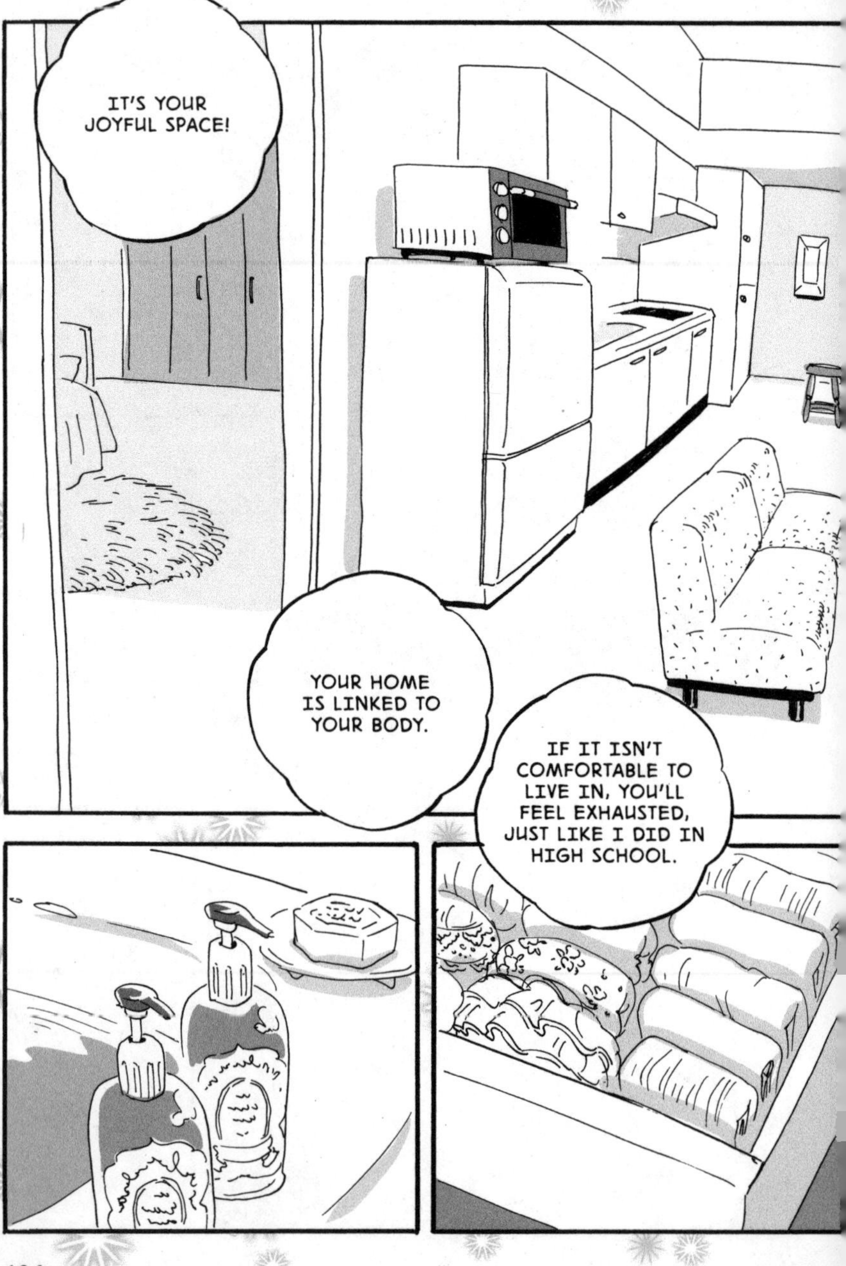

IT'S YOUR JOYFUL SPACE!
YOUR HOME IS LINKED TO YOUR BODY.
IF IT ISN'T COMFORTABLE TO LIVE IN, YOU'LL FEEL EXHAUSTED, JUST LIKE I DID IN HIGH SCHOOL.

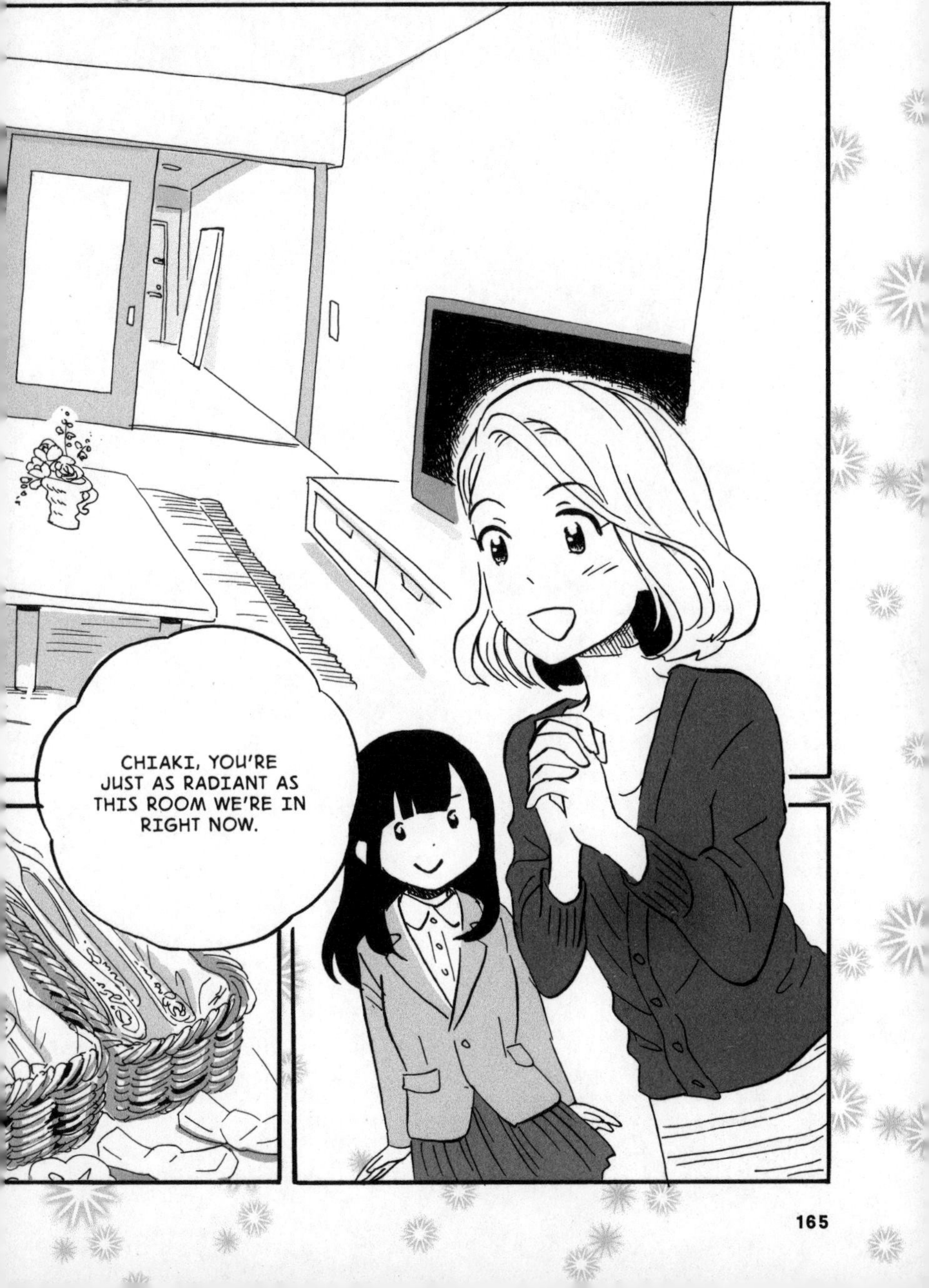
CHIAKI, YOU'RE JUST AS RADIANT AS THIS ROOM WE'RE IN RIGHT NOW.

Designate a "home" for each thing and store it where it belongs.

———

Although we may not be aware of it, our belongings work hard to support us every day. Just as we like to come home and relax after a long day's work, our things breathe a sigh of relief when they are returned to where they belong. It's very important to give our things the security of having a place to come home to.

Things that are returned each day to their designated place are different. They have a special glow. If we take good care of our possessions, they will take good care of us.

10

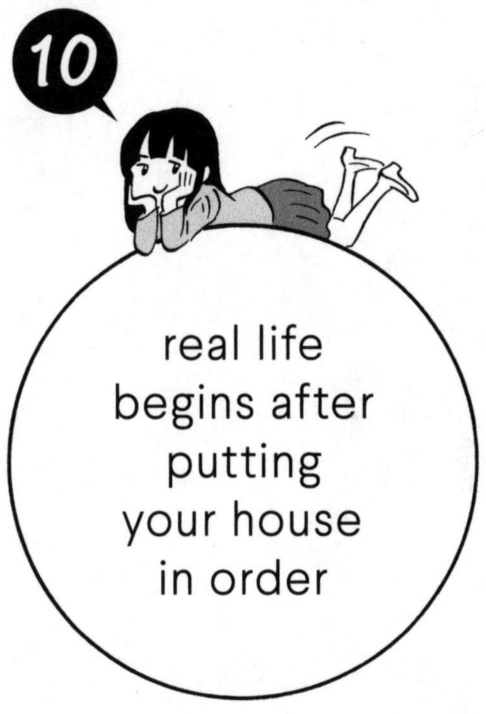

real life begins after putting your house in order

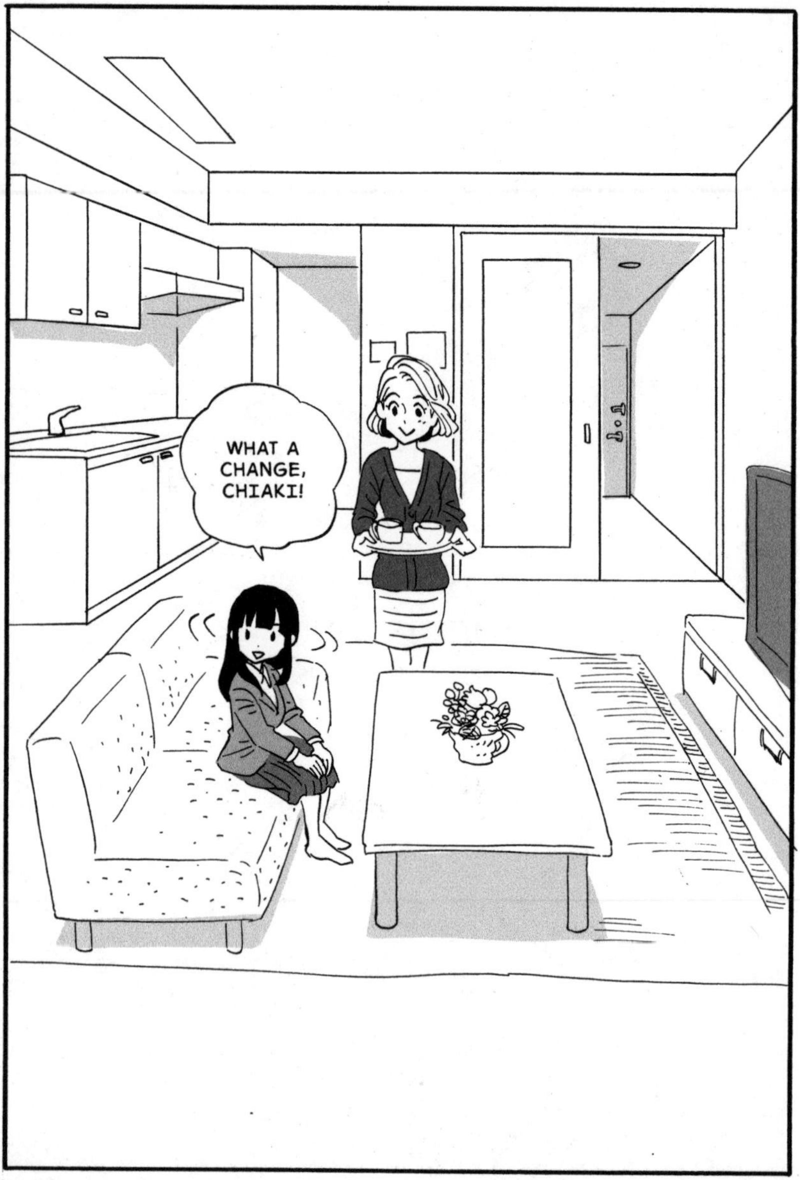
WHAT A CHANGE, CHIAKI!

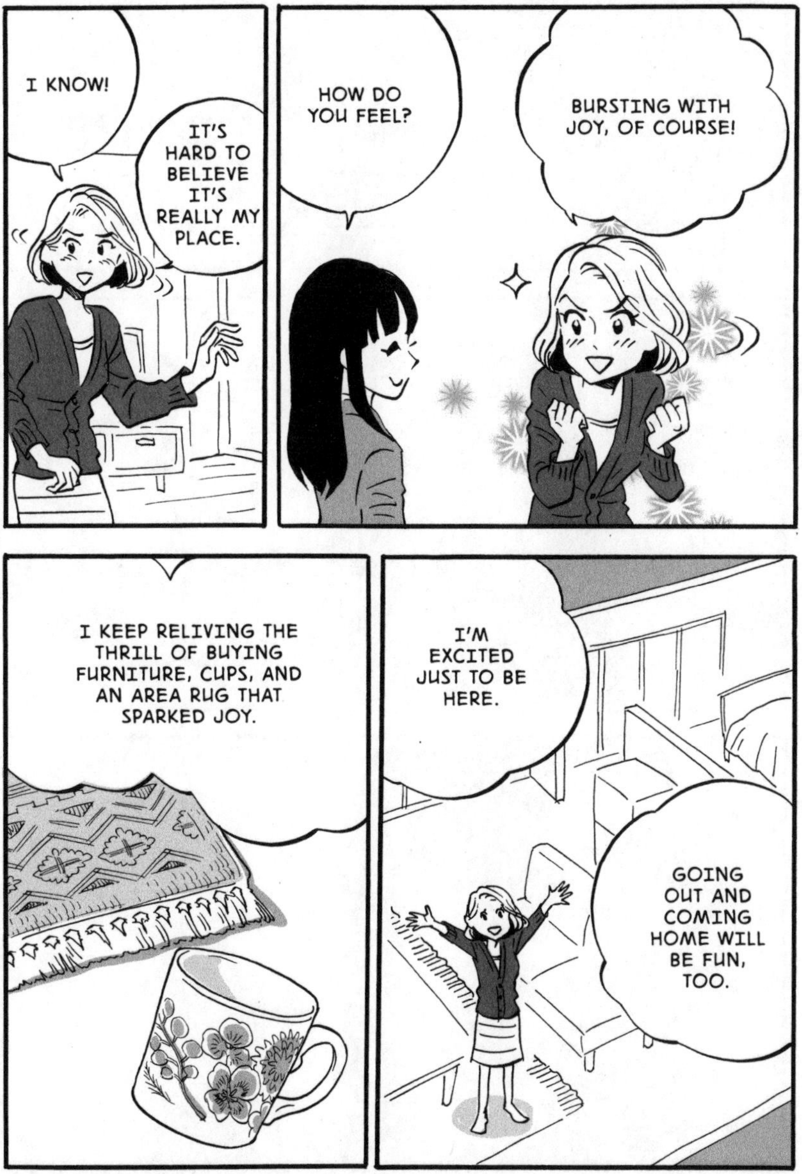
I KNOW!
IT'S HARD TO BELIEVE IT'S REALLY MY PLACE.
HOW DO YOU FEEL?
BURSTING WITH JOY, OF COURSE!
I KEEP RELIVING THE THRILL OF BUYING FURNITURE, CUPS, AND AN AREA RUG THAT SPARKED JOY.
I'M EXCITED JUST TO BE HERE.
GOING OUT AND COMING HOME WILL BE FUN, TOO.

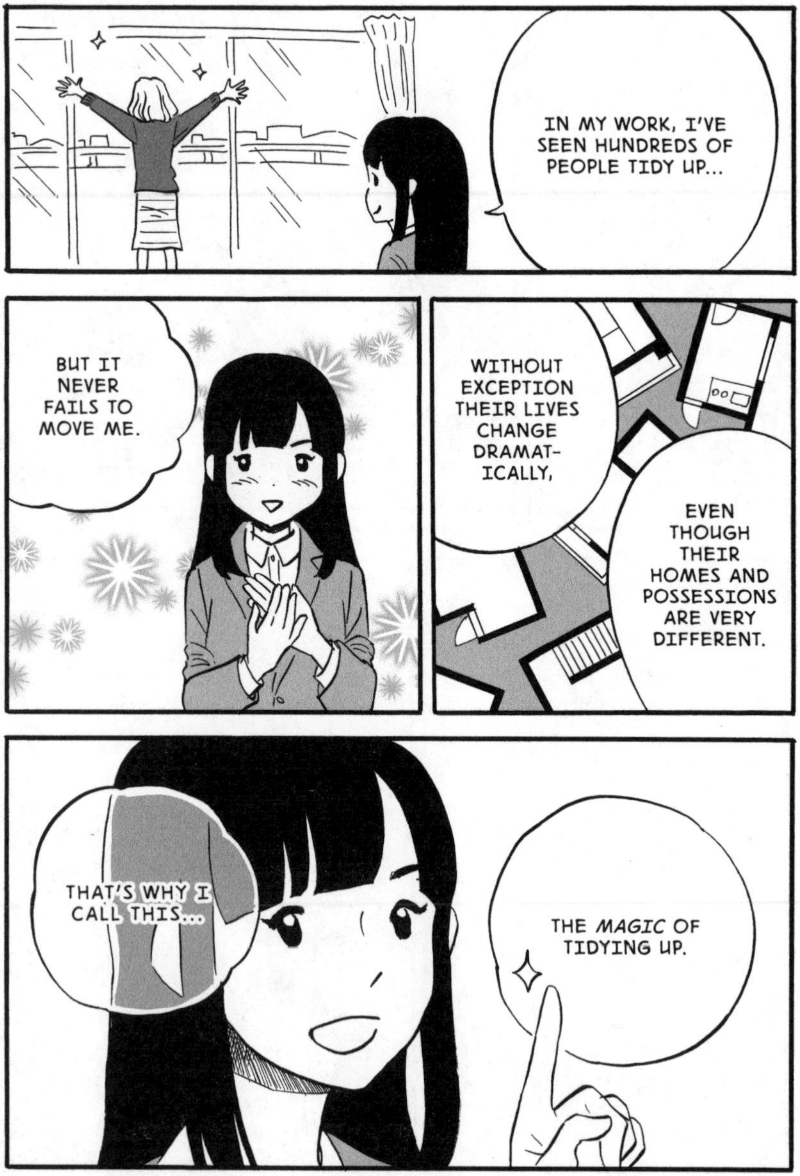
IN MY WORK, I'VE SEEN HUNDREDS OF PEOPLE TIDY UP...
BUT IT NEVER FAILS TO MOVE ME.
WITHOUT EXCEPTION THEIR LIVES CHANGE DRAMATICALLY,
EVEN THOUGH THEIR HOMES AND POSSESSIONS ARE VERY DIFFERENT.
THAT'S WHY I CALL THIS...
THE *MAGIC* OF TIDYING UP.

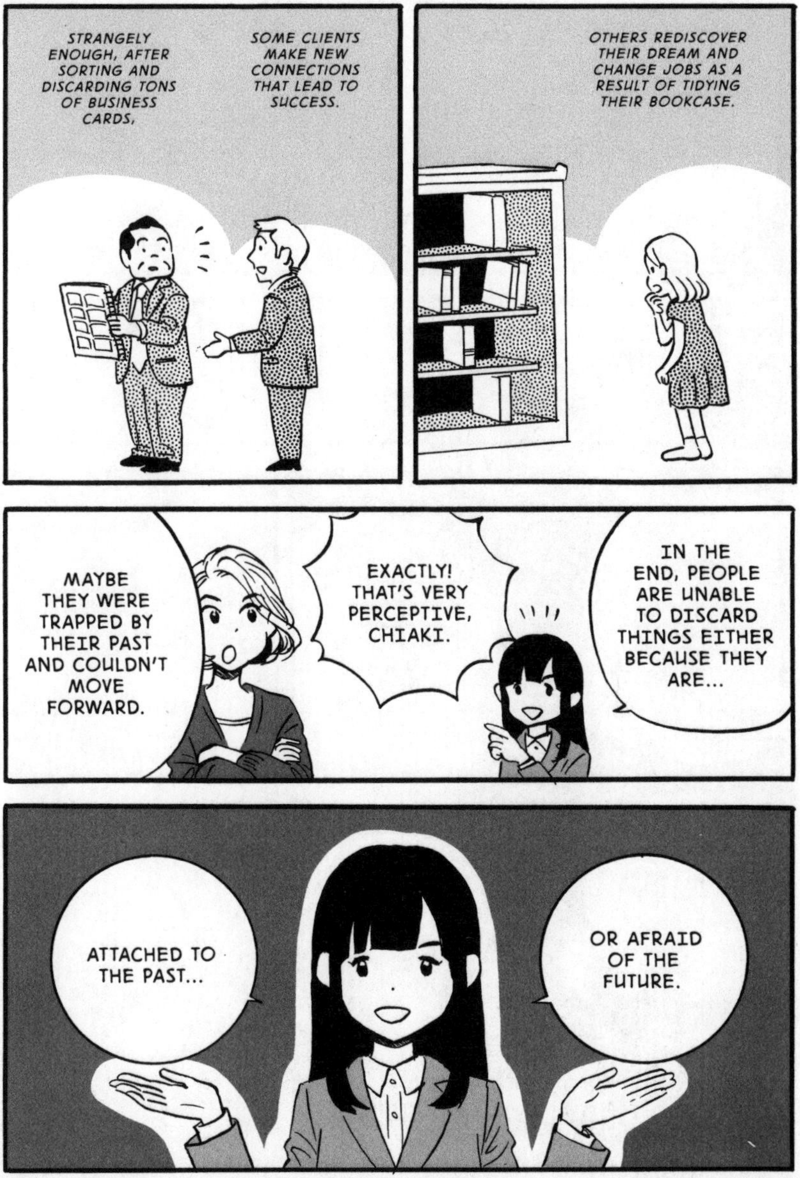
STRANGELY ENOUGH, AFTER SORTING AND DISCARDING TONS OF BUSINESS CARDS,
SOME CLIENTS MAKE NEW CONNECTIONS THAT LEAD TO SUCCESS.
OTHERS REDISCOVER THEIR DREAM AND CHANGE JOBS AS A RESULT OF TIDYING THEIR BOOKCASE.
MAYBE THEY WERE TRAPPED BY THEIR PAST AND COULDN'T MOVE FORWARD.
EXACTLY! THAT'S VERY PERCEPTIVE, CHIAKI.
IN THE END, PEOPLE ARE UNABLE TO DISCARD THINGS EITHER BECAUSE THEY ARE...
ATTACHED TO THE PAST...
OR AFRAID OF THE FUTURE.

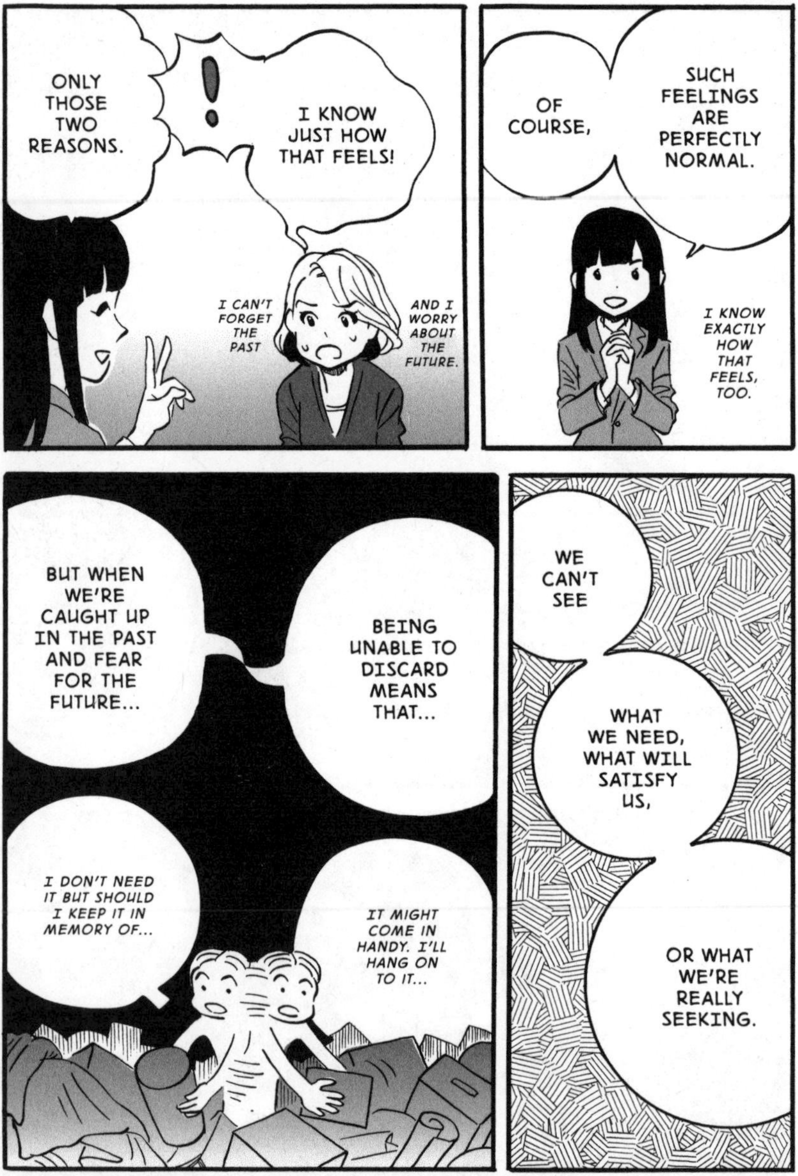
ONLY THOSE TWO REASONS.
!
I KNOW JUST HOW THAT FEELS!
I CAN'T FORGET THE PAST
AND I WORRY ABOUT THE FUTURE.
OF COURSE,
SUCH FEELINGS ARE PERFECTLY NORMAL.
I KNOW EXACTLY HOW THAT FEELS, TOO.
BUT WHEN WE'RE CAUGHT UP IN THE PAST AND FEAR FOR THE FUTURE...
BEING UNABLE TO DISCARD MEANS THAT...
I DON'T NEED IT BUT SHOULD I KEEP IT IN MEMORY OF...
IT MIGHT COME IN HANDY. I'LL HANG ON TO IT...
WE CAN'T SEE
WHAT WE NEED, WHAT WILL SATISFY US,
OR WHAT WE'RE REALLY SEEKING.

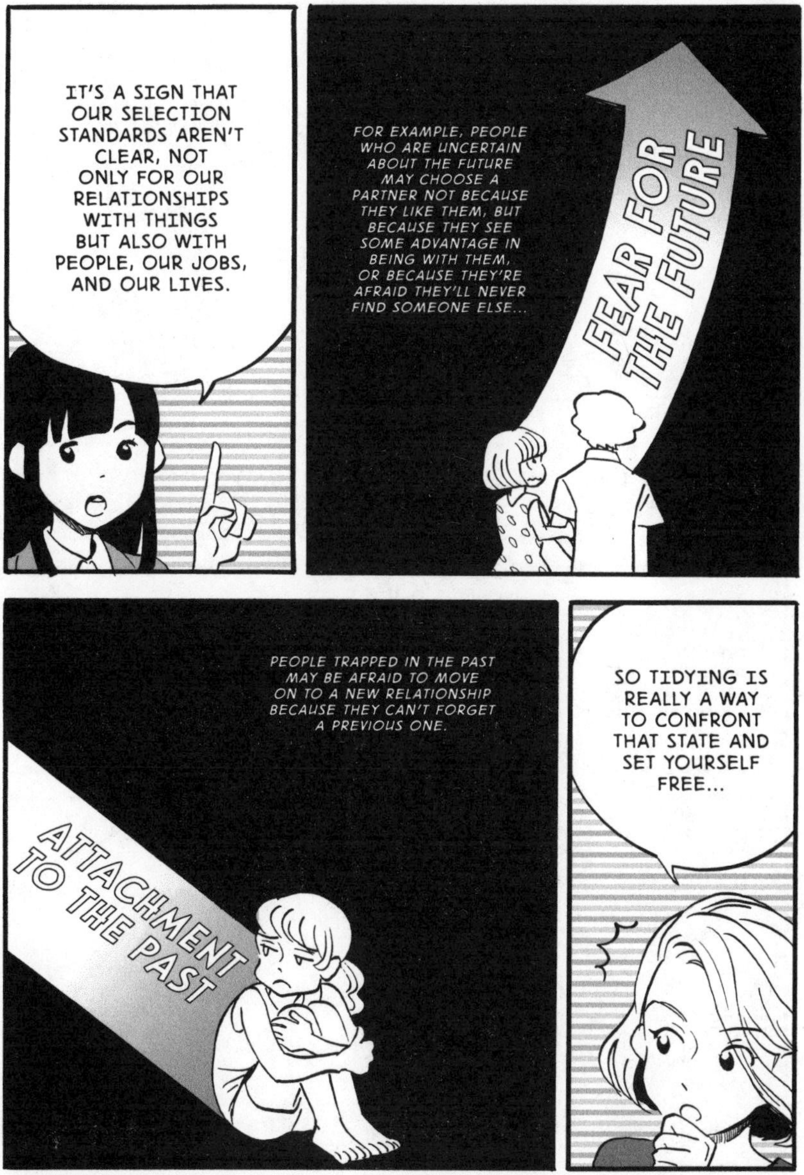
IT'S A SIGN THAT OUR SELECTION STANDARDS AREN'T CLEAR, NOT ONLY FOR OUR RELATIONSHIPS WITH THINGS BUT ALSO WITH PEOPLE, OUR JOBS, AND OUR LIVES.
FOR EXAMPLE, PEOPLE WHO ARE UNCERTAIN ABOUT THE FUTURE MAY CHOOSE A PARTNER NOT BECAUSE THEY LIKE THEM, BUT BECAUSE THEY SEE SOME ADVANTAGE IN BEING WITH THEM, OR BECAUSE THEY'RE AFRAID THEY'LL NEVER FIND SOMEONE ELSE...
FEAR FOR THE FUTURE
PEOPLE TRAPPED IN THE PAST MAY BE AFRAID TO MOVE ON TO A NEW RELATIONSHIP BECAUSE THEY CAN'T FORGET A PREVIOUS ONE.
ATTACHMENT TO THE PAST
SO TIDYING IS REALLY A WAY TO CONFRONT THAT STATE AND SET YOURSELF FREE...

THANKS TO TIDYING, I WAS ABLE TO FACE THINGS THAT I'D ONLY DEALT WITH "FOR THE TIME BEING" OR HAD PRETENDED NOT TO SEE...

THE THINGS I VALUED, THE THINGS I REALLY WANTED TO DO, WERE ALL RIGHT HERE. THERE WAS NO NEED TO TRAVEL IN SEARCH OF THEM OR TO BUY NEW THINGS.

TO BE HONEST, I WAS DOUBTFUL ABOUT USING "SPARK JOY" AS A CRITERION.

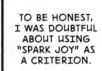

AHA-HA-HA

YOU WONDERED WHAT ON EARTH YOUR HOME WOULD END UP LIKE, RIGHT?

BUT JOY IS AN IMPORTANT AND VERY PERSONAL CRITERION.

IT'S NOT SOMETHING I CAN TEACH ANYONE THROUGH TIDYING LESSONS.

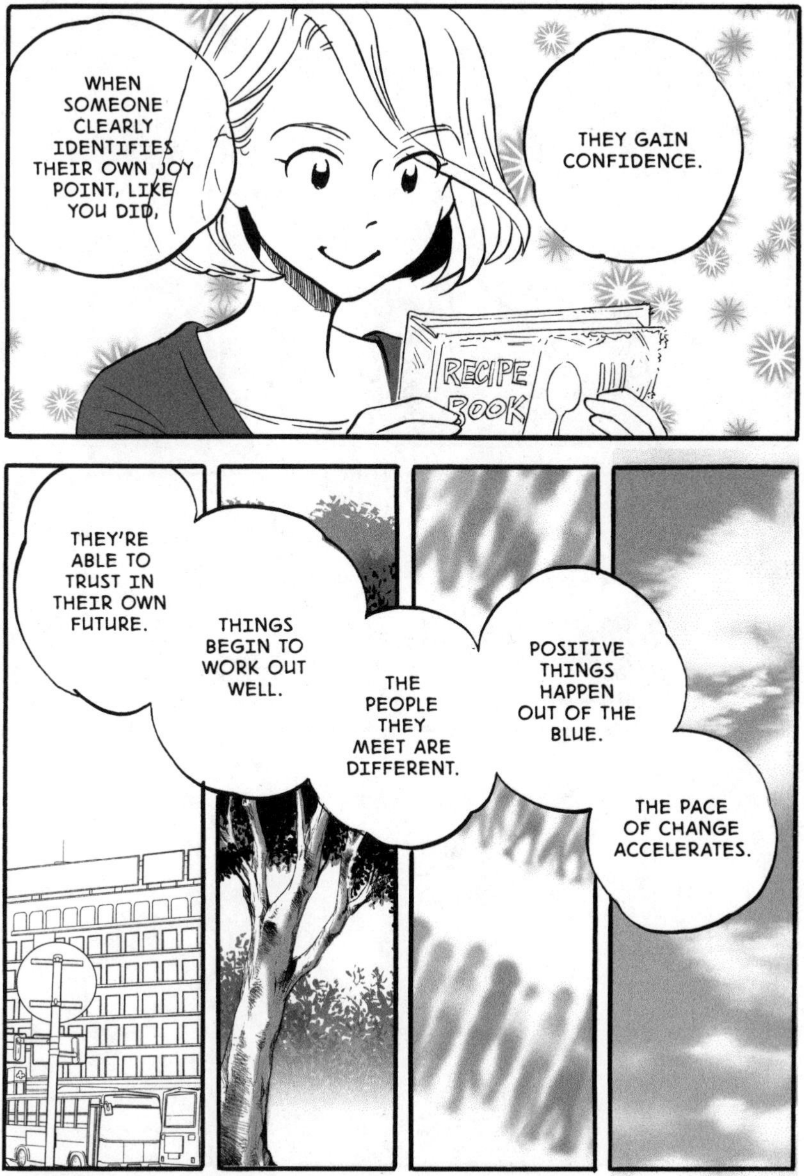
WHEN SOMEONE CLEARLY IDENTIFIES THEIR OWN JOY POINT, LIKE YOU DID,
THEY GAIN CONFIDENCE.
RECIPE BOOK
THEY'RE ABLE TO TRUST IN THEIR OWN FUTURE.
THINGS BEGIN TO WORK OUT WELL.
THE PEOPLE THEY MEET ARE DIFFERENT.
POSITIVE THINGS HAPPEN OUT OF THE BLUE.
THE PACE OF CHANGE ACCELERATES.

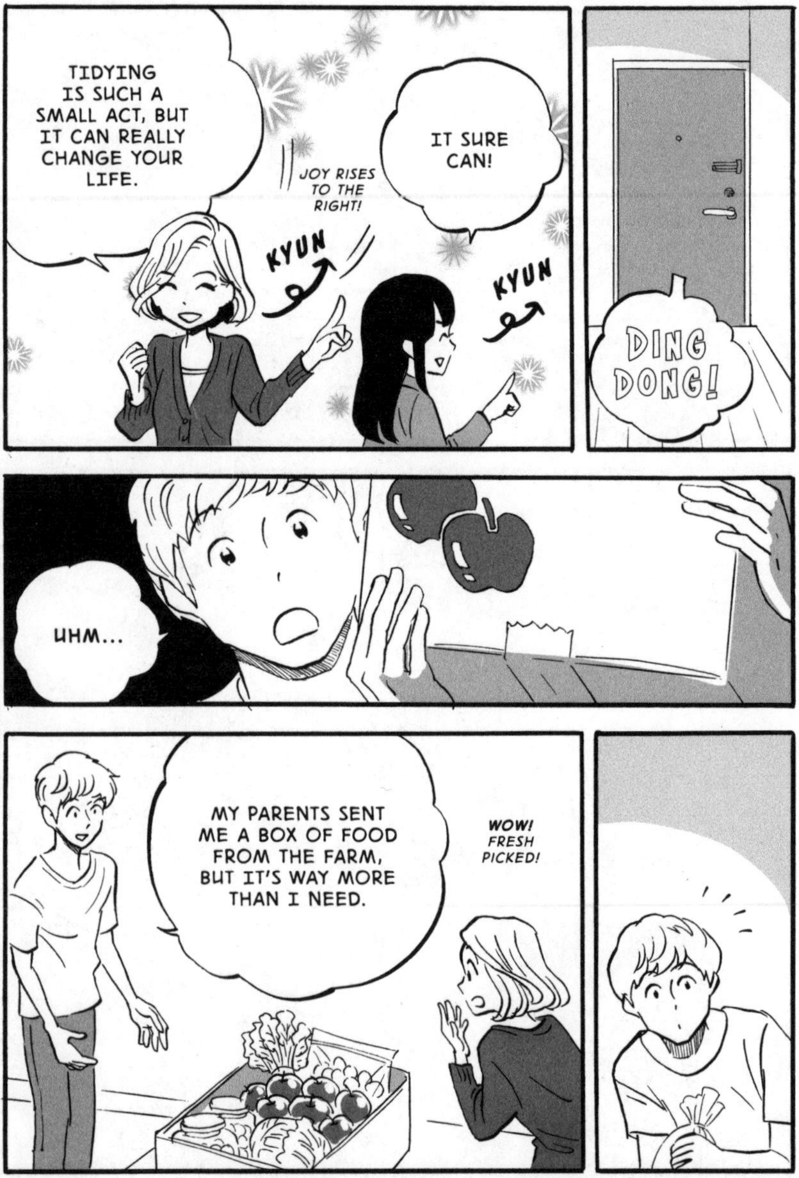
TIDYING IS SUCH A SMALL ACT, BUT IT CAN REALLY CHANGE YOUR LIFE.
JOY RISES TO THE RIGHT!
KYUN
IT SURE CAN!
KYUN
DING DONG!
UHM...
MY PARENTS SENT ME A BOX OF FOOD FROM THE FARM, BUT IT'S WAY MORE THAN I NEED.
WOW! FRESH PICKED!

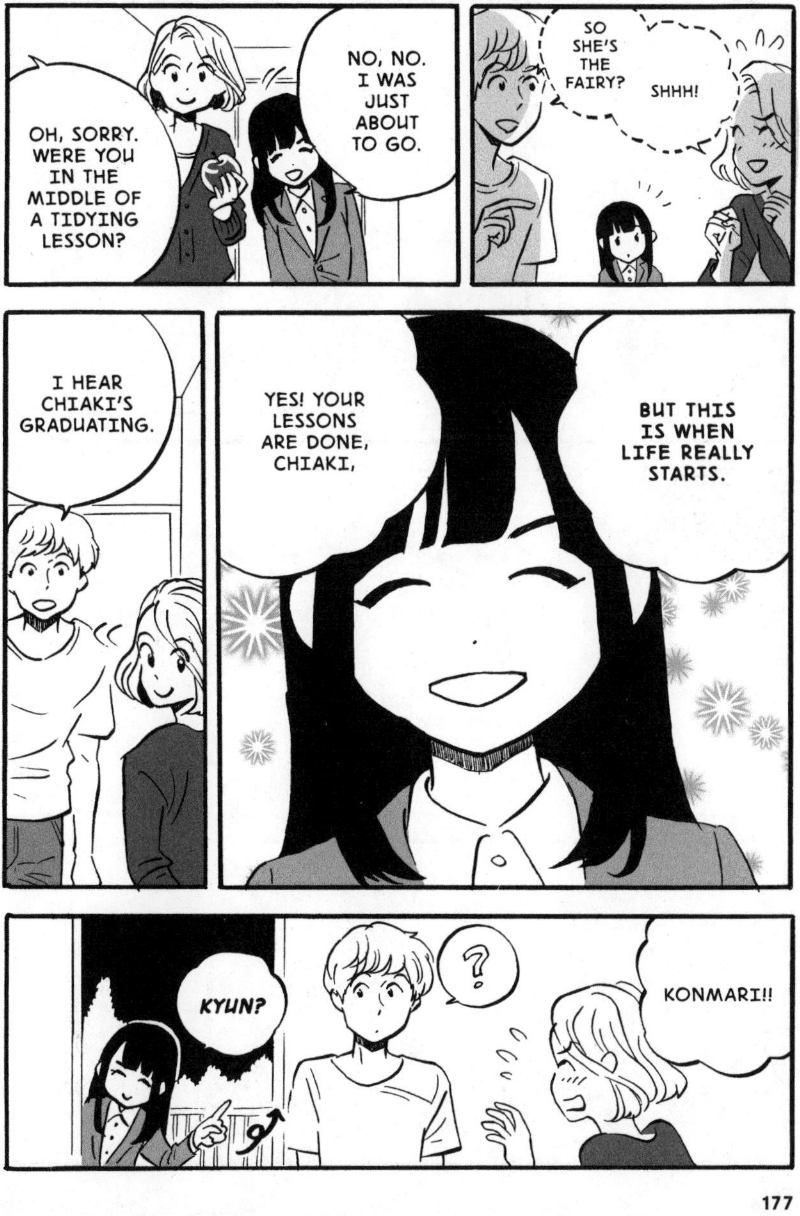
OH, SORRY. WERE YOU IN THE MIDDLE OF A TIDYING LESSON?
NO, NO. I WAS JUST ABOUT TO GO.
SO SHE'S THE FAIRY?
SHHH!
I HEAR CHIAKI'S GRADUATING.
YES! YOUR LESSONS ARE DONE, CHIAKI,
BUT THIS IS WHEN LIFE REALLY STARTS.
KYUN?
?
KONMARI!!

JUST LIKE KONMARI SAID, "REAL LIFE" HAS STARTED.

I LOOK FORWARD TO BREAKFAST SO MUCH THAT I'VE BECOME AN EARLY RISER.

SHOULD BE GOOD WEATHER TODAY, TOO.

THANKS TO MY TIDY DRESSER

EXTRA CARE FOR THE DISTRIBUTOR MEETING TODAY.

I DON'T JUST SLAP ON MY MAKEUP "FOR THE TIME BEING."

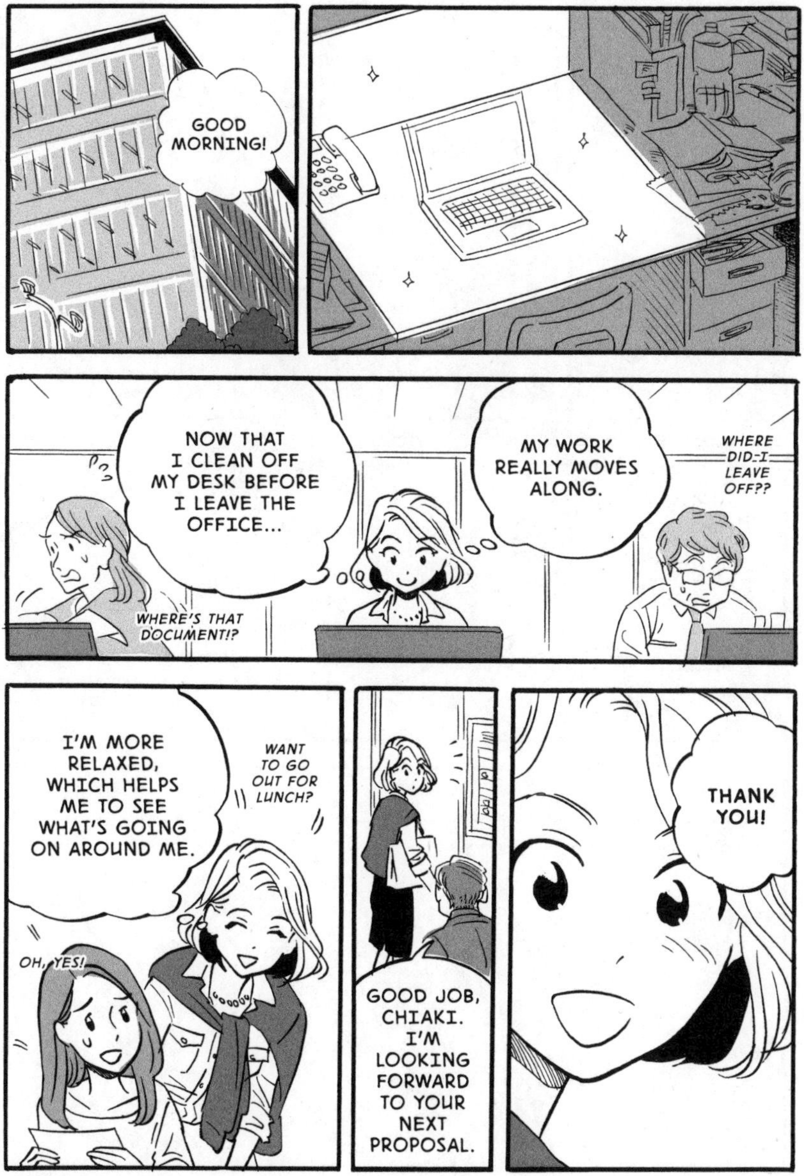
GOOD MORNING!
NOW THAT I CLEAN OFF MY DESK BEFORE I LEAVE THE OFFICE...
WHERE'S THAT DOCUMENT!?
MY WORK REALLY MOVES ALONG.
WHERE DID I LEAVE OFF??
I'M MORE RELAXED, WHICH HELPS ME TO SEE WHAT'S GOING ON AROUND ME.
WANT TO GO OUT FOR LUNCH?
OH, YES!
GOOD JOB, CHIAKI. I'M LOOKING FORWARD TO YOUR NEXT PROPOSAL.
THANK YOU!

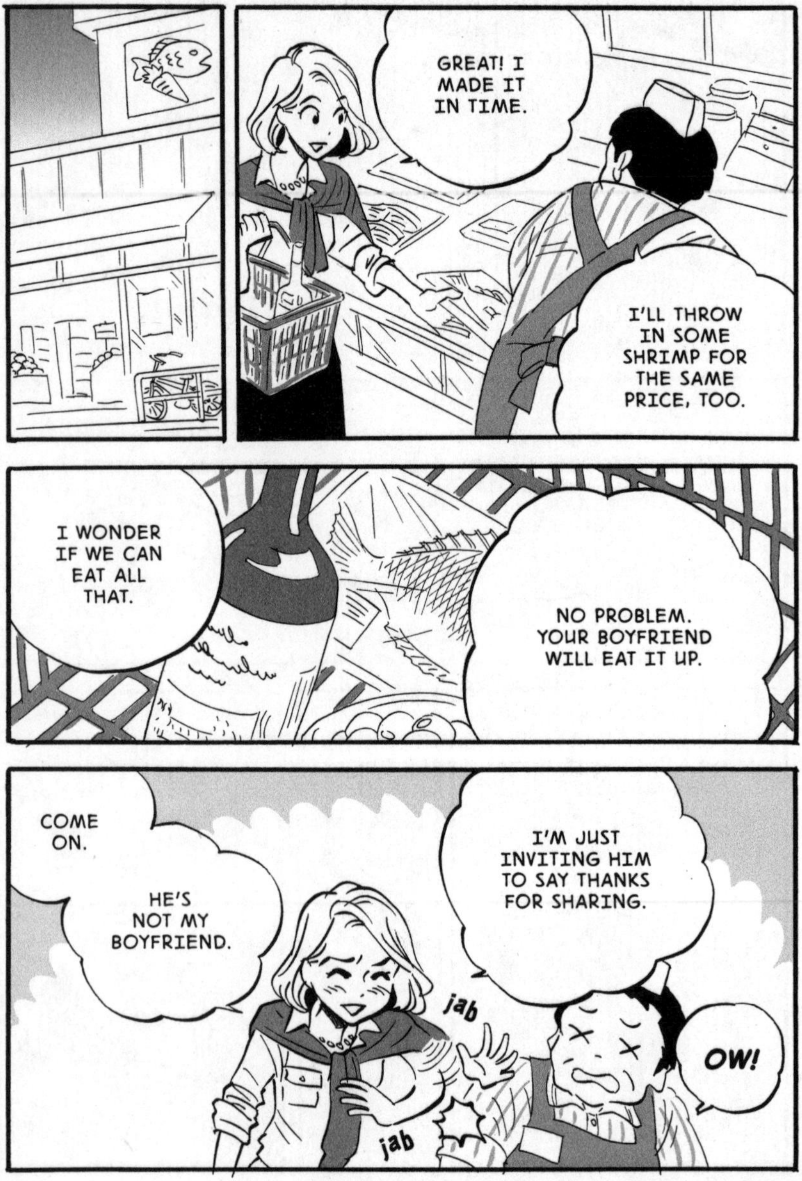
GREAT! I MADE IT IN TIME.
I'LL THROW IN SOME SHRIMP FOR THE SAME PRICE, TOO.
I WONDER IF WE CAN EAT ALL THAT.
NO PROBLEM. YOUR BOYFRIEND WILL EAT IT UP.
COME ON.
HE'S NOT MY BOYFRIEND.
I'M JUST INVITING HIM TO SAY THANKS FOR SHARING.
jab
jab
OW!

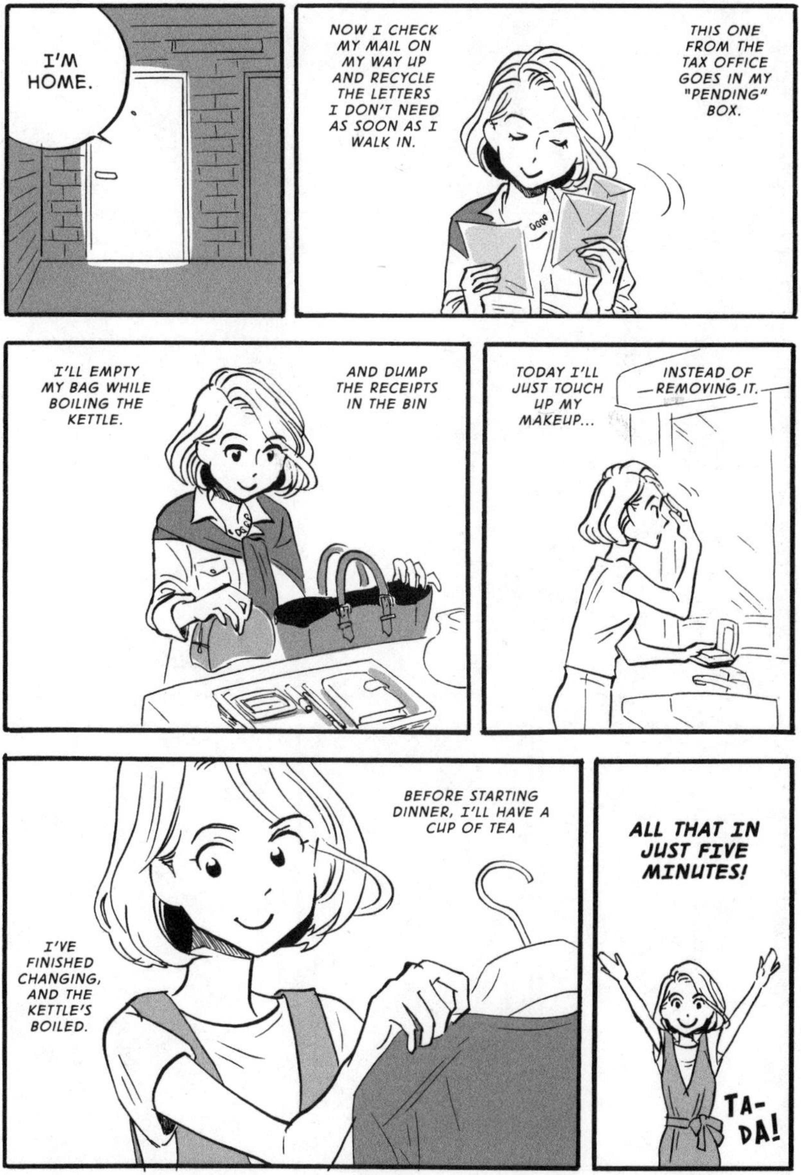
I'M HOME.
NOW I CHECK MY MAIL ON MY WAY UP AND RECYCLE THE LETTERS I DON'T NEED AS SOON AS I WALK IN.
THIS ONE FROM THE TAX OFFICE GOES IN MY "PENDING" BOX.
I'LL EMPTY MY BAG WHILE BOILING THE KETTLE.
AND DUMP THE RECEIPTS IN THE BIN
TODAY I'LL JUST TOUCH UP MY MAKEUP...
INSTEAD OF REMOVING IT.
BEFORE STARTING DINNER, I'LL HAVE A CUP OF TEA
I'VE FINISHED CHANGING, AND THE KETTLE'S BOILED.
ALL THAT IN JUST FIVE MINUTES!
TA-DA!

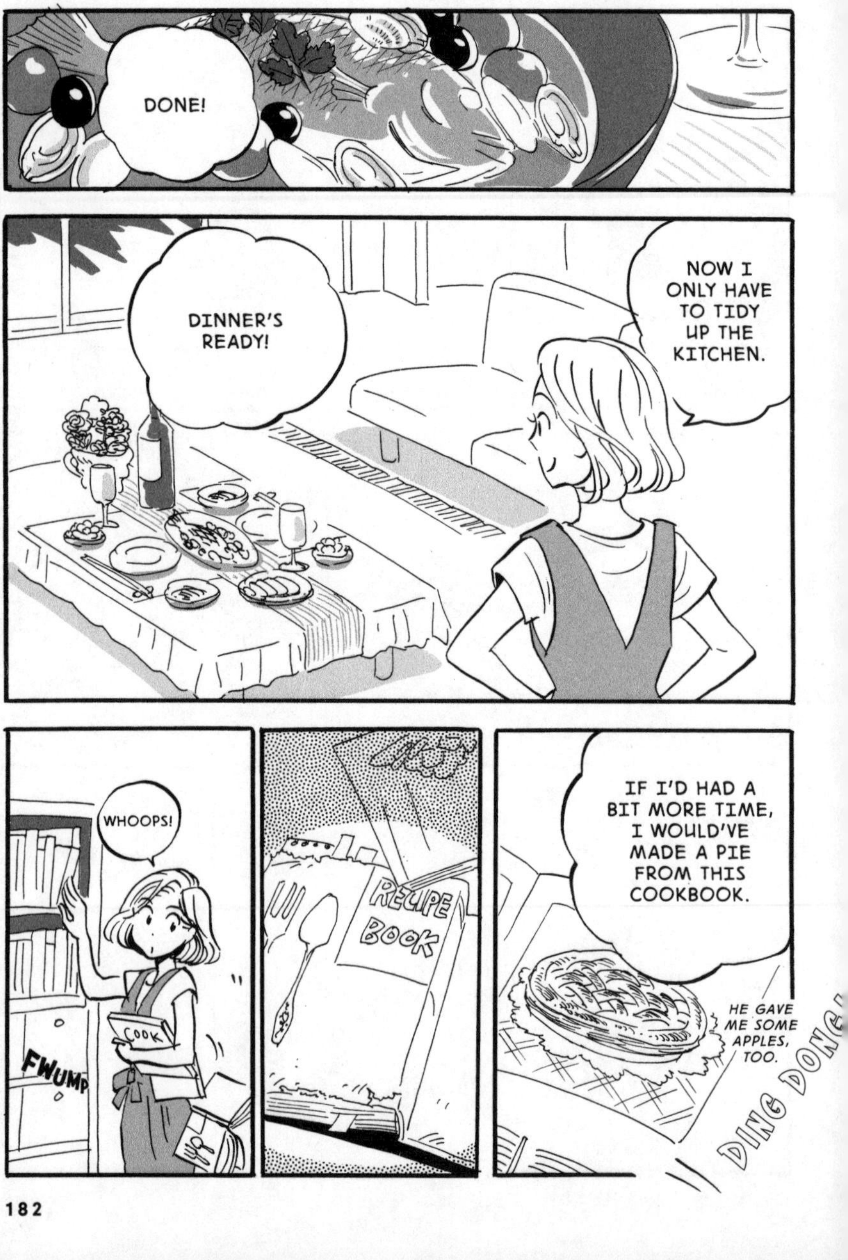
DONE!
DINNER'S READY!
NOW I ONLY HAVE TO TIDY UP THE KITCHEN.
WHOOPS!
COOK
FWUMP
RECIPE BOOK
IF I'D HAD A BIT MORE TIME, I WOULD'VE MADE A PIE FROM THIS COOKBOOK.
HE GAVE ME SOME APPLES, TOO.
DING DONG

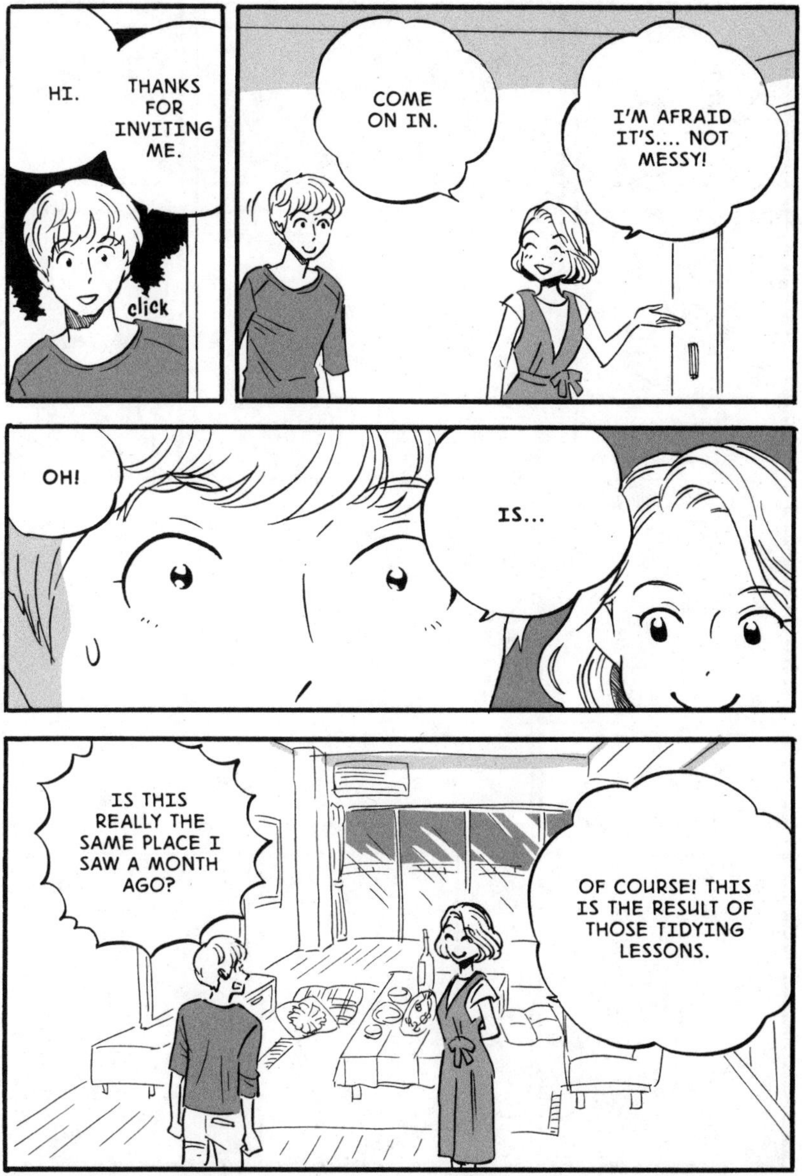
HI.
THANKS FOR INVITING ME.
click
COME ON IN.
I'M AFRAID IT'S.... NOT MESSY!
OH!
IS...
IS THIS REALLY THE SAME PLACE I SAW A MONTH AGO?
OF COURSE! THIS IS THE RESULT OF THOSE TIDYING LESSONS.

SO? LOOKS GOOD, RIGHT?

YES!

IT'S GREAT!

IT'S AWESOME AND ATTRACTIVE... IT REALLY SUITS YOU.

KYUN

REALLY. YOU SHOULD'VE ASKED FOR HELP.

I LIVE JUST NEXT DOOR. THIS MUST HAVE BEEN A HUGE JOB.

NO, NO. THERE'S NO POINT TIDYING UP UNLESS YOU DO IT YOURSELF.

HERE, HAVE A SEAT.

HERE. I BROUGHT A LITTLE GIFT.

OH!

THANK YOU. I WONDER WHAT IT IS.

BLUSH!

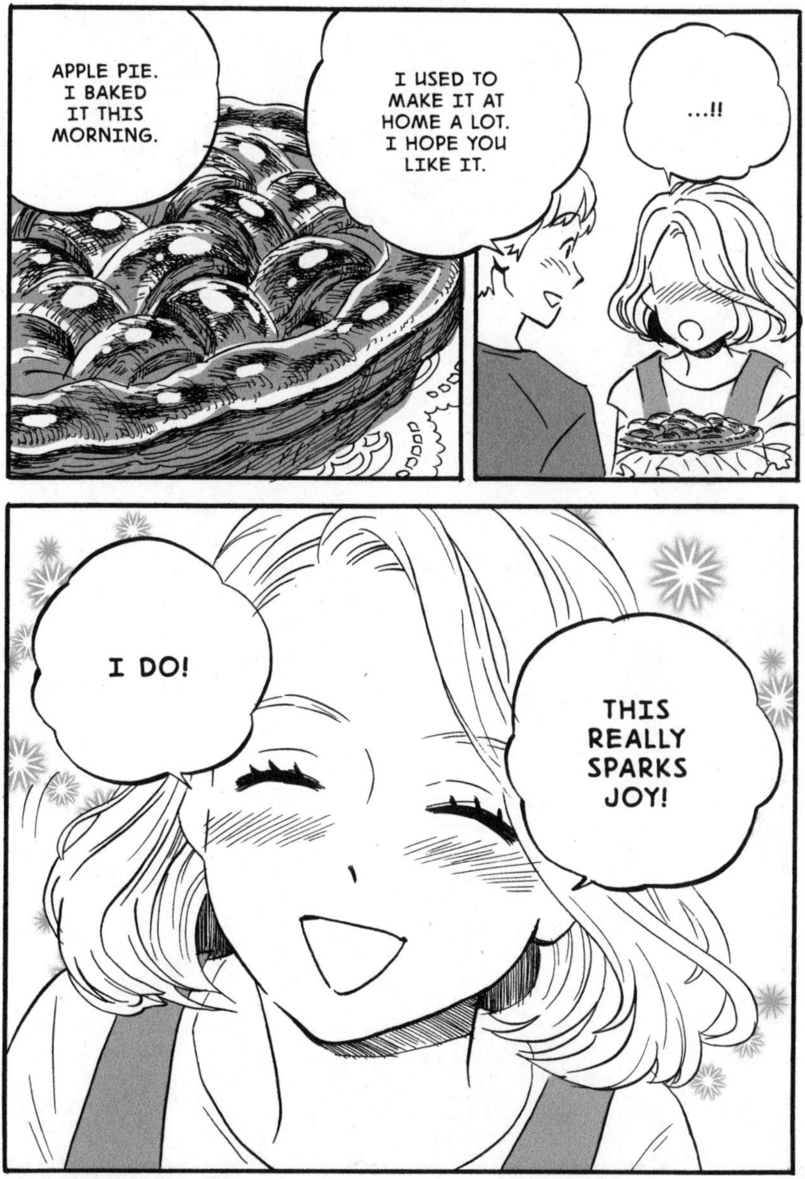
APPLE PIE. I BAKED IT THIS MORNING.
I USED TO MAKE IT AT HOME A LOT. I HOPE YOU LIKE IT.
...!!
I DO!
THIS REALLY SPARKS JOY!

afterword

As a tidying consultant, I have seen how tidying up sparks joy in the lives of many people.

Work, relationships, falling in love . . . the magic of tidying up positively impacts every aspect of life.

If you want to spark more joy in your life, try tidying up by following the advice in this manga. The effect will be even greater than you expect.

I hope that through tidying you will experience joy in your life every day.

about the author and illustrator

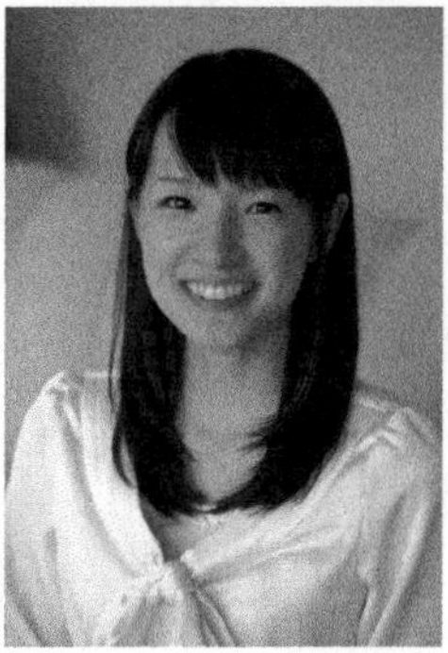

©NATSUNO ICHIGO

MARIE KONDO is the founder and chief visionary officer of KonMari Media Inc. and author of the #1 *New York Times* best seller *The Life-Changing Magic of Tidying Up*, which has sold more than six million copies worldwide, has been translated into over forty languages, and has been turned into a Japanese television drama. She is also the author of *New York Times* best seller *Spark Joy* and the companion journal, *Life-Changing Magic: A Journal*. Kondo has been featured in the *Wall Street Journal*, the *Atlantic*, the *New York Times*, *USA Today*, and on the *Today* show, and has been named one of *Time* magazine's 100 Most Influential People. Visit www.konmari.com.

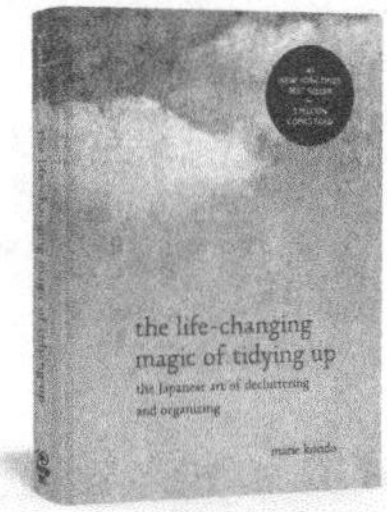
the life-changing
magic of tidying up
marie kondo

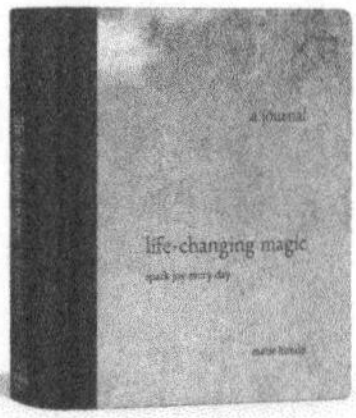
a journal
life-changing magic

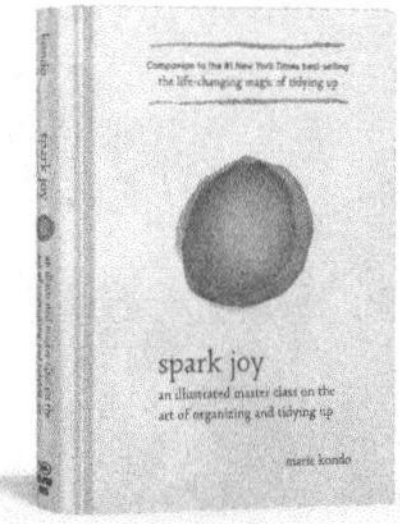
spark joy
an illustrated master class on the
art of organizing and tidying up
marie kondo

YUKO URAMOTO is a renowned manga artist who was born in Fukuoka, Japan. In 2011 she was awarded the Grand Prize in the Shueisha Aoharu Manga Awards. Her works include *Kanojo no kabu* (Her Curves), *Tsubakiso* (Camellia House No. 101), *Kabantoridori* (Different Bags), and *Hanayome miman* (Less Than Married).

All rights reserved.
Published in the United States by Ten Speed Press, an imprint of the Crown
Publishing Group, a division of Penguin Random House LLC, New York.
www.crownpublishing.com
www.tenspeed.com

Ten Speed Press and the Ten Speed Press colophon are registered trademarks
of Penguin Random House LLC.

Originally published in Japan as *Manga de Yomu Jinsei ga Tokimeku Kataduke
no Maho* by Sunmark Publishing, Inc., Tokyo, in 2017. Copyright © 2017 Marie
Kondo and Yuko Uramoto. English translation rights arranged with Sunmark
Publishing, Inc., and KonMari Media Inc. through InterRights, Inc., Tokyo, Japan,
and Gudovitz & Company Literary Agency, New York, USA. English translation
by Cathy Hirano.

Library of Congress Cataloging-in-Publication Data is on file with the publisher.

Trade paperback ISBN: 978-0-399-58053-6
eBook ISBN: 978-0-399-58054-3

Printed in the United States of America

Design by George Carpenter

10 9 8 7 6 5 4

First American Edition